# Your
# School
# Music Program

*A GUIDE TO EFFECTIVE CURRICULUM DEVELOPMENT*

# Your School Music Program

A GUIDE TO EFFECTIVE CURRICULUM DEVELOPMENT

FRANCES M. ANDREWS
*Professor of Music Education, The Pennsylvania State University*

CLARA E. COCKERILLE
*Assistant County Superintendent of Schools, Armstrong County Pennsylvania*

*Illustrated by Joe Smith*

*Englewood Cliffs, N. J.* **PRENTICE-HALL, INC.**

LIBRARY OF CONGRESS
CATALOG CARD NO.: 58-10632

*First printing . . . June, 1958*
*Second printing . . . January, 1959*



PRINTED IN THE UNITED STATES OF AMERICA

98071

# • Preface

*Your School Music Program* has been written for you, because you are in some way concerned with children, music, teachers, schools. It has been written as a guide for teachers, supervisors, and administrators of music; it has been written for school administrators.

The book represents the experience and thinking of a music educator and a school administrator, both of whom have worked with, taught, and discussed problems of schools and problems of music education with thousands of individuals interested in both.

The teaching staffs of our schools are made up of just such individuals, each working to accomplish something that will add to the usefulness and value of education in the lives of boys and girls. Music education has a place in this overall pattern; its objectives are compatible with those of the school as a whole. But the great potential of music in our schools will be more readily achieved if we think of it not only as a subject or an area, but also as involving people and their working relationships.

Schools are made up of human beings. This book is written in terms of human beings. It shows, in addition to the music program's planning and implementation, how school personnel can work together to make this planning effective in successful action.

This book will help music specialists and administrators create a music program that is readily understood and accepted by other teachers and community members, and that is highly functional in the lives of children. We hope it will help you build a better school through music education's contribution as an integral part of that school.

The attitudes and opinions of hundreds of teachers find indirect expression in portions of the following pages. No one individual's or group's opinions or attitudes are cited, however; all individual and group names, all illustrations, all expressions of opinions, and all school and town names are purely fictitious. Any similarity to real persons, places, schools, or events is purely coincidental.

FRANCES M. ANDREWS
CLARA E. COCKERILLE

# • Table of Contents

# 1 · A town talks music

"SCHOOL BOARD ADOPTS BUDGET—MUSIC PROGRAM TO BE EXPANDED"

The banner headline of the *Evening Chronicle* was being read with keen interest and with mixed emotions in the homes of the residents of Stone City.

"The ladies of the Tuesday Afternoon Music Club will be *so* pleased when they read of the amount of money the Board plans to allot to the music program," said Mrs. Peters to her husband, a member of Stone City School Board. "Only last week they were saying that the high school students needed to hear good music and learn to appreciate it. Now they can add more high school classes in Music Appreciation and buy some really good recordings."

Suzanne and Mary were in the midst of their regular after-dinner telephone marathon. "Did you see what the paper said? I'll bet next year we can have that girls' drum and bugle corps we want. Mr. Ross said the other day we could have one if the Board gave enough money so that they could hire another man to help with the band. We can show up Oceanport High next summer in the Firemen's Parade."

Paul Ross, member of the music faculty of Stone City Schools, remarked to his wife as he laid down the evening paper, "This will give us the chance to do what we want to do. We can buy some really good new instruments and step up our instrumental program in the elementary school. In a few years we'll have an orchestra here that will be a sure thing for the State Music Festival. You wait and see."

"More nonsense," growled Jonathan Nelsen, president of the Taxpayers League of Stone City, to his golfing partner, Ben Luther. "Those Board members should have their heads examined. There are too many kids going around blowing horns now. What we need here are better laboratories for our science classes. The country is crying for scientists and we increase the budget for music so more kids can make noise."

"Hey, Dick," called Tim as he brought his bicycle along the curb. "What do you know! It says in tonight's paper that we are going to have all the money for music that we want—I'll bet we can get old Roberts to let us have a dance band this year. That's what we need—a good jazz band to put some life in the school. Polish up your trombone, boy—we'll show them what music is."

The women teachers' bridge club gave attention to the headline when they assembled at Jane Foster's for the bi-weekly game. "Wouldn't you know, girls! The music budget is increased—and us with every Latin book in shreds and not a cent of money to send a student to the Classical Language Convention this spring."

"What do you expect? Every time this town has anything going on the music teachers get a chance to show off the chorus or the band. No wonder they get all the money. Whoever gets to hear the debate team and the oratorical contests? A handful of parents and aunts. It's disgusting."

"It was bad enough this year having students out every other week to go to some music affair or other. I suppose next term we'll have to ask permission of the music department to hold English classes."

"Cheer up, girls," said Betty Perry, principal of Central Elementary School, "think of the fate of the poor grade school teachers. I can just hear all those Junior Bands we are going to have thumping and tooting around the schools and all the mothers calling me to know why their darlings aren't in the band and if I don't think it would be cute to dress the kindergarteners as majorettes!"

Connie and Sonya were sitting on the top step of the Walters' front porch. "I think I'll get yellow, with a real full skirt," said Connie.

"I'm going to get pink," said Sonya. "Without straps, too. Won't it be wonderful? When we have this wonderful music program I know the Concert Choir will be the most important thing. We will probably be asked to sing at all the important things in town!"

Butch Barber, Stone City football captain, voiced his disgust to his father at the dinner table: "Wouldn't you know that dumb school board would do something like that? More money for music. It makes me sick. Why couldn't we get a new assistant coach for backfield? That would mean something to this town. Who needs more music? I tell you if we don't get some more good help for Coach we aren't going to have any kind of a team next fall and then this town will see."

Thoughtfully, Frank Roberts, head of the Music Department of Stone City Schools, looked at the headline. "Music Program to be Expanded." It was a dream come true. Ten years before, he had come to Stone City, a beginning music teacher. Ten years of getting the bands ready for parades, ten years of school shows, concerts for the Tuesday Afternoon Music Club, special numbers for Civic Club luncheons. Always with a minimum of money. Here was his chance at last—a decent budget. And yet Frank Roberts sighed deeply.

"For heaven's sake, what's wrong?" asked his wife. "Isn't this what you wanted? Isn't this what you've talked about and planned for? Why that sigh? You sounded as if the soprano soloist in the Easter cantata had just gotten laryngitis."

"Sure it's what I want, Bess, but I get it the year that Leon List retires as superintendent here, and now there's the new superintendent to think about. If Leon were to be here I know what we would do. But what about this new man? Does he believe in music and what it can do for the school and for the town and for the students? Does he know anything about music education? The music program isn't a one-man show. It is a total staff proposition and the superintendent is the key man. I ought to be elated over the board's decision, but I'll feel better when I can talk to the new superintendent and learn how he feels about things."

Two days later and two hundred miles away, George Fredrick, Ph.D., State University, principal of Bayside High School, and newly-elected Superintendent of Stone City, sat in his office reading the *Stone City Evening Chronicle*. "Expanded Music Program," he mused. "It can be good or it can be trouble. That is a problem that can't wait. It may be the first big thing I must face on the new job. There are things I wish I knew." These he noted on a memo pad:

(a) how the students feel about music.

(b) what the town believes about music.
(c) how the faculty feels about an expanded music program.
(d) what the music teachers believe about music education.
(e) how music fits into the total education program.

When he had finished the list, George Fredrick added, "Make early appointment for conference with Frank Roberts, Music Director at Stone City. Begin to think through music education program."

The little dramas enacted in Stone City are not isolated incidents peculiar to one town or one area. To some extent, in some degree, and with their own local coloring, they are reflected in every school system in our country.

The question of the place of music in the public schools is a question that must be faced and solved by a team, not by an individual. The way in which music instruction came into the public schools has resulted, in all too many places, in a situation in which there is a school with a music program as a sideshow, colorful, entertaining, and attractive, but not a true part of the main event; the School Superintendent runs the main show, and the Director of Music runs the sideshow.

To have music education a part of the school is a different thing. Music then is not a side attraction operating almost independently; it is a part of the total school program, believed in, planned for, and integrated. The School Superintendent and the Music Director work together with teachers, pupils, and the community to achieve the goals which have been set in harmony with the philosophy of the school.

The succeeding chapters of this book have been written for specialists in music education and school administrators, working cooperatively to establish music as a part of the total educative process whose aim is to enable all children to reach their maximum potential in well-integrated, productive living.

## • FOOD FOR THOUGHT

1. What would be your first reaction to a proposed expansion of

the music program in the school system that you know best?

2. Where do teachers, pupils, and lay people get their ideas about music programs?
3. What groups of people in your community would be interested in an expanded music program? What do you think their opinions would be?

# 2 · Music: A part of the total school program

## *Music Is a School Subject*

The question, "Is music a part of your school program?" would receive an affirmative answer from school administrators today. "How much a part of your school program?" would bring a greater variety of responses.

"Have you heard our band?"

"We had a first chair at state orchestra."

"Our spring concert is the big affair of the year."

"Too big a part. The music director is always asking for more time, more money, more pupils. The other teachers resent it."

A few administrators might tell of the music classes and of the learning experiences in music planned for all the pupils. The answers would indicate one of the basic needs in building an effective program of music education; the need for the acceptance of music education as a part of the total school program for the education of children and youth.

## *Problems in Administration of Music Education*

One of the common sources of difficulty in providing for music education is the failure to recognize that school music is a subject to be learned before it is something to be performed. This means that in one of its phases music must be considered an academic subject, taking its place with English, mathematics, and the social studies. For that reason the administrators and music directors have many joint problems of administration which require coordinated action.

## *Planning Time for Music*

Is a weekly visit of forty minutes by the special music teacher to the third grade room adequate for music instruction? One forty-minute period a week for learning any subject in a primary room is a practice contrary to what we know about children and how they learn. Will they learn music that way any more than they will learn arithmetic or spelling?

At the secondary-school level, does a weekly class provide education in music? Does it give the teacher opportunity for anything more than isolated plunges into the vast field of music? What happens to the values junior high school pupils place on music when they can say, "We only have it once a week, so it isn't important"?

## *Finding Room for Music*

An auditorium is an excellent place to stage a concert; is it an equally satisfactory place to teach music classes? In many schools music and the auditorium seem to be inseparable. Is there no need for chalkboards, good lighting, and ventilation in rooms where music is taught? Is it enough for new secondary schools to be built with band rooms and good storage for instruments and uniforms? Or do music departments need practice rooms and small rooms where ensembles can rehearse? Can music be well taught without good teaching materials? What materials and tools are needed for music education? Can they be provided for in the regular budget or must they depend on generous band mothers and community tag days?

### *Determining Class Size and Teacher Load*

A chorus of 125 students with each member having some skill in music and each one interested in singing and wanting to be in the chorus is one teaching situation. Is a comparable situation found in a general music class the same size, of whose members perhaps a quarter have no skill in music, a half, no interest in music? In many schools the music director is assigned large classes in general music because he has skill in handling large choruses and large bands. Where music is believed to be important in the total development of the pupils, what consideration should be given to the size of the music classes?

Because music teachers are people, not mechanical robots, they have definite limitations, one of which is strength. What happens to a music teacher when he must travel to elementary schools in the morning, teach classes in general music in the afternoon, rehearse the girls' chorus, practice with the marching band after school and lead the group singing at a PTA meeting in the evening? What happens to his teaching? Teacher load is frequently heavier in the music department than in any other part of the school, not alone in number of pupils worked with, but also in the wide variety of work to be planned. What factors cause this overload? Is there a solution that is mutally satisfactory to administration and music education?

### *Providing Music Experiences for All Pupils*

At the senior high school level the over-all participation of the students in the music program comes to an abrupt end. General education and exploration are left behind in the elementary and early secondary schools, and the time of specialization begins.

Jane has thoroughly enjoyed music. She sang well and was in the Junior High Chorus. She plays the piano in her church youth choir. But Jane has chosen the Business Education

Course, and as her teacher says, "The employers of our town criticize the school if we turn out secretaries who are not skilled in the business subjects. We need every period of the day to teach these skills to our pupils."

Tom was in the elementary school band. He likes drums; he played them for three years in Junior High School. But Tom has chosen the vocational course in high school. The shop schedule, together with state requirements in English and social studies, leave him no time for music activity at the high school level.

George plays the violoncello. He and his older brother and his mother and father have a string quartet and enjoy playing together. George would enjoy being a part of the Riverview Senior High School Orchestra, but George's family lives on a farm and George wants to continue to live on a farm and be a farmer. He has chosen the vocational agriculture course, and with school work and out-of-school projects, he cannot play in the school orchestra.

These three high school students are typical of thousands in the high schools of the nation who love music, and who, because of a vocational choice they have made, cannot hope to participate in the music activities of their high school. This might be dismissed by saying, "Well, in this life we just have to make choices. No one can do everything," were it not for one important truth: Jane and Tom and George have chosen for their life work vocations in which they will have increasing amounts of leisure time. Automation is bringing to the world of work the prospect of a four day week and a six hour day. Jane and Tom are representative of that great group of workers who will have more leisure time than any workers have had in all the history of man. Labor saving devices on his farm will give George evenings when he will not be physically exhausted from his day's work.

Have we provided for the needs of these young people when we have given them no opportunity to continue their interest and develop more skill in music during their last three years in high school? Can we say that music is a part of our schools for these pupils? Whose responsibility is it to do the forward planning which will make music activity possible for these students?

## *Music and School Public Relations*

It is necessary to go no farther than the columns of the local newspapers to recognize the place of the school music program in the life of the community. Bands parading in volunteer firemen's activities, soloists at local music club meetings, boys' quartets singing at Rotary Club luncheons, brass ensembles leading in community Christmas carol sings, the girls' chorus singing at the Woman's Club banquet, the marching band performing between halves of football games—is this the school music that the community knows, supports, and demands? Is this a tangible way that the schools return to their communities service for the taxes by which the school is supported? This is the part of the music program that can win public acclaim for the school. What happens when it becomes the part of the school program that is "the tail that wags the dog"?

When a chorus is constantly performing, how can it have time to learn new music and new techniques? Can a school band with the need to have a show between football game halves every Saturday in the fall develop skills in other types of performance? Will a music teacher or director who has to meet constant public demand to supply music for meetings, banquets, parades, and luncheons have time or energy to devote to the development of a program of education in music? Every administrator today is required to face up to the problem of the relation of the public performance activities of the high school to the music program of the school, keeping in mind the relationship of school and community. How can he do it?

### *The Music Specialist Helps the Administrator*

School administrators need to think through the meaning of music as a part of the school program. Most administrators have not been trained as music educators. Their knowledge of music education many times is limited to what they have seen in schools as students or as teachers. The teacher or director of music must assume some responsibility for helping the administrator to see the broad implications of an effective music program. The music teacher can plan ways to show the general administrator that music in the school is part of the total education—not just a colorful, entertaining interlude, directed by a teacher who is constantly asking for uniforms, books, records, pianos, and a "day off" to go to the district chorus meeting.

### *The Administrator Helps the Music Specialist*

As the general administrator needs to be helped to realize that music IS part of education, so the music specialist needs to know that music is only a PART of education. Interested as he is in one special area, he may be frustrated and unhappy in his work because he has not considered the relationships implicit in a total school program.

### *Music Is One Subject Among Many*

In the elementary school the music supervisor finds that some elementary school teachers have only a limited knowledge of how to teach music, others have limited talent for music, and a few have no interest. Nevertheless the supervisor is confronted with the problem of depending on these teachers to carry on the music program most of the time. The special teacher of vocal or instrumental music may find that the teachers are jealous of any encroachments on reading, arithmetic, spelling, or writing time. There is resistance, if not open rebellion, to spring concerts and May Days whose preparations upset the school routine. There may be a conflict of educational philosophy between the music specialist who believes that only

children who can sing well should be in the chorus and the elementary teacher who believes that there is no place in elementary education for any activity in which all children cannot participate. These problems, which harass both music specialists and administrators, have no easy solution but become less vexing and frustrating to the music educator who can learn to say, "This thing which I see as my total job is only twenty minutes of the daily job of this classroom teacher." How are the viewpoints of music specialists and classroom teachers reconciled?

## *Every Subject Is Someone's Specialty*

In the secondary school the scheduling of music is one of the biggest areas of dissatisfaction. There are many music educators who believe that in secondary school, because music activities cut across grade levels in a way that no other subjects do, the music activities should be scheduled first and the other subjects scheduled around them. This sounds reasonable and it no doubt is—except to the teachers of English, mathematics, speech, physical education, Latin, or art, and sundry people such as coaches, principals, and superintendents. Each of them has a valid reason why something else should be scheduled first and everything else scheduled around it. To every teacher his subject is most important; that is why he chose the teaching of it as his life's work. *At best a schedule will be a working compromise with no teacher realizing his own conception of the optimum schedule*. How is the compromise reached?

All teachers want to have the best pupils; music teachers are no exception. In high schools the competition for the best students is keen, frequently producing a handful of students who are in everything, every minute of their time scheduled, while many other students have an abundance of so-called "study halls." Guidance personnel are recognizing this problem and are helping the students to make choices. Music teachers must be prepared to accept the fact that some good students will choose dramatics instead of chorus. This is not a plot of the guidance director and dramatics coach to weaken the music program. This is what happens because music is a *part* of the school program, not *the* program.

### *Budgets Have Limitations*

Every subject that is taught in school requires good teaching materials. Every school budget has definite limitations. There are few, if any, schools where every teacher can receive all the material he orders. How can working agreements be reached in a year when purchase of dictionaries leaves no money for recordings? Administrators would like to eliminate the headaches caused by teachers who do not receive all the supplies they recommend. Few indeed are the administrators who capriciously disregard teachers' wishes. How does the administrator help the faculty realize that its many needs must be met with a limited budget?

### *A Music Program Can Be Built*

The problems that plague administrators and frustrate music educators develop when school administrators fail to include music as an integral part of the total school program, and when music educators fail to realize that music is only one of many facets of education. As both groups look at the total school and at the music curriculum and find ways of working together, the design and action of the music program emerge.

#### • FOOD FOR THOUGHT

1. What factors have made music an "extra" in many schools?
2. What are the music problems in the school you know best?
3. Choose one of the problems and describe it as it exists in the school.

# 3 · Establishing lines of communication

## *Planning Communication*

To achieve the rapport essential to building the school music program, the music director and the school administrator must know each other's point of view. Each must attempt to see the school program as the other sees it. This is not easy, because of different background and education and the involvement of each with his own job during the school year. Unless plans are made and ways of communication definitely sought, the administrator and music director may find themselves moving farther apart with more and more minor differences growing into major problems.

## *Written Philosophy of Education*

A philosophy of education is more than just a part of graduate work in education. A written philosophy of education is a basis for program building. A music director who accepts a position in a school without knowing what that school believes about education should not be surprised if at a future date he finds he cannot do what he wants in his music program. The school administrator who employs a music director without learning the music director's philosophy of education may some day discover the music director working in a direction that is foreign to his own views. Good interpersonal relations are easier to achieve when both the school administrator and the music director have compatible philosophies of education—and each knows what the other believes.

Ed Preston has written a short statement of his philosophy of music education; a copy of the statement was included in his application for the position of music director. He feels that part of the statement was responsible for his losing out for election at Twin Oaks: "I believe that in elementary school music there is no place for the special chorus or band or orchestra. I believe that at the elementary school level all music is for all children." However, he knows that what he believed about elementary music was the reason he was chosen at Lake City. He knows now that had he been elected for the Twin Oaks job he would have had to work in opposition to established practice or he would have had to direct a program which was against his beliefs and distasteful to him. In Lake City they want the program he believes in. He has assurance of acceptance.

Falls High School faculty in preparation for a regional evaluation cooperatively wrote the philosophy of education of their high school. A copy of that philosophy is attached to the application blank sent to prospective applicants for positions in the high school. The principal says he believes this practice has attracted teachers whose philosophy fits into the philosophy of the school and thus the amount of faculty turnover has been reduced.

In school systems where no written statements of philosophy of education exist, the preparation of such a statement can be a project for a year's faculty meetings. It takes time, but once completed it saves time. Many problems which take hours of consideration to solve when there is no established school philosophy are solved quickly when there is a written philosophy.

The music director can lead the music teachers of a school system to formulate their beliefs about the music program in writing, so that they have a basis for solving problems and planning learning activities, even though the school as a whole may not have such a statement. An individual music teacher can write his beliefs about music education and evaluate his professional work in the light of his expressed beliefs.

## *Staff Conferences*

As schools are involved in a nationwide movement toward larger administrative units, planning for regular meetings of the staff becomes essential. When the school system was small, the music director and the superintendent or principal might see each other several times a week and casually discuss their mutual concerns. As the school system grows it is possible that months may go by with the music director having no opportunity to see the administrator. The same situation can exist where there are several members of a staff in the music department. The music director should plan for regular staff conferences for the music teachers, inviting into those conferences the general administrators of the schools. If the general administrators do not attend, a summary of conclusions or recommendations can be placed on their desks. "A little leaven leavens the whole lump." A music director, through effective use of staff meetings, can lead the school into the use of this technique for developing understanding and cooperative endeavor.

## *Professional Meetings*

It is common in American education for specialists in one field to gather together periodically to talk among themselves about problems that cannot be solved without involving other people. School superintendents meet and talk to other school superintendents about the problems they have with school principals. In another part of the state, the school principals are meeting to talk about the problems they have with superintendents and with classroom teachers. In a third conference the classroom teachers are talking to other classroom teachers about their problems with superintendents, principals and supervisors. Next month the supervisors will meet to talk to more supervisors . . . and so on.

There is a need for pioneers to break through this barrier of specialties. Could the music educators of your city or county plan a joint meeting with, for example, language arts or art

educators? Do you have some common problems? Can the physical education specialists meet with the English teachers? If they can't, we may expect to keep on in our uncomfortable rut of organizing meetings to talk about the same old problems, failing to enlarge our vision by asking to our meetings those other people whose understanding and help are essential for solving mutual problems.

### *Written Curriculum Outlines*

The fact that "Band-Chorus-Orchestra" *is* the music program to most citizens, and even to educators who are not working directly in the music field, is not surprising. That is what they see; that is what they know. In many respects they are like the people of Europe, Asia, and Africa who believe that all Americans are rich, drive Cadillacs, own swimming pools, and divorce their mates. They know it because they have seen it in the movies. People have seen Band-Chorus-Orchestra on the stage, and they accept it as the music program.

We must be realistic and accept the fact that many people are not interested in looking beneath the surface of the program. But music educators should be willing and able to show those people who are interested what the complete music program includes. Because this program does not lend itself to public performance, the written music curriculum guide is probably the best way to assemble the true picture in such a way that it can be understood. To write out such a guide is not easy. It is a job that can be readily pushed aside by saying, "It is more important to do than to say." But when we are considering understanding and communication, the importance of a written guide makes the work worth while. School administrators, supervisors of other fields, school board members, and PTA's need to know about the music activities they do not see or hear. Your course of study or curriculum guide can give the needed information when it is well prepared and plans are made for presenting it to the school and community.

### *Understanding Is a Two-Way Street*

We have been talking about ways in which the music educator can open the lines of communication so that administrators and others in the school will understand the aims, philosophy, and scope of music education. The music educator has the obligation to avail himself of every available means to learn about and understand all the other phases of the school curriculum. Among other things, this means he does not miss staff meetings "because I had to accompany a soloist for the Music Club."

He participates in the local teachers' organization, and does not refuse committee assignments "because I always have so much night work with the music program."

He reads the course of study outlines of other areas of work so that he knows something of the total school program and cannot say, "I just don't have time to visit in the rooms and see what others are doing, so I can't correlate music with other subjects."

At a general convention he attends one meeting, at least, in a field other than music so that he will no longer be heard saying, "But our problems are so different from theirs."

Administrators have learned much in recent years about the dynamics of working together. Music specialists have long known good techniques for transforming individual performers into ensemble members. A planned application of that knowledge and those techniques to the administrator-music director relationship is needed for advancement in music education.

## • FOOD FOR THOUGHT

1. Plan to present the picture of a school music program to:
   (a) An elementary Parent-Teacher Association in a fifteen-minute speech.
   (b) The School Board in a ten-minute talk.
   (c) The public in a 500-word newspaper article.
   (d) A high school faculty in a five-minute presentation as a panel member.
   (e) The local music club in an address.
2. Write your philosophy of music education in 300 words or less.
3. Make a collection of written courses of study in music education.
4. Plan a program for an educational meeting for high school music teachers and high school principals.

*Check List*

In the schools you know best:

1. Is there a written philosophy of education?

2. Do the various departments have the opportunity to explain their work to the school boards?
3. Are the school people asked to talk about their programs to various lay groups in the community?
4. Are some faculty meetings devoted to learning about the work of different departments within the school?
5. Do the teachers in various departments and on various grade levels have opportunities for exchange of ideas?

# 4 · Elementary music teachers

## *Job Descriptions: Meet the Teachers*

John Brice is starting out on his rural mail delivery route when he passes the Stuartville one-room schoolhouse. What he sees makes him slow down and smile, for Betty Smith has stopped her small coupe in front of the schoolhouse and four boys are running from the building toward it. John leans out his car window and calls, "Hi there, Betty! My boy says you're bringing an Autoharp today!" By the time she emerges from her car, the boys are ready to help, and she loads her equipment into their eager hands. "I've got the Autoharp," Billy says happily. Jim can't wait for the new songbooks—"Now we can learn that two-part song you told us about last week, Miss Smith!" Harry is lugging a portable phonograph, while Tommy, arms full of records ("May we keep these all week, Miss Smith?") tries to read all the labels as he goes back to the building.

Hurry up, Miss Smith! Your class has been waiting for you since you left them Monday at 10 o'clock—waiting for music. And somewhere in this same county, classes in twenty other rural schools are waiting their turn. During the week, through rain, snow, mud or dust, the old coupe will pull up in front of their schools and other boys will rush out to help Miss Smith as she brings music to the children and their teachers.

At 9:15 A.M. on the same Monday in a city hundreds of miles from the parking site of Betty Smith's car, Helen Jones waits for her cue. Materials are ready—chalkboard, resonator bells, pictures, phonograph, songbooks all in the right places. Cameras wheel into place. The director gives a signal. Mrs. Jones is on the air! On the television screens of a hundred classrooms, music comes to the city's children. "Hello, Mrs. Jones!" exclaims a third grader; Mrs. Jones is really in the classroom to him . . . and to all the children. They look to see whether she is wearing a new dress, whether she has changed her hairdo. They notice everything. But most of all, they are waiting for the new song Mrs. Jones promised them for today—and the resonator bells. When the camera pans around to include a view of these, "There they are—we're going to learn a tune on them! Remember, Mrs. Jones?"

Whether through the electronic miracle of twentieth century television or in the one-room tradition, music in today's schools is a lively and potent area of education. Why? How? What other jobs do teachers hold in the elementary music program? Is music a vital force in the lives of children today, or is it an unnecessary expenditure of taxpayers' money, a furbelow in the school budget? To find some answers to these questions, let's explore the function of music teachers today in your school program.

## *The Traveling Teacher*

Go back to Betty Smith and her rural school route. Betty's job is to teach music in twenty-one rural schools in one county. This job can be called by various titles; "traveling music teacher" probably describes it best. Betty travels almost as much as she teaches. The job itself is not an unusual one. No one school could afford the services of a music teacher, but under a county organization, twenty-one schools can. The schools Betty services are elementary schools, usually including grades 1-8. Not all of these are one-room schools; several are larger, and probably with the passing of time the one-room schools will be incorporated in a larger organization.

Betty does not take on the entire responsibility for teaching all the music in these schools. She encourages the elementary classroom teachers to carry on with classroom music to the best of their ability and interests. In fact, she makes them feel that *she* is assisting *them* in developing music as one aspect of the total program, rather than isolating it in a dubious hour of glory once a week. She hopes that this way music will touch and enliven many facets of classroom activities; she seeks ways and means of helping the classroom teacher work with music so that this may be accomplished. When the forty-niners and the California Gold Rush are a topic of study, she brings recordings of the songs that went west with them. It is likely that she will help George, who plays a little guitar, work out a simple accompaniment to several songs the class is singing.

Betty is something like the old time peddler with his wagon

of household supplies; she knows in general what materials and methods will be useful in all the schools, but she must inquire as to the specific needs of each "household" and each "housewife," filling their orders next time around.

In addition to this, the general outline and content of the music curriculum are her responsibility, for each child deserves an opportunity to explore and enjoy music; whether he is in the newest consolidated school or the oldest one-room building makes no difference to her. Perhaps the things that keep her going through mud, sleet, snow, and rain are the eagerness of the boys and girls and the responsiveness of their teachers. This is a job that never really pays off in honor or glory. It pays off in the faces of the children. Betty thinks that's plenty of reward.

### *The Supervisor of Teachers*

Agnes Piper is a Supervisor of Music in a city of 50,000 people. Agnes has been "supervisor" for thirty years. Her job, as outlined by her administrator—and Agnes has not tried to change it during her tenure—is to visit the classroom teachers from first through sixth grades, distribute lesson plans, observe the classroom teachers as they teach music, and report on their work to the principals. Agnes would like to spend more time with each classroom teacher, but she is the only music supervisor, and in order to get around to all the classrooms she has to hold to a tight schedule.

Agnes isn't too happy about her job; she feels that the teachers accept her on sufferance rather than with active cooperation. Most of the time she finds that she is telling them what *not* to do instead of making workable suggestions. She realizes, too, that when she enters a room both teacher and children "tense up." The children go through their paces in terms of the lesson plans their teacher is supposed to follow, Agnes has a brief conference with the teacher at the classroom door, and that is "it" for another two or three weeks. Once or twice Agnes has had bad moments when new teachers asked her to *show* them how to teach the class or invited her to take over, but it's been so long since Agnes has taught that she is afraid to try. She wonders whether the teachers realize this. But then, she tells herself, she is a "supervisor;" she does what she has always been expected to do.

What Agnes suspects, but doesn't really want to investigate, is that concepts of supervision have changed. When she is tempted to try some changes, she reminds herself that it won't be too long until she retires, and after all, you can't teach an old dog new tricks. Or can you? And who would help her learn? Sometimes she almost wants to try, though.

### *The Music Helping Teacher*

The job Agnes Piper holds is the product of an older philosophy of music education. Today many "supervisory" jobs are recognized in terms of less formal titles. Among these is the job of "music helping teacher." Tom Overton holds such a job; he is one of four "helping teachers" in a city system about the same size as that in which Agnes works. Tom works in a system where classroom teachers, as in Agnes' system, are expected to carry on the music program. But Tom does *not* observe and report on teacher efficiency. His job is to help the classroom teacher find ways and means of using music effectively in terms of children's growth and needs. Thus he is actually more concerned with the nature and growth of children than with a set music curriculum in terms of weekly coverage. He is also concerned with the classroom and school program as a whole. And he is interested in the classroom teacher as an individual, her attitude toward music, her feelings of adequacy as she helps children in musical activities, her ability to see the implications for music in relation to each child's development.

With the entire picture of children, teacher and classroom program in mind, Tom, after he is sure of the rapport between teacher and himself, will encourage the teacher to ask for materials, methods of presentation, and actual help in teaching children music. He welcomes requests to do some teaching, but when doing so, it is never with the attitude that the teacher must imitate. Rather, it is on the basis of a partnership in which he and the teacher work together for a richer and more adequate classroom program.

Tom's visits may be on a regular basis, but if a teacher prefers that he visit more or less frequently—for example, if the class is engaged in a project where music plays a large part—he will change his schedule to accommodate her. Since Tom is highly successful at his job, the teachers with whom he works think of him as a friend, and an unexpected visit is welcomed rather than looked upon with suspicion and antagonism.

Tom and his fellow music "helping teachers" hold open in-service workshops for the classroom teachers; attendance at these is not compulsory, but the real problems and situations that form the basis of discussion and investigation at these sessions attract many teachers, even at the end of a busy day.

### *The On-Call Music Teacher*

Less structured yet is the position of Susan Drake, "on-call music teacher." As the position title implies, this teacher visits the elementary classrooms on call from the classroom teacher, who, when she feels the need of help, asks for a visit. Perhaps a teacher needs materials, or suggestions for helping with creative music activities, or perhaps the class needs help in transcribing a song they have created. The services of the "on-call music teacher" are always at the disposal of classroom teachers, but the hidden part of this job lies in revealing the many ways music may be a lively and rewarding experience for children, and persuading teachers to explore these ways and use them.

To a classroom teacher brought up in the tradition of simply teaching "rote" songs and working with syllables, newer ways may bring about insecurity unless they are carefully initiated and implemented. Yet basically, this job and the "helping teacher" job are rooted in the belief that every teacher has a definite potential for contributing to children's musical growth;

the music specialist's work is to identify this potential so the teacher recognizes it, and to build upon it in terms of confidence and security.

### *Why So Many Titles?*

Sometimes music positions similar to those described as "helping teacher" or "on-call teacher" carry the title of "music consultant," "music coordinator," or "resource teacher." Although these positions vary in their exact responsibilities from system to system, it is safe to say that there are more similarities than differences, particularly as to their purposes. These positions have evolved through classroom teachers' resistance to and resentment of the traditional music supervisor as a narrow-field specialist. Of all the positions in education, that of the elementary classroom teacher is one of the most demanding. No one can be a specialist in everything; today we hope that our elementary teachers will be, primarily, specialists in children. And of course we hope that they will have a knowledge of subject matter. But to expect them to be *experts* in music and art, as well as the basic areas, is out of the question.

Consider Mrs. Olsen, a third grade teacher. She likes teaching, likes children, enjoys her life as an educator. But in her first job she had a supervisor of music who discovered that Mrs. Olsen was lacking in musical experience and background; in fact, Mrs. Olsen herself thought that she just wasn't able to sing "in tune." The result was that for one entire school year Mrs. Olsen's day was ruined when the supervisor came—not that the supervisor tried to make her uncomfortable, but just being observed while teaching a subject in which she was insecure *made* her uncomfortable. Finally music was taken out of Mrs. Olsen's hands, and her class was taught by another teacher.

Although this may have been a relief, it was also, in Mrs. Olsen's mind, open recognition of inadequacy as a teacher. In her next job she worked with a music helping teacher. "I can't sing," she said at once when they met. "We might as well get this straight right away." To her surprise, the helping teacher showed no signs of shock, or even disappointment. In the talk that followed, Mrs. Olsen learned that teachers were encouraged to carry on many types of musical activity in the classroom. It was suggested that she drop in for visits in other classrooms to observe the music program in action. The various ways in which this teacher grew in musical confidence and participation were many. Mrs. Olsen became a positive contributing force in music education due to the difference in basic approach, a difference that can be summarized in a few words: "Let's help you find out what you can do," instead of ". . . what you can't do."

### *Why Can't the "Mrs. Olsens" Sing?*

Few individuals do everything equally well. The few who do are usually tempted into fields more remunerative than the classroom. As a matter of fact, the music specialists don't do everything equally well. Some sing, some play the piano, some the trombone; each has a "major." Some play two or three instruments extremely well. Even within one field, however, individuals do not perform equally well in all peripheral areas of that field.

All this is leading up to the fact that there is little reason for music specialists to expect stellar music teaching from all classroom teachers. With the countless variations in talent, training, and professional education that exist from state to state, city to city, college to college, individual to individual, why should we?

Some specialists say, "But their certificates state that they can . . ." Whoever is saying this should remember that although his (or her) own certificate may state that he is duly authorized to teach music, this may include certain phases that would be somewhat embarrassing if the letter of the law were interpreted literally. Would each specialist be able to teach counterpoint? Bassoon? Teach a gifted child to write a motet?

Look at it this way: we must expect different strengths from different individuals. And in spite of one or two college courses in music education, there will always be classroom teachers who feel lost when it comes to music. (In fact, as the demand for elementary teachers increases, there may be more of them.)

There are good reasons why this is so. To college instructors working with future classroom teachers, such reasons are an old story. A student stops at the desk after the first class meeting. "I think I should tell you I can't sing very well," she says. "I've never been able to stay on tune. I expect to have trouble with this course." Having delivered herself of this, she is obviously relieved. But around the "confession" hangs an aura of guilt heavy enough to stem from robbing poor boxes or assaulting one's aged grandmother with a deadly weapon.

Ask this student, "What makes you think you can't sing?" She'll answer, "When I was in second grade, my teacher told me not to sing with the rest of the children . . ." She may say first grade, second, third, or fourth; other students mention similar experiences at these grade levels.

The result seems to be the same. In the thinking of the child, it emerges this way, "The teacher says not to sing. So I guess I don't sound good enough. She doesn't want to hear me. I'd better not try." Sensitive and impressionable, many children regard such instructions as final. So . . . they stop singing.

But it isn't always the teacher who administers the blow. Some students say, "My mother (or it could be 'my older sister') has a beautiful voice. She always said it was too bad my voice wasn't like hers." Perhaps it sounds strange to say that a boy or girl could be discouraged by a beautiful voice, but we must realize that this isn't the point . . . it's the fact that the individual's own voice doesn't measure up to the voice he admired, even loved, in the case of the mother. This is an example of a goal far beyond the child's reach. He gives up.

Or the discouraging element may be the peer group. Here's the seventh grade boy who was a non-participant in most music classroom activities; definitely so in singing. After giving him several weeks in which to adjust, the teacher asked him why he didn't join in singing with his classmates. He replied briefly, "I don't like it. I tried it once in third grade and they laughed at me. I've never sung since." Out of curiosity, the teacher checked. Back throught his sixth grade, fifth grade, fourth grade teachers—sure enough, he had maintained his silence. Busy teachers, heavy pupil loads—no one with time enough to figure out why Sammy didn't sing, but held fast to his clam-like attitude in the face of the passing days of music and singing. Sammy moved away before he really grew to like singing—if he ever decides to be an elementary classroom teacher, he may be another who stops at the teacher's desk with the familiar story.

One boy came into a college methods class with an obvious chip on his shoulder where music was concerned. He went through all the motions in class, but his heart certainly wasn't in it. Moreover, he didn't even want to discuss it. He was the sort of student who causes the teacher to think of tearing up all teaching plans, looking desperately for new "stimulators" or other "blood-transfusions" for the course, and searching his conscience in the small hours to see whether he has fallen into the wrong vocation. Finally, the last day the class met, the teacher ventured to ask him to come in for a final conference. "Let's have it," he said. "I know you haven't liked the course, but I don't know why. For the sake of those who follow you, it might help if you'd come right out and tell me. You've passed the course, so you can afford to be honest."

Suddenly the student decided to take the plunge. "Well, you're right. I don't like music," he blurted out. "When I was in fourth grade, the music supervisor organized an elementary school choir. Each member was to have a red robe, and I surely wanted one of those robes. But—only ten members of our class were chosen, and I wasn't one of them. I've disliked music ever since!"

Now who would think a small boy could want a red choir robe so desperately that his failure to obtain one would follow him, in the form of an obvious attitude, for years? Yet the robe wasn't the important thing—it was his failure to succeed, to gain group status, which made him turn against the cause of his failure.

These incidents may seem minor, as you read them over. But each one was a heartache to the child it affected. Who's to blame? The teachers who thought it was better to ask a child not to sing than to have her sing the wrong tune? The mother, father, sister, or brother with the better voice? The little boys and girls who laughed at the child with a "funny" voice? Or the teacher who was told by a supervisor to "pick ten children from your grade to be in the new choir"? None of these individuals set out to create a dislike of music in a child; that we know.

We also know that we cannot control home situations. We can, however, do something about the schoolrooms in which we teach.

To begin with, it really isn't the way a child sounds when he makes his early musical attempts that is of primary importance; it's the spirit in back of that effort. Adults who understand children know this. Some singing is almost technically perfect, but it isn't music. On the other hand, certain groups of first graders sing their songs with joy and abandon, and all kinds of tune approximations . . . and it *is* music!

An absent-minded musician tells how she was given a beautiful compact when she played for the wedding of a friend. For two years, she remembers, whenever she felt low in spirit, she would take out the compact and powder her nose. One day an observer said to her, "But Helen, there isn't any powder in that compact!" Helen comments, "All at once, the truth dawned upon me—there never *had* been any powder in it! Nevertheless, it served a purpose in my life!" So the singing of the first graders, although far from perfect technically, may fulfill the real spirit of music.

Needless to say, not everyone understands this. In one school a high school language teacher, blitzed during the summer by new ideas, decided to descend into the first grade and teach the children some Spanish songs. She was a well-meaning and kindly person, of forceful personality, so away she went. After the first session, she came storming in to the principal and exclaimed, "They can't sing. Why can't they stay on the tune?" The principal and the music specialist tried to explain to her that not only had many of the children never been to school before, but that it was not unusual, early in the first year of school, to find a rather large group of children who wandered from the melody occasionally.

Whether or not she believed this is relatively unimportant. The point is that she was trying to use music only as a means to the end of reaching a skill goal—learning a language. Building enjoyment of music was the goal for the children.

It should be obvious to the majority of readers that, in any area, learning progresses from diffuse, crude efforts to comparatively refined achievement. The fatal blow to such progress is dealt if we keep children from making these efforts. By such action we destroy self-confidence and undermine security in the learning situation, defeat attempts to gain prestige in the eyes of teacher and peer-group, and thus stifle motivation.

And to what end? We all know that children are learners, not performers. No one would think of saying to a child, when he first attempts walking and falls, or even to a handicapped child after repeated falls, "stop trying!" Yet the equivalent of this has happened to some of the students and teachers who say, "I can't sing—never could!"

Such individuals *can* improve their singing. But it takes much more time than would have been necessary had they been encouraged to keep on singing instead of being made to feel that their efforts added nothing to the musical achievement of the group. In the meantime, too, they have lost years of singing pleasure, and in many cases have acquired a negative attitude toward musical activities as a whole.

Here is a revealing feature of remedial work with "out-of-tune" singers at the adult level: fully as much time must be spent in restoring their self-confidence as in actually working with problems of pitch and voice. So, with good reason it can be said, "Don't stop them singing. Accept what they have to offer and keep them participating. This is the way they learn."

## *Who Should Teach Elementary Music?*

In certain school districts all the music is taught by a music specialist, often called the music supervisor. She visits each classroom regularly, as often as time permits. Music starts when she arrives, stops when she leaves. It is really a "special" subject in these cases, although she may try to relate it to other classroom activities. In such cases music is often completely removed from the realm of the classroom teacher.

It definitely seems advisable that each classroom teacher should have much assistance available to her where music is concerned. But the wisdom of removing it from her teaching province seems questionable. Let's look at this problem in the next few paragraphs.

It is a subject of much discussion. "Music specialists should teach all the music!" says one group. "Not enough time!" retort others. And all stages of betwixt and between.

While the law is being laid down in such theoretical dialectics, we have only to look about us to see that the job is actually being done by music specialists alone, by classroom teachers alone, and by combinations of both in various places and degrees. Very likely it will continue so for a long time.

In this case we can proceed by attempting to agree on what is best for the children. Years ago wise minds decided that obviously the classroom teacher knew the most about the children in her room and what their total learning experiences were, while the music specialist knew the most about music. But since the latter saw relatively little of the children in each room and had only a limited opportunity to become acquainted with their areas of learning, her knowledge of each classroom situation was limited.

Therefore the two individuals should make a strong teaching partnership *if* they were willing to pool their efforts. The combination of knowing the children, the music, and the total classroom experiences would be an excellent basis for teaching.

This still makes sense. We can't bypass the classroom teacher and say, "Hands off—this is private property." Neither can the classroom teacher bypass music and say, "This is none of my business." Whatever is the business of the pupils is the business of both teachers. Can music flourish in an isolated twenty-minute period, daily or weekly?

Actually, the main difficulty in getting the teamwork going between music specialist and classroom teacher lies in a pathetic lack of interest in what is best for the pupils themselves.

Music teachers cite the attitude of classroom teachers: "She leaves the room as soon as I come in," or "All the time I'm there she sits at her desk correcting papers."

Classroom teachers cite the music teacher's attitude: "You don't know enough about music to teach it, so why don't you leave it to me?"

Who is to teach music should be a matter of *policy,* not happenstance. It should depend on the general supervisory policy of the school, who plans it, how it is planned, *and who agrees to it.* If teachers don't agree to a policy willingly, they will find more ways to get around it than can be countered by any supervisory force.

If a teacher leaves his classroom when the music teacher arrives, even though he's supposed to stay, he's obviously disinterested in music. Suppose he is asked to stay and *help* her the next time she comes—asked, in advance, to help demonstrate the workings of the piano, carry in a bass drum, distribute the bell blocks . . . any legitimate reason will do. Chances are he'll agree to help.

This is simply one example of getting the classroom teacher into action, simply one approach. The music teacher must be resourceful and tactful in enlisting the cooperation of diffident or negative individuals.

The administration must help by supplying in-service assistance. Don't say to your teachers, "What do you want in the way of help?" and shrug off the whole matter if they don't tell you. It's likely that they don't know, or can't pin-point the kind of help they need. "Sink or swim, then, we've given you a chance to ask for help," doesn't accomplish much. Help them analyze their strengths and weaknesses, find out what they need in the way of in-service training. But remember—a two or three-day workshop may be a good initial shot, but it needs several boosters in the way of intelligent follow-up to make it effective.

Yes, it's a big job. But isn't it better for children to have teachers working together?

Specific ways in which the classroom teacher can help with the music program are listed in Chapter 6.

## • FOOD FOR THOUGHT

1. Either talk with several elementary classroom teachers and ask what kind of help they would prefer from music specialists, or outline the kind of assistance a music specialist may furnish in the way of singing, listening, rhythmic, and correlating activities.
2. List five ways in which a music specialist can help a classroom teacher who is unable to sing "in tune" carry on a vigorous music program.
3. What characteristics must a music specialist have in order to work successfully with elementary teachers?
4. If you know any individuals who say they cannot sing, ask them when they first became conscious of this. Do all children learn to sing at the same age? To walk, talk, or read?
5. Should elementary teachers be expected to teach their own music? Can a music specialist ordinarily spend enough time in each classroom to develop music successfully?
6. Do the elementary music teachers you know devote most of their time to teaching or supervising? Is the designation "music supervisor" an official title in most of the schools you know?

# 5 · Why do we have music in the elementary schools?

## *Origin: It Must Have Begun . . . But How?*

Thousands of years ago man discovered music. We don't know exactly how, although we wonder. Was some primitive man prodded by a sharp stick, and did he respond with a wail covering a range of pitch? Was he curious about the sound; did he try it again? Or, did he accidentally light upon a hot coal from a burning tree and give forth in vocal anguish a crude approximation of a scale, and did his observant children at once imitate him in a delighted fashion? Did he stumble over a hollow log and notice its tone? Did he listen to the wind singing through the trees and try to imitate it?

No one can be sure, because early man never carved on the surface of a cliff any message to the effect that "Today I discovered music. Tomorrow I shall practice. I believe it to be an art!"

## *Today's Musical Environment*

Children do not discover music and realize it at any particular moment of their development in today's world. For however dictators may try, it is impossible to regiment even a way of life, much less individual growth. But, unlike primitive man, children today are born into a world where music is part of their environment. Think in terms of figures alone: over three thousand radio stations operate in the United States, continually pouring music into the ears of adults and children throughout the day and much of the night. Add television and phonographs to this, and there is no difficulty visualizing a musical environment—of sorts.

"Of sorts" is intended to mean "of dubious quality." Probably primitive man was more interested in the nature of sounds he discovered than in an examination of their quality—that is, it is unlikely that he pounded the hollow log and immediately exclaimed, "This is a *poor* tone—let's make it better!" Preschool children are not primarily concerned with the quality of music they hear. We as *teachers* may complain about the quality of music poured out by radio and television—we think we have a legitimate "beef." But on the other hand, we say that children must have a background of musical experiences, so we can build upon it in terms of appreciations, knowledge, and skills. Obviously they have the background, and it is probably at least a beginning if we choose to use it.

One fact stares us in the face—when children come to school, they like music. Yes—they like different kinds of music, because they are different as individuals. Let's not quibble over the kind they like; instead, let's concentrate on the main fact and say, "Good—they like music. We take it from there."

## *Transition to School Music*

Now we can, if we wish, accept these facts: most children have plenty of music in their environment. Children like music. And children differ in their reactions to music. They cross the school threshold and become involved in a school music program. Now things change. For music, to justify its inclusion, must become part of education, must have aims, objectives, and outcomes in a tangible sense. Nothing is wrong with this, unless the child is required to ignore his musical background in the transition to school music.

Let's suppose the teacher wants a class to sing a song appropriate to the opening of school in the morning. So she teaches a greeting song to the first grade; the class greets the teacher by singing "Hello" or "Good Morning"—a kind of primary "Hail

to the Chief" type of song. Most of the children may accept this, because they don't question what the teacher does. But if you see a disinterested look on a few faces, don't be surprised. Why sing a greeting? Who does? For five or six years these children have been arising every morning and *no one* has ever sung to them any formal kind of salutation. Why now?

Remember, you have to expect thinkers, even in the first grade. One of these may think of singing a good, lively tune he has learned from the radio. He generously suggests to the teacher (possibly thinking she needs help) that the class sing *it* instead of "Hello" or whatever. He may even suggest a singing commercial.

*Now* what happens? The teacher says this is not the kind of music we sing in school. Back to "Hello." Well, the thinker figures, who needs to sing "Hello" when everyone says it? He stays mum on this number. But more important, he and the rest of the class may have found that they can write off their background of music—the teacher doesn't want it, there's something wrong with it. Trouble is, they can't write it off—they like it. It's musically more potent and exciting than "Hello" or "Mary Had a Little Lamb." (For that matter, how many urban children have seen a lamb?)

### *Bridging the Gap*

You can see at once that a gap exists between music many children have experienced *before* entering school and music they experience *after* entering school. Yet the basic answer to why music is included in the elementary program is that it is a natural activity for today's children and adults. It is a basic part of our environment, and the school seeks to use the child's environment as a basis for his education. The big job of today's school is to keep it a natural activity for children while at the same time turning their interest toward better music than most they experience on radio and television.

The world of music, like other aspects of the children's world, is an area to be explored, an area of experimentation, an area of self-fulfillment. Johnny, the thinker who feels that singing "Hello" is somewhat phony, may change his mind if he understands that music is an interesting and effective way of conveying a message, a mood, or idea. He may already know that Indians used "drum talk"—now he is learning a whole new world of song—"sound language." But the wise teacher, bridging the gap, will help Johnny discover for himself how people sing salutations; will explain, perhaps, that music is frequently used as a means of greeting.

Yes, music is part of Johnny's environment, as the entire literature of folk and composed music bears witness, but Johnny needs to discover this in his own way, although his method may be far from the accidental discovery of our aboriginal ancestor.

### *Music as Self-Expression*

Another reason why music is part of the curriculum is that it is a means of self-expression. Since the school seeks to help children express themselves, individually and in groups, music falls within the scope of its responsibility.

Ideally, this should be a creative process. But the history of public school music reveals that in the process of organized teaching, creativity all too often vanishes. If we are willing to assume that children are both creative and musical to a degree, we must face the unpleasant fact that the school is at fault for failure to tap these characteristics and start them flowing in the direction of true self-expression.

Children frequently create songs spontaneously as they move in and explore their world. Linda sings in the sandbox, "It is sticky stuff!" when the sand is wet. David, gathering a pail of small stones by the shore and dipping them in the water sings about their shiny, wet smoothness. Mary watches a bird fly and sings, "High, high up!" Is this creative? Yes, for it is a new discovery for each, a translation into song, however naive, of an individual reaction. Who worries about range, pitch, tone? Not Linda, David, or Mary, but the teacher. And when this worry is translated into action concerning improved singing, children become self-conscious and anxious; their spontaneous approach to music vanishes, if indeed it has not already disappeared under the impact of radio and television music.

Somewhere between the early spontaneous music of young children and their conditioning to the dubious music of mass media, interference with an evolving aesthetic sense begins. Yet it is not difficult to stimulate the aesthetic reaction of children during the first few years of school—time and again teachers have noted that children react well to "good" music. This happens chiefly in situations where the teacher does not interfere with the process: she sets up a situation in which children can absorb such music and invites them to listen. The urge toward self-expression in music and an aesthetic reaction to it are part of the same human response.

### *Music Is a Social Art*

Still another reason music is part of the curriculum is that it has social values. This is not limited to participation in a chorus, band, or other performance group. Music is a key to understanding people everywhere, to learning that we are much alike. Children singing a lullaby are transferring the feeling of a parent toward a child, and although they may not understand it in a mature sense, they understand the feeling of affection and security gained through singing the music. In singing of home, family, and all the familiar aspects of everyday living, these same children identify with their world. Singing games, informal play with music through drums, chants, spontaneous rhythmic movement—all these are social in their origin, all these bring about the interplay of one child with a world of children and adults—and this through sound and motion. Here is something to do with a minimum of talking and a maximum of doing. Later these same children will know their world better through pooling their musical resources in the making of music, or through the skilled efforts of certain individuals who give their talent for the enjoyment and understanding of the group. And this is social, for it is the product of a people or of many peoples' musical heritage.

### *Music Belongs to Everyone*

Music is a part of the school curriculum because it belongs to all the children of all the people. This may become another stumbling block to music education, however. In the effort to produce skilled performing groups, the music program is often centered around those children who show the greatest talent or interest in music. Does the music curriculum really belong to the children? Within the framework of the public schools are we able to build a music program that will take care of the entire range of musical talent, taste, and interests of all the children? If we are to do so, it means changes in our thinking. Facing facts, we cannot remain on Cloud 90 and at the same time plant two feet solidly in the classroom of Jefferson School where 35 eight-year-olds are waiting for music. The very strength of music in a democracy is its ability to assimilate the various contributions of many national and ethnic groups—drawing them into the circle instead of shutting them out. The school music program must evidence this same broad scope.

### *Music Is a Real Subject*

Finally, music is part of the school curriculum because it is a subject with its own discipline—a subject through which children may gain knowledge, skill, and appreciation. No need to be apologetic about this, either; just a need to keep the process from becoming a deadly bore. This, too, is a teacher responsibility, for no subject is more interesting than the teacher helps it become *in the minds* of the children she teaches.

#### • FOOD FOR THOUGHT

1. How do children acquire their musical values?
2. Listen to a sample of music from four or five radio stations in your locality, tuning in for a period of several days, six or seven times a day. What percentage of classical music do you hear from such sampling? At what age do you think listening to music on radio and television affects children?
3. Observe small children as they play. In what ways do they express themselves in music?
4. Why does music deserve a place in the curriculum? Should it be considered an extra?
5. Do you believe that school music really can change the musical values of children for the better? How?

# 6 · Elementary school music: Content and method

## *Music Is a Creative, Self-Expressive Art*

The newborn child cries at the moment of his entrance into the world. This is an act of self-expression: the utterance of a sound. It is this self-expression we have noted as a most important reason for including music in the school curriculum. The approach to music as a self-expressive art is closely related to the creative approach in children's musical development.

But look at your school music program—how much evidence of self-expression and creativity in children's musical response can you spot? Probably not much. For it is precisely at this point that we often fail to distinguish between group performance of music and self-expression in music. Let's attempt to discover how we *can* place the emphasis where it belongs—on music as a self-expressive and creative activity in the elementary school.

We want to build for children a program of music activities through which they can express themselves. Now, do you notice that when we talk in terms of schools we tend to speak of groups, of children in the plural? This may be a trap, for it causes us to forget the individual's reactions and think in terms of more or less rigid group reactions.

For example, teachers often ask what they should expect of children at a certain grade level. The answer to this is at once the only possible answer and also no answer at all—it depends upon the group of children being considered, and as every teacher knows, groups of children vary almost as much as individual children vary. "I have a *good* class this year," a teacher will report to her principal, or, "This third grade is certainly not as good as last year's." What she means is that she has fallen into the habit of expecting every class to fit a picture she has built up over a period of years. But children just don't fall into neat patterns, and teachers are forced to notice the differences.

Unfortunately, the more teachers attempt to make children conform to a pattern, the more resistance they are likely to meet. And this resistance may be the very core of the self-expression we are discussing. In the plural, it should be handled as group expression growing out of, but not identical with, individual expression. The group influences the individual in either of two ways—it may repress him, or it may free him. In the one case we usually find the child failing to express *himself* and trying to imitate. Creatively speaking, this is not what we hope for. The imitative pattern is useful, but not for this. But when the group climate and behavior is such that it encourages the child to be himself in music activities, the reaction is much more likely to be a creative one.

Therefore the teacher, if the function of music is to be an expressive one for children, must strive to maintain a classroom climate in which children may "be themselves" both in group and in individual activity (within, of course, the boundaries of acceptable social behavior). In the following discussion of the music program, we shall be specific about ways and means, but right now let's face one fact: if music is to be accepted as an expressive art we have been giving little more than lip service to this concept where children are concerned. Why? The simplest way to put the answer is that we have been too concerned with making the music *sound* good to ask whether the children *feel good* about making it.

### *Ready for Music?*

Have you ever noticed that it seems to be the fashion to dissect each curriculum into many categories when writing about it? Sometimes it appears that we are thinking, "The more dissection, the better the curriculum," so we chop finer and finer. We will avoid the "chop-chop" procedure here; for our purposes, let's say that we will base music curriculum content on two major divisions which continually overlap; these are making music and listening to music.

(Now unless you notice that qualifying *"which continually overlap,"* you'll miss the point of the whole philosophy underlying the approach—for music can't really be dissected, even though the curriculum can. If dissected, it ceases to be music; it deteriorates, very likely, into musical busywork.)

Let's see how this works out. Take the situation in which Tommy, a pre-school child, is given (or comes upon) a drum. The first thing he does is investigate it. He may sit on it, roll it around, or feel it as preliminary steps. But sooner or later, Tommy hits it, particularly if there is a drumstick or mallet handy; otherwise he will use his hand or fist. The *sound* is one that further stimulates Tommy's native curiosity, so he continues to hit it for a while, *but not necessarily with a musical purpose.* Still, something about the sound may arouse a musical impulse; Tommy may chant or sing as he "plays" the drum.

This is not "cute" as some adults might say should they be watching. Nor does it reveal musical talent. It is simply a free activity. To turn this in the direction of a musical experience, does Tommy need guidance? Or will he, if left to his own devices, proceed independently toward a musical activity?

In answering this question we come face to face with a concept known to every educator, but not necessarily understood—the concept of readiness. In the simplest terms, let's look at it this way:

Children, at any given point in their development, are ready to achieve through experiences. *The primary emphasis should be on what they can achieve at the present.* It should be on getting them *ready* for future achievement as a secondary emphasis. This secondary emphasis should grow out of the primary emphasis. Nothing complicated about it—we are simply saying that Johnny is all ready to do certain things today, that he *can* do them with satisfaction, enjoyment, and mastery, and that doing them will prepare him for doing other things tomorrow, next week, next month, next year. Our job is to identify the things he can do now, and help him use them in learning to do others.

If the concept of readiness at times has been shot at but missed in educational implementation, could it be because we have been so busy getting children *ready to do things* that too often they have not *done* much of anything? Does the tomorrow we are getting them ready for always come? Let's avoid the mistake of assuming that it does as we develop their music program. Instead, *let's try to make sure it does.*

## *Basic Concepts*

Making music—listening to music. Trimming this down to basic concepts, we come up with the following:

1. *The Concept:* The music program should include many opportunities for individual expression of the *child's* feelings about music.

*An Illustration:* Take that business of drums. Children in the early grades should be given opportunities to investigate these fascinating instruments. Use them often. Let children take turns playing them. (In the interest of sanity you won't turn a whole class loose upon ten or twelve drums!)

If Tommy hits the drum *hard* and says, "Bang! bang!" as he does, don't stop him. He won't do this forever; he will watch other children with drums and learn that there are other ways to use them. But for the time being, this is Tommy's way of expressing himself through a new voice. Yes, the sound may be very crude music, if music at all, *but*—accept it. In doing so, you are accepting Tommy, giving him solid ground upon which to stand.

Where will he go from the "Bang! bang!" stage? Perhaps toward expressing the movement of people, animals, machines; perhaps toward translating speech into drum sounds. He will move in the same way children move when they acquire a language and a vocabulary; from crude, unrefined noises into coherent speech, learning loud, soft, fast, slow, long, short sounds, *and their associated meanings.*

Over a long period of time his aural and muscular control of these sounds will refine as his *understanding of their meaning* becomes more comprehensive. He will be able to produce more nearly the sounds his ideas and feelings are telling him to produce. This is emerging technical skill. Still later he will learn to produce the *exact* sound a composer tells him to produce through the printed page, the musical score. This is the music reading skill.

But notice! The whole growth sequence originates in Tommy's own feelings about the drum and its voice, in *making* and *listening to* sounds—musical or otherwise.

2. *The Concept:* The music program should include many opportunities for the *group's* expression of musical feelings.

*An Illustration:* How can a group express its own musical feelings? Here, unless we move delicately, we may get from the class a distorted image: what they think the teacher wants in the way of *her* feelings about music.

Yet young children can express a mood, a spirit in music, very well indeed if we don't let details of technical performance interfere. Remember, expression here should come from the inside; from inside the children into the song.

How can children sing a lullaby? From their own realization of the importance of love and security as they have learned these from their parents, grandparents, other relatives; even if they have not, simply from their own deep need of such qualities.

Now of course no teacher would try to explain this to children in so many words. What she *can* do is help them visualize, feel, understand the situation in which a lullaby is sung, thus tapping an emotional release that, although naive, is valid.

Children are not likely to achieve choral perfection in the way of tone, phrasing, and so on. In fact, the more the teacher presses for such perfection, the more likely she is to have an artificial response.

But why should we expect young children to sound like a trained chorus? Simply because some of us still have a mental image of first and second graders as a kind of angelic choir, looking sweet and otherworldly? Remember that in the situation where all children are singing at their own level of musical achievement—and this includes control of the voice—there will be quite a few different sounds. Some will come from children who have not yet learned to sing "in tune," others from children who do not yet have the concept of a pleasant vocal sound.

Yet these same children may be expressing themselves through a song. Do you want to slow down—even put an end to—their musical growth? If so, an effective way is to make them so aware of their shortcomings that they will be afraid to "join in" with group expression experiences. As with the individual, the procedure is to accept, recognize what is good through honest praise, give each child a secure basis of participation, and provide a wealth of singing experiences through which the group may mature.

3. *The Concept:* Both of the above should encompass a basic creative approach in which the integrity of children's attitudes toward music is preserved. The children's impulse to create music of their own, however crude the efforts, should be encouraged.

*An Illustration:* This basic creative approach implies much leeway in encouraging children to interpret the music they sing and hear. It also implies care and understanding on the part of the teacher in selecting suitable materials. Is it necessary, for example, for each class to sing a song about a policeman just because it is in the book? What about the first grade rural child who has not seen a policeman guarding the school crosswalk or directing traffic? Obviously he cannot interpret such a song. Or the city child who has never seen the mountains, the inland child who has not seen the ocean—how can they express themselves in songs about these? Remember, if we want children to make music creatively they must first sing about things familiar to them.

And what blocks children from making songs of their own? Usually the fact that as teachers we consider their attempts crude, not musical enough, not patterned or technically good. Yet this is true of the beginning efforts of most creative artists. Is it necessary to come out with a miniature art song written on the chalkboard to have a valid creative experience? The early efforts of children should really be no efforts—they should be spontaneous song-like response minus the net scooped about to capture the result. Encourage children to sing about the things they know, the things they do, let the process go on for a long, long time, help when help is needed and welcome, and the technical end of the process will grow. Remember, though, that these may be children who can't yet spell, read, or add in some cases; please refrain from expecting their songs to sound like the Brahms' "Lullaby."

4. *The Concept:* A broad experience in appreciative activities, through listening to and making music, should be continually in progress.

*An Illustration:* Appreciation of music differs for each child as his values differ, as his stage of development differs. Now appreciation embraces, in its various connotations and implications, sensitivity and responsiveness, along with a developing understanding.

Each teacher can help children here. Provide many opportunities for them to absorb music—recognize their responses to it. This is not a highly structured process in its early stages. It is a matter of helping the child become aware, a matter of helping him build and vitalize his musical concepts. Some of these concepts, for example, might have to do with good singing tone, sounds of different instruments, the rhythmic swing of music.

A child develops his concept of "house" as he notices many houses, of "day" as he becomes aware of the differences between day and night, or the passing of many days. He gains a concept of flight by watching birds and airplanes fly. In much the same way he builds his concepts of music—but with the emphasis on the aural experience. If a young child listens to many songs sung by different singers with good tone quality, he will form a concept of desirable singing tone, through his response to these experiences.

Nor does the teacher need to say, "*This* is what is good." She needs only to provide it in sufficient quantity. The child will make his own mental labels.

5. *The Concept:* The re-creative experience, in which children bring into play their own feelings toward music composed by great musicians, is close to the "pure" creative experience.

*An Illustration:* Both the creative and the appreciative aspects are brought into play when children "re-create" music. Where the creative and the re-creative diverge is difficult to say, with young children, and it doesn't much matter. What does matter is keeping the artificial parrot-like performance of music out of the classroom. If you want an example of this latter, take a look at some of the child "stars" who perform adult music on stage and television.

6. *The Concept:* Children's participation in the music program may be active—making music—or absorptive—listening to music. Either may be *abortive* if the teacher interferes with, instead of nurtures, the child's true musical values, whatever these may be.

*An Illustration:* When children are making music, it is active participation. When they are absorbing music by listening to others, it may not be active in the sense of physical muscular participation. But the process of musical participation may be taking place, even with the child who is just sitting. To interfere with this may be disturbing; at least wait and see what emerges from each child's participation.

7. *The Concept:* Building skills in music is a legitimate function of the school music program. Such skills should be based upon *cognitive perception of the musical experience* and the objective to which the skill is related.

*An Illustration:* From the time a child first hears music he is building skills. He is learning the *sound* of music. When he has acquired a broad base of musical experience, it is the teacher's job to help him use what he already knows and to point out or help him acquire in a functional way further musical skills. What do we mean by "cognitive perception?" Simply that the child gains the musical skill through a *thinking* and *sensing* process. And, of course, the functional part of the process is that his skill must emerge from the experience he has with music, and must be used for an acceptable—to him—and satisfying musical end.

## *Scope of the Elementary Music Program*

If the music program in our schools is satisfactory, it will include *at least* the following:

1. Singing many songs, not only during "music period" but at other times during the school day. The singing experience can be a relaxing one at times when children are tense, it can be stimulating when children are fatigued, it can promote the development of insight if thoughtfully used in relation to other subject areas and activities.

2. Using classroom rhythm, melody, and harmony instruments for song accompaniments, rhythmic interpretations and dramatizations, creating melodies and dances, and exploring tonal and rhythmic relationships. Instruments include drums of various kinds, castanets, maracas, tuned glasses, bells, Autoharps, Harmolins, flutes, and so on.

3. Copious use of live performances and recorded materials for both "quiet" and "reactive" listening. "Quiet" listening is often employed to mean that children simply listen. "Reactive" listening is purposeful in terms of participation—children listen to, notice, and react to instruments, melody, rhythm, harmony, form, or any combination of these and other musical factors.

4. Classroom programs in which children have a cooperative experience in contributing or pooling their musical interests and abilities for the benefit of each other.

5. Experiences in translating (a) musical action into notation and (b) the musical score in terms of musical action. Such experiences should be directly related to making or listening to music. The goal is making possible greater enjoyment of music through increased facility.

6. Music used in association with other areas and experiences.

7. Opportunity to learn band and orchestra instruments and to play these instruments in ensembles. (Informal use in the classroom when appropriate is also desirable.)

### *How Do the Classroom Teacher and the Music Specialist Work Together?*

No two individuals will have exactly the same pattern of working together. The work of each, however, should complement the work of the other.

(A) Miss Burns, a third grade teacher, finds her class interested in fire engines. She arranges to take them on a trip to a local fire house where they see several fire engines and other equipment. The firemen show how the ladders work; they explain how they put out fires. When the class returns to school they talk about the trip, and among other things, decide to relive it through a musical interpretation. As they describe and act out the sounds and actions, they develop a musical version with drums, voices, Autoharp, piano, bottles:

1. Miss Burns and the class describe the trip and write a list of sounds and actions on the chalkboard as they do so.

2. They write a note to the music teacher asking that she help them with their project on her next visit. Included is a list of instruments they think they would like to use.

3. The music teacher brings the materials requested plus any others she feels may be useful.

4. After exploring the ideas of the children in group discussion, she helps them sound the various instruments to see how they may be used.

5. Classroom teacher and specialist help children interpret from chalkboard description the sights, sounds, and activities of the fire house. Some outcomes in rhythmic and sound interpretation might be:

(a) Child blows fire whistle—empty pop bottle.

(b) Firemen run for trucks—irregular drum beats, using various size drums.

(c) Firemen climb in trucks—using lower-pitched to higher-pitched drum sounds to indicate climbing.

(d) Trucks drive off—children show how they move, imitating sounds. Sirens are imitated with voices.

(e) Truck drives over bumpy road—big drum imitates.

The above are only a few of the motions and sounds children may suggest. The teachers should be careful to stimulate but not dominate the flow of ideas as children express their interpretation of the experience. The key to this activity is to accept all ideas and try them; some will be found more appropriate than others, but each child should be given the opportunity to participate, and the ideas of each child will find a place somewhere in the group's discussion.

(B) The question of when to place songbooks in the hands of children often perplexes both music specialist and classroom teacher. Here is an opportunity to combine the knowledge of both in the interests of the children. One group handled it this way:

1. Classroom teachers (or a committee of teachers) met with music specialist. *Various viewpoints* were expressed:

(a) All children should be given books in first grade to familiarize them with the look of the printed musical score.

(b) Children should begin to learn to read music at the same time they begin to read language.

(c) Some children lack the background of musical experiences that should precede the use of the printed page. Extensive aural experience should precede the visual.

(d) The musical score is complex. Each page contains a multitude of notes, clefs, bars, staffs—this is confusing to the child and beyond his visual comprehension. It becomes a meaningless experience.

(e) Premature introduction of the printed music may be frustrating to the child who does not understand it, thus causing negative attitudes toward music.

These viewpoints represented diverging opinions. In some situations friction might have resulted, causing an impasse to effective planning. But in this situation, a general supervisor conducted the meeting. He encouraged the expression of all viewpoints, then asked the group to consider the basic reason for the use of songbooks.

After considerable discussion, it was agreed that the songbooks were used to help children develop skill in making music through the assistance of the musical score. Learning a song, furthermore, implies both the reading of words and the reading of music when books are used. But the group decided that the reading of music grows out of the broad objective of providing a wide range of musical experiences and should not be separated from the actual making of music. Once having agreed upon this, it appeared obvious that emphasis upon developing reading skill was insignificant unless grounded in the larger development of understanding the whole art of music as it functions in children's lives.

This group of teachers decided that the basic factor in deciding when to introduce songbooks was the ability of children to *translate abstract symbols into meaningful musical action.* This means that one indication of the right time would be language reading ability. Another indication would be the children's ability to express themselves easily and fluently through music—songs, rhythmic motion, listening—both creatively and re-creatively.

Jane Horn, a fourth grade teacher, brought up the familiar question: "How shall we manage to keep children at an approximate level of learning experiences when it looks as though different classes may receive books at different times?" Immediately another teacher pointed out that this was a reason for putting books in the hands of all classes at the same time. But Miss Horn, having thought a bit more, said, "If we could agree to be flexible in what we expect a class of children to know when they enter a higher grade, this business of books would not have to be handled so rigidly. After all, a book should not dominate a child. It should be a tool to assist in his development."

In effect, this was the viewpoint adopted by the group as a working agreement. No teacher should expect children to meet rigid musical standards upon admission to a higher grade level. And for the sake of a broad type of uniformity, these teachers further agreed that in their particular situation songbooks could be introduced, using exploratory techniques, sometime in the second grade, probably in the last three or four months of the school year. By this time all children would have sung many songs, listened to much recorded music, participated in rhythmic activities. The group suggested that children might be ready for songbooks when:

1. They had a large repertory of songs.

2. They had learned to notice the "ups" and "downs," the "longs" and "shorts" of melodies.

3. They were sensitive to the mood of music and the ideas of music as expressed in songs, rhythms, records.

4. They had had some experience in creating songs and "rhythm stories" (such as the one described in the firehouse field trip) and had worked with putting these in a rough musical code, for example, using dashes of different lengths and at different heights on the chalkboard.

5. (See preceding discussion of language reading ability.)

While songbooks may be used occasionally as interest-arousers fairly early in the school experience of young children, these teachers decided that actual translation of musical notation should be postponed until:

1. Children could read language with such a degree of facility that this would not interfere with their attention to the notation.

2. Children could use and recognize printed numbers with enough facility to locate pages in the songbook.

*In the actual reading of music, it was agreed that the main focus should be on the recognition of a musical idea.* In other words, emphasis that concentrates on the recognition of a single tonal pattern of two or three notes will have little significance musically. A composer *says something* musically in a phrase or a period. Just as children learn to look for an idea as they read language, they should look for a musical idea as they read music; they should try to recognize what the notes say in music. Concentration on the recognition and performance of smaller units of tonal or rhythm patterns grows out of the "big idea"; these units contribute to the whole idea and should be used as drill or emphasis areas as they increase recognition and musical translation of the idea.

If you had attended the meeting at which the foregoing discussion took place, you would have noticed that there was no dividing line between the classroom teachers and the music specialists. Perhaps this was largely due to the skilled leadership of the general supervisor who chaired the meeting. Basically, however, it grew from the confidence music specialists felt in the classroom teachers and vice versa, and from an atmosphere free from tension. No teacher felt that, having stated his viewpoint, he would be attacked by another. Each was genuinely interested in finding a solution to a perplexing problem, each was willing to explore and perhaps compromise a bit in order to arrive at a working solution. In the end, although there was not unanimity of thinking in one direction, these teachers arrived at a working agreement. Perhaps it is better that there should not be one-hundred-per-cent agreement, for this might imply an unwillingness to change in future years. What is important is that a sound basis for procedure was formulated with the assent of all interested parties.

## *Helping Children Improve Their Singing Voices*

The reasons why children fail, in their early school experience, to sing "in tune" or to repeat a melody accurately are well known and have been cited by many authors and lecturers.

Chiefly, these are lack of interest in or responsiveness to pitch, failure to relate singing voice and aural perception, and lack of confidence in ability to sing. Sometimes, but rarely, a child has a physical handicap in the way of hearing loss or nasal and/or throat obstruction that is a significant cause of inability to progress in the singing experience. Since these latter two are only susceptible to help through medical attention, the teacher's function is simply to notice signs that indicate their presence and refer the matter to the school nurse. A closer look at the first reasons and some suggestions are:

1. Kenny's musical background appeared to be sharply limited when he entered first grade. He sang lower than the other children, and seemed to have little concept of the "tune."

The teacher helped the entire class notice the different pitches of various sounds such as bells, train whistles, voices (speaking and singing), and helped children make a picture chart of these sounds with high, low, or varying degrees of pitch represented. She called their attention to the sound of a whole tune—the way it "stayed together" and compared it with a spoken sentence that had an understandable idea. She did not single out Kenny for special attention, but encouraged him to participate naturally with the other children as they explored these activities. As Kenny acquired more musical experiences, he began singing normally.

2. Jane, a second grade pupil, did not sing "in tune" with the rest of the class. In general she seemed to have a sharply limited attention span—this applied to all her school work. The teacher described her as withdrawn at times and easily distracted. The teacher felt that Jane was probably inattentive to the sound of a melody. Instead of making an issue of this, the teacher saw that Jane had opportunities, along with the other children, to participate in activities that aroused a high degree of attention and interest; for instance, playing the melody on bells.

3. Richard's home background was musically good, but

this was not much help to him since he had often heard his mother, who was an accomplished singer, tell her friends that "Richard just can't sing at all." Actually, Richard's singing was not at fault; he sang like many children, but often did not repeat a tune exactly as he heard it or in the same key. Since Richard had been discouraged from singing by his mother, his confidence had to be restored before he was willing to join wholeheartedly in the singing activities of the class. This was a case where the home had set standards of achievement too high for a child to reach. Richard was encouraged to participate in many musical activities besides singing, and proved to enjoy rhythmic play particularly. Gaining approval and security through this, he gradually gained the experience and security he needed to improve his singing.

Notice that at no point in the three cases cited did a teacher single out a child for remedial work. Instead, the individual variations of children's musical behavior were accepted, just as their variations in other areas were accepted. They were noted, and something was done about them, but without embarrassment to the child and without demanding immediate conformity to a set, rigid standard of performance. In each case the teacher explored until she found areas in which the child could succeed, and through these successes built toward further success in areas of weakness.

Children succeed through believing that they *can* succeed, and with regard to this principle, music is no different from other subjects or activities. When a teacher understands this, every child will be able to find a satisfying place in the music program.

Have you ever watched a group of first grade children running home after school? How often they are waving papers in their hands as they run! Why? Some teacher has said, "These are *good!* Take them home and show them to your mother." And each child runs proudly along the street, just a bit more confident and secure. The accolade of praise is a magic touchstone to continued efforts—use it often.

## *Listening to Music*

Children soak up music as a sponge soaks up water. Music is everywhere in their world—radio, television, movies, juke boxes, phonographs. Yet they never become saturated with music as a part of their free environment. Perhaps this is why many teachers have found that playing records of music in the classroom at various times, while children rest or while they are busy with other things, seems almost a normal activity.

Although we have said that music is everywhere in their world, we have not said that it should be *their* music. For much of the music children hear is popular music, music designed to attract and stimulate adult attention. True, children pick up and sing the songs we have in mind. But it is not music intended for children—and this is the point. Certainly we do not intend to divide music into "child" and "adult" categories; some very poor music has been written particularly for children. We are saying that since children may hear too much of one kind of music outside of school—and not necessarily music intended for them—the school should balance their diet. Young children have an affinity for what we loosely call "good" music; they can absorb this as easily as music of lesser quality. Here are some of the ways in which the music listening experience can be handled as part of the elementary program:

1. In the primary grades, non-directed (absorptive) listening experiences should be provided frequently. These may be for purposes of relaxation or, when indicated by children's behavior, for stimulation. The Bach "Air for the G String" would be appropriate for the former; by contrast, "Scheherazade" by Rimsky-Korsakov might serve as a "pick-up" for a class in low spirits.

Would playing a record (for example "Scheherazade") as background music while children work at their desks be distracting? Since children are largely accustomed to music as a background for other activities outside of school, the answer is probably, "No—it will not be distracting." However, the teacher can determine this by observing children's reactions, and by considering the type of work they are doing when the record is to be played.

2. The interpretive (re-creative) listening experience helps children develop a sensitivity to music. In this we encourage children to listen for a mood, to talk about, draw about, or move to music as it affects them. Since children differ, a wide variation in response to music is to be expected. Some children will be more articulate than others in listening, some more imaginative in their interpretation. Basically, this may be considered to be a self-projection into and an identification with music.

3. Building listening skills is the third (re-active) phase of the experience. Here children, after a broad basis of listening to music, direct their attention to listening for instruments, voices, form, composers' styles, and so on. This activity develops gradually from the kind of listening mentioned in (1) and (2). Gradually, remember! To force it is to kill the spirit of the music.

From all of these (and certainly they are never entirely separated one from another) children build a sense of values concerning music.

Here is one example of a listening experience plan. Many ways of possible development are noted, although certainly not all of these would be included in any one experience, due to limitations of time and material.

The objective of the plan? An interesting musical experience for children, leading to greater understanding and appreciation of music.

### A Plan for the Use of Records in the Elementary Classroom

Name of Record: The Cat's Fugue, *by Domenico Scarlatti*
Grade Level or Age Group: *9-11 years, approximately*

Probable Appeal to Children: *The music is lively. The tune is easily recognized. The idea of the cat discovering the tune is appealing and arouses interest. Teacher may read story of music either before or after class hears music.*

Rhythmic Activities: *Dramatizing rhythmically the walking of the cat.*

Singing Participation: *The use of any round will aid in understanding way the fugue is built.*

Songs To Be Used with Lesson: *Choose from songbooks used in class. Look for melodic, rhythmic, structural, or subject similarities.*

Subject Correlation: *Add words to spelling list; for example, "fugue" and "Scarlatti." Scarlatti lived during our Colonial period. Did we have a King then? Were we friendly with Italy and Spain? Locate on map.*

Classroom Activities Correlation: *Make a bulletin board with appropriate material.*

Out-of-School Correlation: *Watch a cat walk. How does he move his feet? Tell the story of "The Cat's Fugue" to your parents or your friends.*

Activities for Advanced Children: *Read more about the life of Scarlatti. Listen to another fugue—"The Fugue in G Minor" by Bach. Look up material on the harpsichord. How is it different from the piano? Did Scarlatti play piano or harpsichord?*

Activities for Slow Learners: *Find pictures for bulletin board. Participate in rhythmic activities as above.*

Other Activities: *Discuss why some keys have higher pitch than others. Does the "cat's" theme always begin on the same pitch?*

Musical Learning: *Use of theme notated on chalkboard; point out differences in ascending and descending passages. Point out pattern of fugue and meaning of term. Discuss time signature and tempo.*

Questions to Put on the Chalkboard: *Listen to the music of "The Cat's Fugue" and try to discover answers to these questions:*

1. *How many times do we hear the tune?*
2. *Is it always exactly the same?*
3. *Does it ever begin on a lower note than it does the first time we hear it?*
4. *Is it like a round where the parts not only begin one after another but also end one at a time, or do all the parts end together?*

Other Chalkboard Material: *Differences between harpsichord and piano:*

1. *The strings of the harpsichord are plucked by leather "quills." The strings of the piano are struck by felt hammers.*
2. *The harpsichord often has two, and sometimes three, keyboards. The piano has only one.*

Excellent notes on "The Cat's Fugue" will be found in Lillian Baldwin's *Music for Young Listeners, The Blue Book.**

## *Singing in the Upper Elementary Grades*

Sometimes we have to make an assumption, and a general one at that. Our general assumption at this point is:

Children will be interested in beginning some part-singing by the time they are in the fourth grade if they have had a good music experience in the first three grades. (Of course, they will continue singing many unison songs.)

This point of departure can give or take several months or even a year. Part-singing is harmonizing, so remember that this means singing one part with another, not *against*. All of us who have taught music in the schools are familiar with children who attempt to sing one part *against* another by stuffing their fingers in their ears. The minute you see this, a red light should flash on in your mind. It means that the child with the stuffed-up ears is not listening to the other part and singing

*Morristown, N. J.: Silver Burdett Co., 1951.

with it—it means that he is battling it, trying to escape from it.

Now in singing, as in every other music activity, we have to listen before we can reproduce. Music is an *aural* art; even Beethoven, totally deaf so that he coud not hear the actual sound of the Ninth Symphony as he conducted it and had to be turned around so he could see the audience applauding, heard it in his "inner ear."

Just as we can think without speaking aloud, so children develop the ability to listen for and hear the sound of music without singing aloud; they then extend this skill by singing one part while listening to another . . . literally fitting together the sound of the two parts. This calls for the fine coordination of actually hearing two parts and singing one . . . and children can do it well, with satisfaction and musical enjoyment. Except, of course, when they lack the background of musical experiences that makes it possible for them to sing in harmony with sufficient ease and facility to enjoy the music they are making. Or when the teacher drills so long on first one part and then the other that they seem like two separate musical entities instead of one *whole.*

Now—how are today's teachers developing satisfactory part-singing in accordance with the above philosophy? Here are some of the ways:

1. Singing rounds—listening to recordings of rounds.

2. Accompanying a round with any one part of the same round. For example, "Three Blind Mice" may be sung straight through by one group of children while another group harmonizes by singing only the first line: "three blind mice."

3. Harmonizing certain melodies a third above or a sixth below. (If this use of interval terms bothers you, try singing the last three notes of "Drink to Me Only . . . "; now sing them three notes higher. This is harmonizing in thirds. Move this harmony part down an octave and you will be harmonizing in sixths.)

4. Chording with the 1st, 4th and 5th notes of the scale as they sound right.

5. Trying all the above with sets of bells, piano, tuned glasses. Children enjoy this—furthermore, it is generally agreed that such reinforcements of the vocal experience are particularly effective with children who lack confidence in their singing ability.

Have you observed, in reading these suggestions, that they are all aural in approach—"by ear"? The making of music is rooted in the hearing of music, the "listening for and to" of the music maker. It is *not* rooted in the reading of notes, for that is the visual-mechanical aspect of the experience. It is rooted in the aural aspect.

Newer song texts incorporate all these approaches to the development of part-singing. In addition, there are recorded songs from each book in albums available to the teacher and children so they can hear the sound of the harmony. It is certainly desirable for each school to have these recordings available for use. They are stimulating and revealing to children and teacher as well.

Should children try to imitate these records? No, of course not; why set an impossible goal? And imitation would bring about an artificial result. The records are best used as part of the listening-singing process. And, of course, to help classroom teachers who lack confidence in their singing ability. But don't over-use—you may stultify initiative and spontaneity in the children's singing.

## *Elementary Teachers Can—and Do—Teach Music*

"Go ahead and teach it," says the principal to the classroom teacher. "Oh, come on now; you can certainly teach some music the days I'm not here," says the music helping teacher to Mrs. Lucas.

But although Mrs. Lucas may smile weakly and seem to agree, she is thinking to herself, "I won't. Because I can't. And I'm not going to make a fool of myself trying."

The trouble is, no one is giving Mrs. Lucas definite suggestions to help her skate across the thin ice of teaching music. Just saying to her that she can, she should, and implying that she must, won't help a bit.

There are ways, however, in which every elementary teacher can carry on the music program in her classroom. And all of the ways are as desirable for the teacher with a strong background in music as for Mrs. Lucas and her apprehensive rebel company.

1. Many songs from the basic song texts are available in recorded albums. Children can learn the songs by listening to these records. Mrs. Lucas can ask for the albums and a small phonograph.

2. Many free, imaginative, and creative musical activities are possible whether or not the teacher can sing in tune, read music, or play the piano. Rhythmic activities are attractive to all children.

3. Every teacher can do competent work in the area of listening experiences.

4. Every teacher can relate the musical activities of the class to other areas; art and social sciences are two good examples.

5. Every teacher can ask to have musical instruments brought into her classroom for demonstration.

6. Every teacher can borrow a set of bells and pick out a few tunes on them, then use them in class to add simple harmony parts, help children make up tunes, devise two or three-note introductions to songs.

7. Every teacher can use rhythm instruments to dramatize a story. The clippety-cloppety of a horse's hoofs can be a wood block, coconut shells, or even cupped hands pressed together. From such simple steps the teacher, growing in confidence, may have her class moving to drums, tambourines, and other instruments.

8. Every teacher can help children collect objects to be-

come part of a classroom musical collection. A horseshoe is used in some classrooms as a triangle; a piece of metal with a good musical sound serves the same purpose. Bottles, empty or filled with various amounts of water, will produce tones of definite pitch. Teachers can also help children make rhythm instruments such as drums, sand blocks, shakers, or jingle sticks. (Remember that such instruments should have good tone.)

9. Every teacher can locate the wealth of material available on teaching music—if she wants to.

10. Every teacher can attend in-service workshops or lectures on ways to teach music.

11. Every music teacher can look for ways to help. Every classroom teacher can *ask* for help. *Every teacher can teach music—if she wants to!*

### *The Instrumental Program*

The sparkle of the gold, silver, nickel, brass, the gleam of the wood on musical instruments is never as bright as the eyes of the children who gaze upon them. What do they see—a musical extension of themselves, the sharp, smart colors of the band marching down the street, the massed instruments on the stage before a receptive audience, eager to applaud? Do they hear in that "inner ear" we mentioned the strains of music to be made? Do they somehow feel the joy of "belonging" that comes from membership in a musical group, the feeling of identity with something bigger than the individual? Is it the desire for self-expression that shines in their faces? Whatever it is, seldom is there a dearth of eager aspirants to play instruments. And whatever it is, we believe the instrumental part of the school music program is rooted in the same philosophy as is the general or classroom portion of the program.

Any normal child can learn to play an instrument. The embryo instrumentalist, then, is not a specialist in any sense of the word. Nor is he necessarily more talented than his fellows. Some children, of course, do possess a high degree of musical talent; they will become more skilled as musicians, given the same opportunities as the less talented. The basic premise here is to expect that children will progress and achieve differently as they study an instrument.

When should we introduce the instrumental program in the elementary school? A few guiding principles are:

1. When the child is mature enough to understand the 'discipline' of caring for an instrument, bringing it to school, practicing.

2. When the child is physiologically able to handle the instrument. This means in terms of size of child in relation to instrument, coordination, jaw and dental development in the case of wind instruments, eye development in relation to reading music.

3. Since most public school instrumental instruction is class instruction, a limited amount of individual attention is possible for each child. Children must be of adequate intelligence to benefit from this particular type of instruction.

4. A reasonable effort should be made to screen from the beginning program children whose desire to play an instrument is only a passing fancy. Genuine musical interest is the best safeguard against a high dropout rate. Those who seem not to possess such interest should be advised to postpone instrumental work.

5. A specific grade level at which to introduce the instrumental program may be either fourth or fifth. Although it is sometimes placed at third grade level, the greater maturity of fourth and fifth grade children seems to indicate faster progress and a more rewarding musical experience.

6. If the school offers instrumental instruction, it should be a regular part of the school program. No charge should be made,* the instruction should be available to all qualifying children, and it should be provided on school time.

* This does not apply to the rental of school-owned instruments.

A sound instrumental program contributes to the development rather than the exploitation of children. There will be many degrees of progress, and we cannot afford to set rigid standards if we are to keep children achieving in the program. This certainly has implications for performing groups in the elementary school.

### *Correlating Instrumental and Vocal Music*

Too often these areas operate on independent schedules. Too often Mickey, who in sixth grade is playing fine trombone, sings a song along with the rest of the class and looks at an instrumental arrangement of the song, wishing the teacher would ask him to bring in his instrument and play the trombone part some day. And Linda with her flute; a flute descant is written in above the notes of the Indian song the class is singing—why doesn't the teacher suggest that she bring her flute to class and play it? Linda has already borrowed the songbook and played the descant at home. But not in school. Wilma plays the cornet. She was quite excited the day Miss Turnet, the music teacher, showed the class pictures of cornet and trumpet. Wilma wondered why Miss Turnet didn't ask her to show the class a *real* cornet; Tom, across the aisle, could have shown them his real trumpet. "The kids could have *heard* what the instruments sound like, too," thinks Wilma to herself.

Everything you're thinking makes sense, Mickey, Linda, and Wilma. Trouble is, the teachers have not planned together. We need a team working here—the instrumental teacher, the classroom teacher, and the music specialist or supervisor. They could inquire about the musical resources of their pupils, discover who plays instruments, including guitar, accordion, harmonica, ukulele, as well as the standard band and orchestra instruments. And they could include these human musical resources in their teaching.

A picture may be worth ten thousand words, but the real thing is worth ten thousand pictures. What do you have in the way of real musical resources in your classrooms? Are you using them? You'll enjoy it; your pupils will, too.

### *The Rhythm Band*

The Occasion: Parent-Teachers Meeting. The Place: stage of the high school auditorium. The Activity: audience listening to first grade rhythm band. The Reaction: applause, laughter, amused comments of parents, teachers, friends.

But no matter how amused the audience, rhythm bands, as they are usually organized and conducted, often bear little or no resemblance to a musical experience. They are more in the nature of a mechanical activity, with children striking various instruments at particular times in a fashion reminiscent of marionettes banging instrumental facsimiles and with just as much understanding. What pleases these adult viewers, apparently, is the children's miniature or toylike imitation of adults.

Yet even the imitation has little or no value, since the small players are not attempting to learn by imitating. They're just going through automatic motions.

The process of training a rhythm band too often is just that—training children to strike various instruments at certain times, but with no conscious consideration of the whole musical cause or effect. This could be done more efficiently with machines than children.

If an elementary teacher took a reader and assigned one child to read the word "and," another the word "house," and each child another word as it occurred in the story, then had one child start and stop the reading, we would have a situation making just as little sense to children as does the rhythm band. Johnny can strike the triangle on the fourth count of 64 measures without ever having a meaningful musical experience. Certainly he'll enjoy it. He enjoys banging with a hammer, too.

The most successful rhythm band episode ever witnessed by one teacher took place when the small player of the tambourine enthusiastically smashed his hand right through the instrument. This brought down the house.

When you figure out why, you'll have the real reason for classifying rhythm bands as something other than musical experiences.

They come a lot closer to show business, so let's face it. Dress them up, let them hit instruments if you must, but don't call it part of the music program.

The desirable rhythmic experiences emerge from the child's initiative and imagination as part of his response to music. Not from a mass attack on percussion by small children behaving like automatons!

The foregoing comments on stilted rhythm band activities, in which the child has little or no opportunity to use musical instruments thoughtfully and creatively, *should not be construed* to mean opposition to the use of rhythm instruments (drums, maracas, castanets, and others) in the classroom. Such instruments are an excellent means of making music and of enriching classroom musical experiences. Interpretations of rhythmic movement, story and poem dramatizations, song accompaniments, explanation and illustration of rhythmic patterns—all these and many other activities call for the use of such instruments. In fact, their use in today's classrooms, both elementary and junior high, is broad in scope; these instruments (as well as others, such as bells and Autoharps) are used to promote legitimate musical growth through musical means. The child who is helped to consider their characteristics and decide upon constructive musical uses for the instruments, then execute the ideas in terms of musical action, is growing both in skill and appreciation.

• FOOD FOR THOUGHT

1. Describe ways the teacher can create a classroom environment in which children will express themselves naturally through music.

2. How can we help children use their present musical achievements as a means of getting ready for others?
3. Seven basic concepts of elementary school music are listed. After reading the illustrating example given for each, write another illustration for each concept.
4. If classes are varied in their talents and abilities, can teachers hope to cover the same music course of study every year in different classes?
5. Make a list of desirable musical experiences for elementary school children. Which experiences will be best suited to various age groups?
6. Discuss several ways in which classroom teachers and music specialists can work well together. Ask two individuals to illustrate by dramatizing a short scene in which they take the parts of classroom teacher and music specialist.
7. Make a lesson plan for any musical composition you think suited to elementary school listening.
8. Ask your friends whether they took piano lessons at any time. Find out how many stopped within two years, and ask why. Analyze these reasons and try to relate to desirable teaching practices.
9. Teach simple two-part songs to a group, using an aural approach—singing, listening, and singing back. Use no notation.
10. Is it possible to set exact standards of achievement on a grade level basis for the music program? On what basis should teachers and supervisors develop suggested standards of achievement?

# 7 · The administrator looks at the elementary music program

### *"Good Morning, Miss Stevens, I'm the Music Teacher"*

Miss Stevens's reaction to the music teacher at the door of her elementary school classroom will determine the extent of achievement of the music program in the room. The combined reaction of all the "Miss Stevenses" of the school will determine the success or failure of the music teacher in the school system. It is important that the music specialist, who gives guidance to the classroom teacher in her music program, or who is responsible for the total music program in the classroom, recognizes the problems in human relations that arise in the Music Specialist-Classroom Teacher relationship and acquires some skill in solving them.

It is also important for the administrator to be aware of those "between-us-girls" tensions which all too frequently disturb the calm of elementary schools. Where a man teaches or supervises elementary school music, the same problems exist, although the universal desire of women to be at their best before men may keep the problems from breaking out in their most virulent form.

### *What Is Your Correct Title?*

The name given to the music specialist varies from place to place according to custom and duties. "Supervisor" is a commonly used term. In some systems, because "supervisor" has come to have an unpleasant connotation, other descriptive titles are used—"helping teacher in music," "music consultant," "special teacher," and so on. What is the best title? About two decades ago, when there was general disagreement and discussion about the titles that should be given to those people who were designated to lead teachers in the improvement of classroom instruction, one of the pioneers in supervision in education remarked in an address, "It doesn't matter what you call them, in six weeks every teacher will know what they are." His words are true today. The important thing is not what we call the music specialist but what she does and how the program grows under her leadership.

### *The Music Specialist as the Music Teacher*

In large elementary schools the music specialist may be the only one in the building who teaches music. The total responsibility for music may be hers. This means that her relationships are 90 per cent with pupils. But the 10 per cent with other teachers may make or break the music program.

There are a few very simple things the music teacher will need to do to make her an accepted part of the school faculty. The successful music teacher in an elementary school:

1. *Learns to Say "Our Pupils"*—

When a music teacher goes into a classroom for twenty minutes a day it is not easy to think of the pupils as being her pupils. It is easy to think of the pupils as belonging to the teacher in whose room she is working. As a result unfortunate remarks such as, "Your pupils were inattentive today," "What happened to your class?" make a breach between classroom teacher and music teacher. The music teacher who thinks, and therefore says, "our," unites her work with that of the regular teacher.

2. *Learns to Know the Pupils' Names*—

This is not quite as impossible as it seems, or not quite as easy as it is to write. One of the major complaints that teachers make is that special subject teachers make no effort to learn the pupils' names. Small seating charts for each classroom are helpful, and because elementary children love to wear badges, music class name cards are quite acceptable to them.

3. *Learns the Curriculum for the Grades*—

If the music program which is taught entirely by the music specialist is not to be separate and apart from all the rest of the school program it will be because of the effort of the music teacher to know the total curriculum of the school. Studying written curriculum guides, observing bulletin boards and chalkboards, examining textbooks, and attending curriculum meetings are the methods available to all music teachers.

4. *Observes Time Limits Carefully*—

The elementary teacher has seen the scope of her work increase yearly without a corresponding increase in time for teaching. She is resentful of the specialist who is scheduled for twenty-five minutes and keeps the class for thirty minutes. She is annoyed with the music teacher who is scheduled to arrive at 1:30 and comes at 1:45.

5. *Becomes a Faculty Member*—

When a music teacher is assigned to do all the music teaching in a building she has a position as a faculty member. As such she is wise when she assumes her share of the extra faculty duties. If playground, hall, or lunchroom duties are expected of the regular classroom teachers, the music teacher who shows she is willing to accept a proportionate share of those duties will receive a warmer reception for her work than if she remains aloof from such activities because she has no home room assignment.

### *The Music Specialist as a Music Supervisor*

In schools where implementation of the philosophy of education requires that all subjects of the elementary school shall be taught by the classroom teacher in a complete "self-contained" classroom, the specialist in music has a variety of roles she can play. Common among these is the role of supervisor. This position is one in which regular visits are made to the classrooms, usually on an assigned schedule. Course of study outlines are prepared for the various grades. On the occasion of the classroom visit, the supervisor may demonstrate certain music activities, may teach the lesson, or may observe the classroom teacher teaching music and analyze with her the success or failure of the work.

It is supervision carried out in this rather rigid fashion that has resulted in much of the criticism directed at supervision in the elementary school. Yet it does not have to be that way. The music specialists and administrators who are aware of the human relations aspects of this organization of work can achieve rapport with the classroom teachers, with the result that the visit of the Music Supervisor becomes a pleasant, challenging educational experience rather than an event to be dreaded, survived, and forgotten for a month or six weeks.

### *Classroom Teachers Are Seldom Specialists in Music*

The supervisor of music who visits a teacher six to twelve times a year and who must depend on that teacher to develop the music program between visits, needs to accept the fact that seldom will the music program achieve the degree of success that she herself could achieve with the same pupils and the same curriculum guide. Elementary classroom teachers are rarely specialists in music. Where they are specialists in a subject it is quite likely to be in the language arts or arithmetic. In most classrooms the elementary teacher's specialty is the children in her class and how they grow and learn. Dissatisfaction with the progress in many rooms will have to be expressed in carefully chosen challenges to growth, rather than in caustic criticism. Elementary teachers as well as their pupils want to enjoy music. When the element of joy is removed from it the value of music for both teachers and pupils is sharply reduced. The music supervisor who can accept progress toward a goal and not demand arrival at a goal will survive and will see her program survive.

### *Classroom Teachers Want to Participate in Curriculum Building*

The supervisor who spends all summer writing out curriculum guides for teachers to follow often does it with the idea that she has made things easier for the teachers and simplified supervision for herself. Actually neither is true. The elementary teachers who accept a curriculum outline without question usually follow through a course of study with the same nonchalance. Alert, thinking teachers resent being given curriculum guides in which they have had no participation.

"But if they aren't music specialists, how can they help to write a curriculum guide?" The pupils who will be taught are just as important as the content that is in the study. The classroom teacher knows the pupils in her classroom; the specialist knows music and how it should be presented. Together they are a team for teaching music to children. When it is necessary to prepare a curriculum guide in music or change any part of the school curriculum, the supervisor who solves rather than creates problems will meet with groups of teachers. They will evaluate the former program, suggest activities which children enjoy, talk about relationships of music to the rest of the curriculum, plan for equipment and supplies, tell their aims and objectives for music. From this group thinking the supervisor and teachers receive the guidance they need to plan their work. As "ours" the music course of study finds an acceptance which is never received by "hers."

### *Classroom Teachers Have Strengths and Weaknesses*

Sooner or later, and more often sooner, every music supervisor hears, "I can't teach music." Frequently it is said quite hopefully as the teacher thinks, *"Maybe this one won't make me teach it!"* Although some few teachers for one reason or another feel they can't teach music, their number is small. In music as in every other curriculum area there are teachers with certain weaknesses and certain strengths. The supervisor in any field who "tailor makes" his program to play up the strengths of a teacher and minimize the weaknesses will be amply repaid for his efforts. Helen Jack does not sing well but she loves rhythm and rhythmic activities. A program in Miss Jack's room which has a large amount of rhythmic activity and less of singing is a program that the teacher will like and with which she will be successful. Next year the children will be in Tom Gregor's sixth grade. He has a boy's choir in his church. Vocal music will play a big part in his program. By the end of the elementary school, the music work will be balanced if a flexible supervisor acts in accordance with her knowledge that the teachers, as well as the pupils, are individuals with strengths and weaknesses, and they will work hard in those areas in which they experience success.

### *Most Teachers Want to Learn*

The flexible supervisor learns to change the music program from room to room because she recognizes the strengths and weaknesses of the teachers and builds on their strengths. The astute music supervisor has full knowledge of the weaknesses in the teacher's ability to teach music, and plans opportunities for the teachers to learn how to turn the weaknesses into strengths. The supervisor and administrator can plan for the inclusion of some work in music in the in-service education of the teachers. This need not be formal class instruction. A variety of informal activities might better serve the purpose and by its nature be more attractive to the teachers. Such a program was planned by Marie Sampson with and for the teachers of Mapleville—

Sept. *Do You Want to Move to Music?*
Rhythms and Records—Teachers of Kindergarten and First Grade

Nov. *Here We Come A-Carolling*
Carol singing Grades 5 & 6—Learn some new ones—Enjoy singing some old ones.

Jan. *Swing Your Partners*
Singing Games for Teachers of Grades 3 & 4.

Mar. *Be a Disc Jockey*
Using the record player—Teachers of all grades.

These informal meetings which Marie and the teachers participated in were held in the evenings, but they could be after school or on days set aside for in-service education. Their informality attracted a large number of teachers who learned new techniques, gained confidence in their own abilities to direct music activities, and had fun together.

## *The Music Specialist as a Supervisor and Teacher*

Many music specialists have the dual role of supervisor and teacher. Their schedule permits them to be in each classroom one day a week where they teach the lesson. The classroom teachers conduct the lessons on the other four days carrying out the work begun by the specialist. Some schools use this plan as an intermediate step when moving from a situation in which all music is taught by a specialist to one in which music is taught by the regular classroom teacher. The music specialist in this dual role has all the problems of the teacher, plus all those of the supervisor.

### *What Does the Classroom Teacher Do?*

Elementary teachers have few, if any, moments when they are free to be away from the pupils. Many of them look upon the music specialist's visit as a time when they can leave the room. The music teacher faced with the responsibility of leading those teachers in improving their teaching of music feels that the teachers should remain in the room to observe and learn. The administrators usually are in accord with the music specialist's point of view. The music teacher-supervisor has a real opportunity to win teacher support for her program when she is understanding enough to know when to say, "Miss Stevens, for the next ten minutes we are just going to review some songs; would you like to take a break until I start the new part of the lesson?"

Or—"Today we are going to do some rhythm work. You've done this with us before. There won't be anything you don't know about. If you have something else you want to do, you won't need to be here."

If she shows concern for the teacher, then when she says, "In this lesson I am going to start something new that I would like you to continue," she can be reasonably sure of attention and cooperation from Miss Stevens.

### *The Music Specialist as Consultant*

If you were to poll supervisors and administrators to find out their feelings about the ultimate goal for the role of supervisor you would find increasingly larger numbers of them saying, "We want supervisors to be consultants—available to the teachers at their request."

With the improved education of teachers both in college and in service the goal of consultant is one which can be reached by specialists in various fields. The common question raised even by those who believe thoroughly in this concept is: *What if no*

*one wants to consult?* If no one calls for the consultant, does she sit in the office and wait? These questions haunt even the most experienced supervisors when they think of being consultants. Good salesmanship must enter into the picture. Teachers will call the consultant if they know what the consultant has to offer to them. Cleverly prepared bulletins such as the one Mary Keyes prepared for the teachers of Fountaindale will attract requests for help (see page 84). The consultant who is consulted makes it easy to reach her and she takes the initiative in suggesting the activities in which she would like to serve as consultant.

Sometimes she is required to approach the question directly by saying, "May I come to your music class next week to hear your group sing Christmas carols?" Once inside the room the opportunity for evaluation and consultation may come easily.

*Small Problems Clinic*

Are "little things" bothering you? I will be in your building on Tuesday, November 14. Leave a note on the desk in the office if you want me to come to your room.

Mary Keyes
Music Consultant

*Are You Studying Indians?*

I have expanded my collection of recordings of Indian music. May I share them with you?

Would you like to make Indian instruments? I will help!

Do you want to learn a war dance?

Mary Keyes
Music Consultant

## A Common Problem

Supervisor-Teacher-Consultant—when all three are combined, one problem occurs in the special fields with regularity: What do you do when you are just out of school and are to be a consultant to or supervisor of teachers who have taught for many years?

It helps if the supervisor learns to say "experienced" rather than "old"; it helps to listen as well as to tell; it helps to remember that the experienced teacher has survived, which means that she has been acceptable to the school and community; it helps to remember that she is probably a little frightened of you; it helps to remember that there is only one year when you are just out of college.

Time takes care of the rest!

## • FOOD FOR THOUGHT

1. Discuss the advantages and disadvantages, as you see them, of:
   (a) the position of music supervisor.
   (b) the position of consultant in music.
   (c) the position of special teacher for music.
2. Present the arguments of the teacher who doesn't want to teach music, the administrator who thinks all elementary teachers should teach their own music, and the music director of the schools who resolves the conflict of opinions.
3. To what extent do you believe that special teachers of music should participate in the program of the school (Playground, Cafeteria, PTA, Assemblies, etc.)?
4. Describe some in-service education activities that would help create confidence in their ability to teach music among classroom teachers of music.
5. Make a collection of written curriculum guides in use in elementary schools.

# 8 • Secondary-school music teachers and the music curriculum

## *General Music Teachers*

September again! Miss Hall, standing at the door of the music room waiting for the last seventh grader to scuttle in, is greeted by Mrs. Park. "I don't think I'll ever get the clatter of those typewriters out of my ears. You music teachers! Nothing to do but have the class sing a few songs and play some records for them. Now there's a real life. How about changing jobs? See you after school, Sally!"

As Mrs. Park hurries away, Sally Hall glances into her classroom for a quick count. Sixty-two in the class; three missing. Wonder if *anyone* in this school thinks the music teacher works for a living? Smiling to herself, she closes the classroom door.

Sally, we'd like to talk with you about your work. Are you really leading an ice-cream-soda existence inside the door of Room 201; is life a musical merry-go-round of singing songs and playing records?

Since Sally is the counterpart of thousands of music teachers over the country, we can assume that what we might learn from her is fairly typical. What *does* Sally do?

The position is that of general music teacher, with some

choral groups included. She teaches grades 7-8-9. In her present position these classes meet twice a week for approximately 45 minutes, but in other schools they may meet only once a week. Some schools run the general music classes for each group every day but for only one semester of the school year, block plan; still others drop the music classes at the end of seventh or eighth grades. Sally thinks the size of her classes too large. "A class of 65 boys and girls, meeting twice a week—it's difficult to learn much about them as individuals. And with a class that meets *only* twice a week, the size of these classes makes it more difficult to develop desirable behavior without dictatorial methods."

All the children are required to take "general music." Some of them like it, some of them do not. By the time boys and girls reach the age of 12, 13, 14, 15, they have rather definite ideas about music. Sally and her fellow music teachers try to meet all the tastes and attitudes represented in their music classes by using a wide variety of musical materials and methods of presentation, but sometimes they say, "It's like shooting in the dark."

The general music program is the one segment of secondary-school music involving the total school population. It is at once a challenging and complex area. You may think, "Well, the elementary classroom music program also involves all the children, so why pinpoint this secondary general music area as being more involved?" Briefly, the reasons include:

1. Pupils are pre-adolescent or adolescent, and are in a complex developmental stage with regard to family, school, and community. Their attitudes toward music are much more fixed—today we have the rock and roll fans, the jazz devotees, the longhairs, and all stages of in-betweens. The program must satisfy these diversified interests.

2. Pupils are no longer in a single classroom unit or group. They move from teacher to teacher. Greater independence of action exists; they express their attitudes more freely. This affects teaching techniques.

3. Teachers report this expression of attitudes is particularly noticeable where "minor subjects" (usually meaning subjects that do not meet daily during the school week) are concerned. "If I don't like it, why bother? It doesn't count anyhow!" This attitude can be counteracted only by making classes interesting and challenging.

4. General music classes are sometimes regarded as scheduling catchalls where any number of pupils may be assigned for the sake of convenience. This is indicated by the ridiculous size such classes may reach, a size all out of proportion to English or social studies classes, for example. It seems to reflect an attitude that general music is a "poor relation" to the program. This situation handicaps teachers; it has a bearing on their efficiency.

5. At least part of the difficulty is an uncertainty as to the nature of learning experiences in these classes. This may reflect a weakness in the preparatory experiences of the teachers. Too often the classes turn into a choir preparation program with the emphasis on sight-reading, part-singing, and choral techniques. Since these classes usually involve all the pupils in a given school, and since the large majority of the pupils will form an audience or consumer group as adults, the emphasis instead should be as much on appreciative as performance techniques.

6. Many teachers report pupil behavior problems make teaching difficult in these classes. The large size of the classes does not help this situation.

Faced with these problems plus others peculiar to her particular situation, it's easy to understand why Sally is often perplexed about many aspects of her work. She feels almost isolated, at times.

Perhaps her biggest handicap is a feeling of working alone. Yet there are four other general music teachers in nearby schools. Has anyone suggested to them that they pool their resources and work on a positive basis of constructive group action? Or do their supervisors and principals assume that a teaching certificate is a magic sword with which they will be able to whack off the heads of any problems that arise? If so, it's a foolish assumption.

Even outside of the music program itself, Sally needs help in learning to work with other faculty members, needs to know that open channels of communication exist between her and her department head, her principal, the guidance department, and other key teachers and administrators.

Who arranges this? The framework for such communication is the responsibility of administration, but action within the framework depends on the teachers. This may involve a large or small group, depending, of course, on the size of the school system. Who are the music teachers in her particular system, other than Sally?

### *The Instrumentalists*

There are three instrumental teachers. We won't have any difficulty locating Bill Jones, one of these teachers. He holds forth in the junior high building with Sally, and if you open the front door of this building around 8 o'clock any morning you will hear concerted and muffled but unmistakably instrumental sounds coming from a subterranean chamber. Follow the sounds and you will arrive in the band room.

Here Bill is working with a group of sixth grade pupils who play a variety of instruments. They come in before school officially begins and receive class instruction. This is possible through the cooperation of their parents, who either drive them to school early or provide bicycles for transportation. Follow Bill through his day and you will see group after group of young instrumentalists visit the band room.

You will also go with Bill to several far-flung elementary schools where he teaches groups of boys and girls. Watching these youngsters unpack their instruments, set up stands, and produce various sounds, you will sense the excitement that is always present when children are busy making music. At least, it's music to them and to Bill. You may marvel at his patience as he trims clarinet reeds, replaces broken violin strings, adjusts a bent saxophone key. Bill is happy, and certainly busy. Does he have any problems? Yes, he does! Here are some of them:

1. More children want to learn to play instruments than can afford them. Should the school provide instruments?

2. It is difficult to schedule instrumental classes without interfering with the regular classroom activities, particularly on the elementary level. How can this be arranged without treading upon the toes of other teachers?

3. Shall instrumental instruction be provided free of charge to all pupils, as well as instructional materials, or shall a fee be assessed for such services and materials?

4. Shall pupils for the instrumental program be selected on the basis of musical talent, or shall all children be accepted simply on the basis of desire to participate? Is it possible to provide service on the latter basis of operation?

5. How much community and school service shall be expected of the instrumental performing organizations? Do they exist primarily for the instruction and musical growth of the pupils, or as a showcase for school and community?

6. What should the instrumental teacher expect from the pupil in the way of musical achievement at the time he begins instrumental instruction?

Bill would be very frank in telling you that he works around these problems so they are not too much on his mind. He would also tell you that he feels they form an intangible block to a more effective program; he often wishes there were a clearcut statement of policy concerning them. No such policy exists that he can find. You see, he too would like to have, and feels he needs, a working policy such as the one Sally needs.

### *Choral Directors*

Over on the stage of the senior high building, Dave Speres is rehearsing his mixed chorus of one-hundred-plus boys and girls when we walk in on a Tuesday morning. Perhaps this is not a very good time to visit, because Dave is about to blow his stack and therefore once more will be referred to as a temperamental musician. Sometime over the weekend, between Friday's

rehearsal and today's, fifty of the folding chairs that Dave's choir members stack neatly after each rehearsal have disappeared.

In addition, Dave has just received a notice that a photograph of his choir must be taken for the yearbook during his next rehearsal, and that he cannot use the regular rehearsal place (the stage) for that period, since it will be used for taking photographs of other school groups as well. Why does all this disturb Dave?

"Fifty chairs missing means that half the chorus stands. They can do it, but it's a disturbing element for them, and when we have only forty minutes twice a week for rehearsal, there isn't much time to cope with disturbances. As for the photograph, we need every minute of rehearsal time this week; we're trying to learn a program to sing for the Town Boosters Club benefit Friday night. The principal asked us to appear there. And our 'rehearsal hall' happens to be the stage of the auditorium, but we were unable to get on it for two weeks because of a stage set erected by a community group for their play. We were rehearsing 100 youngsters in a room meant for 40." Dave suddenly stops and laughs. "You probably think this is small potatoes. And I keep telling myself not to take it so seriously. Well, I shouldn't. It's all happened before . . . it will happen again, too."

Dave also teaches some courses listed as Music Appreciation I and II, a Music Theory I course alternating on a semester basis with Music Theory II, and directs a Boys' Glee Club and a Girls' Glee Club. Most of the time he does his work in a manner not more or less excited than that of his fellow teachers. When things pile up and he can't predict what will happen next —when at the same time he is under pressure to produce a polished "outside" performance—he builds up steam.

Well, so do his colleagues; we just happened to walk in on Dave the morning his head of steam was building. But the point is that Dave, too, needs the same working agreement Sally and Bill do. Does "the case of the missing chairs" need to be a mystery? Of course not. The chairs are probably in the library, where a group held a meeting last night and needed them. Someone intended to tell Dave, but forgot. If he had known, he could have sent the fellows directly to the library for them.

If . . . if . . . if. It's easy to see that something is wrong here. Can it be that old feeling of every man for himself? Sink or swim . . . no life preservers available?

### *Odd Jobs*

We can drive a short distance from the town where our three friends teach and find some secondary-school music teachers whose positions are more inclusive, overlapping with the elementary program. Now these teachers are in contact with a larger segment of the school system, but this does not simplify the nature of their work.

Take Sue Davis, for example. She teaches the general music classes in Frenchville Junior-Senior High School, directs the school chorus, supervises the elementary music program, and also functions as instrumental teacher. In other words, she's "it" in the music program. Saturday afternoons during football season she fields a forty-piece marching band; in May you will see her high school chorus singing at the Commencement program. Sue is busy, so busy that few people ever see her sit down. And she is doing a fine piece of work, according to the report of her supervising principal.

Does Sue feel that her position is satisfying professionally? In many ways, yes. She knows almost every child in the schools and can call most of them by name. She rarely goes shopping in the local supermarket without being stopped five or six times by parents who are interested in their children's musical progress.

Yet Sue feels frustrated too, because she does have to spread her efforts very thin. Her schedule is so crowded that if Sue stops for a conference with Mrs. Ray, the third grade teacher who is greatly interested in developing her classroom music program, she will be late getting to Mr. Lamb's room, and Mr. Lamb claims that music is completely out of his scope, so he may take her tardiness as a personal affront. She'll have to spend extra time with him explaining this, and it is difficult to keep him interested enough anyhow so that he will not take off for an admittedly-needed break. This will make her late for her chorus period at the high school.

Once she gets off her whirlwind schedule, it appears that the schedule keeps going but she can't get back on. Sue has tentatively planned to talk over such problems, and others, but she hates to bother her supervising principal; he seems even busier than she.

Can a position as broad in scope as Sue's be streamlined without destroying its effectiveness? Is there any solution? The more she builds up the music program, the more she feels that loose ends are lying all over the place. Is another teacher the answer? She often wonders.

In small school systems all over the country music teachers are involved in such positions as Sue's, but with different combinations of duties. Some music teachers also teach other subjects part of the time. Sometimes they are not qualified to teach such subjects.

Contrariwise, other subject teachers sometimes fill in by teaching music classes. So this is not simply a combination of elementary-secondary, instrumental-choral responsibilities; it cuts across subject-area lines as well. These teachers will point out the disadvantages of such far-flung teaching responsibilities, but some of them will also note certain advantages.

In examining music teaching at the secondary level—although as we have seen, the elementary level is involved, too—such problems must be considered.

## *Talking It Over*

It will not be necessary to dig very deep to strike the taproot of the secondary music program. As in the elementary school, this taproot is the *total school system*. Music is only one part of it. If it is a sound program, it is an integral part. But in other instances, it may be under- or over-developed.

Also, secondary music should be rooted in the elementary music program. There should be no sharp division, no splintering off from this elementary program. Too often there is a lack of communication between elementary and secondary music teachers or, just as important, between elementary classroom teachers and secondary music specialists.

Oddly enough, this may occur even in the case of instrumental teachers who are working with elementary school pupils. They think of such pupils only as instrumentalists, not in terms of all the school experiences they have from day to day. Now certainly in this case there is bound to be a lack of communication between the teachers involved. Still, in defense of the instrumental teachers, Bill Jones says this happens because he doesn't have time to observe the pupils in their regular classroom situation, and because he is teaching only a relatively small proportion of these pupils.

Now of course there should be a director of music education who would take care of the problems of Sally, Bill, Dave, and their colleagues. But not every school system is large enough to have a director of music education; in fact, the position exists only in larger city or county systems. So it is more or less normal to have a number of music teachers working in a fairly independent manner in the same system. No one wishes to be accused of "bossing" the others; thus a great deal of uncoordinated effort and waste motion may result. Each teacher may be competent, but conflicting viewpoints and interests may impede the effectiveness of the program.

There is only one answer: group action through organization. Who will object to this? Let's be frank—teachers will object who are "set in their ways" and afraid of change, teachers who fear their weaknesses and inadequacies may be revealed, teachers who are so satisfied with their prowess that they see no need for working with the group. In addition to these, there may be a few instrumental or choral specialists who have built up their end of the program to such an extent that they think a broad-based reorganization will be a deterrent.

All these faint-hearted individuals are, we think, in the minority. But they may be loudly vocal in their protests. The majority of teachers, conscious of the developing strength of the music program when it is built around the musical needs of all the children, will win over the minority.

No sharp break-off between elementary and secondary music should exist. But it does, and to a greater extent in general music than in the instrumental area; instrumental teachers more often combine elementary and secondary class instruction than do general teachers. Neither should there be a sharp division between the instrumental, the general, and the choral programs. And we know there should not be a no man's land between music and other subject areas. Children don't think this way—unless teachers teach this way! We would like to help them integrate their world.

## *Planning Together*

Let's assume that a superintendent of schools has been aware of the music teachers' difficulties—and, of course, of their successes as well—for some time. One morning the music teachers find in their mail a short memo asking them to meet with the superintendent.

This is a general memo addressed to the group, so no teacher will have to ask silently, "Now what have I done?" And within a few days, they gather in the superintendent's office. The aroma of coffee fills the air, a scent that does a lot to promote informality. After a social "mixer" period, the discussion begins with a type of progress report.

Here is a wise superintendent; he already knows much about the music activities in his district, and he comments favorably about many of them, thoughtfully including some from each teacher's bailiwick. He does not dominate the discussion at this session, but by the time it is over, the teachers have talked at some length about the kind of music program they would like to see flourishing in the schools this year, next year, and five years ahead.

Nothing is labeled "impossible" in this session; no limiting factors such as money, personnel, or time are allowed to kill an idea. The result is that everyone speaks freely, and one or two teachers who have been silent at meetings now begin to express themselves. Though it is almost time for dinner when the meeting breaks up, they are a bit sorry to go—time has passed rapidly.

This superintendent knows that his personnel must feel they can contribute to any curriculum project before it is launched. He has helped them to feel this way—confident and useful. Now they leave, but a steering committee has been designated by the group to continue planning. The committee includes an instrumental teacher, a junior high general music teacher, a senior high choral teacher, the band director, two elementary specialists, an elementary classroom teacher, and a general supervisor.

The committee is likely to do a sound, constructive piece of work. Of course John James, the band director, will have his differences with Mrs. Shutz, the choral director, because students in this school have always had to choose between band or chorus, and many of the same students would like to elect both. Now, however, the committee will think through the entire music program, elementary and secondary. So the problems of individual teachers will lose some of their personal implications, and somehow a solution may emerge from the larger framework. This will benefit not only individual teachers, but also pupils who have been in the middle of a tug-of-war.

### *A Teaching Basis for Music in the Secondary Schools*

Turn back to the discussion of music in the elementary school and take a quick look at the reasons listed there for including music in the curriculum. Are there different reasons for music in the secondary school? Basically, the same reasons prevail; the emphasis, the situation, and the children are somewhat different, however.

Children still like music. They like it all through school. But wait: this doesn't necessarily mean that they like it in *school.* The gap between out-of-school music and in-school music has widened in too many cases. Johnny has been taking accordion lessons for five years, Tony plays nice guitar, but they don't tell their music teacher about this. Why? Because they don't hear accordion or guitar mentioned in music class; they hear about violin, oboe, trumpet, and instruments that seem to have more musical importance. Somehow, Johnny and Tony feel a bit inferior.

The truth is that Tony is a better musician than Dave in the same class, but Dave plays French horn and when the teacher mentions this, it takes on an aura of prestige. In this class popular singers and instrumentalists are not discussed. Yes, the gap is wider than it was in elementary school. For boys and girls, as they grow older, develop their own values where music is concerned.

We must accept these values, we must accept everything our pupils do musically, if we are to open their eyes, ears, and minds to the many great musical experiences waiting for them. Bridging from what they know, feel, and like about music to what we teachers think they *should* know, feel, and like is our responsibility as educators.

If children identify themselves with music that we believe is not worthy of our attention, it is because the environment makes it easy for them to identify with such material, makes it difficult for them to know better music. Many art songs say in great and lasting music the basic "I love you" said also in inconsequential popular songs. The difference is that these great songs are not plugged daily over radio, TV, and jukeboxes. Thus the great and good become the strange and rare.

But appreciation is built from knowledge of any music, since all music has the same basic components. Remember a song, popular a few years ago, concerned with the call of a wild goose? Its rhythmic accompaniment throbbed across the country for weeks. Mr. Norris heard it, and heard about it from his teen-age pupils. He played it in class the same day he played a record of Schubert's "Erlking." There is a suggestion of excitement in the accompaniment of "The Erlking" and a feeling of suspense. He provided a situation in which the class compared the two songs. They liked "The Erlking," too. He accepted their choice; they accepted his. He didn't preach values. He showed the merits of each song.

Leonard Bernstein, in discussing the Brahms *Symphony No. 4,* refers to a portion of it as resembling a ". . . huge, mad, German tango."* Immediately to many an amateur listener this segment of the symphony seems more understandable; common ground has been established. Who hasn't heard a tango? "If a symphony can sound like a tango, maybe I can understand it," says John Doe, who always thought of a symphony as being an endless procession of sounds too difficult and unrelated for him to comprehend. Bernstein, too, is approaching the matter by incorporating the familiar and known in a bridge to the less familiar.

Likes and dislikes in music are a means of expressing one's values. "This sends me," says fourteen-year-old Harry, rocking to a solid beat. "I get the message." To prove that he is receiving, he moves, he rocks, he rolls. He expresses himself through music.

Is this bad? No—it may be healthy. But it also may be a steady, limited diet that defeats growth in musical awareness. If so, it *is* bad, for anything that limits desirable growth is bad. (We mean "bad" in a perfectly good sense of inadequate, substandard, injurious; let's not quibble about it.) Of course, there is an obvious relationship between this and our discussion of music and environment. However, adolescent values are growing and developing; this is the good side of the picture.

All great music is the product of human experiences; vital, moving, graphic experiences. It is great music because it continues, generation after generation, to touch the lives, the emotions, the thoughts of people everywhere. For many adolescents, music is an escape into a world where they are not faced with problems. Do they like the loud, beating, swinging, sometimes discordant and violent sounds of modern jazz (and we use the term loosely) because it expresses today's world? Because it releases and distracts them temporarily from their troubles? Because it has an emotional impact? An intellectual significance? All of these are possible answers. We know that a small per

---

*Leonard Bernstein, Analysis Record to the Music Appreciation Record of Brahm's *Symphony No. 4 in E. Minor, Opus 98.* New York: Book of the Month Club, Inc. © 1957 by Leonard Bernstein.

cent of our youth express themselves well in performing music brilliantly; a larger per cent on a less spectacular level. And many try, but succeed on a performance level that would never bring joy to the heart of a musician.

Nevertheless, they express themselves as best they can. The music program that encourages them to do so, through creating, performing, exploring, listening, and discussing, is serving youth's need for self-expression. The program that takes them *where they are* in this process of expression and *leads them further* (in desirable directions) justifies its inclusion in the school curriculum.

### *Music for Everyone*

"I just *have* to be in Choir. It's my senior year. When we come in from football practice and the fellows begin singing, I feel left out. I've got to be able to sing with them." So says six-foot, 180-pound Lefty on a fine September afternoon. His plea is addressed to Mr. Hande, Choir Director at Smith High. Now Lefty won't add much to the musical prowess of this 100-voice group, but Mr. Hande juggles the bass section a bit and Lefty gets in.

Why? Because Mr. Hande knows that this is an example of Lefty's need to get a bit closer to his classmates through music. Miss Ring, over at Tower High, would say Lefty should have decided three years ago that he wanted to be in Choir—he'll pull down the performance level of the group. But to Mr. Hande, the social value of his organization is almost as great as the musical value. He takes them as they come, whatever their reasons, if they can sing reasonably well, and his limit is the number he can get into the rehearsal room.

How do you see the social values of music? Every society is reflected in its music; Haydn's patterned society, Beethoven's thunderous challenge to kings and emperors, Debussy's kaleidoscopic shadows of things real and unreal. Was Carmen a delinquent struggling to escape into a better world than her cigarette factory? Was Tosca, entrapped in a world of conflicting political forces, very different from thousands in Europe yesterday and today? Is the folk song of love, sorrow, birth, or death relating an experience different from that shared by men and women, in every corner of the earth?

Music needs no justification here. It reveals the very substance of life—its inclusion in the curriculum on this basis alone would be more than sufficient. And the secondary school is an ideal time for developing such understanding. Not only are teen-agers highly receptive to the social and emotional implications of music—they are better able to intellectualize their responses.

In discussing the elementary music program we stated that music belonged to all the people. Believing this, we can say that the music program of any school belongs to the pupils as well as the teachers. No teacher planning group, then, can say, "We alone know what our pupils should do, like, and experience in the music program." For in such situations, we are likely to lose a large group of boys and girls who really like music but feel the school program has little to offer.

Do you believe the secondary program should concern itself chiefly with those who are already embryo musicians by vocation or avocation? Do you believe your program should concentrate on twenty or thirty per cent of the school population? Are you willing to disregard the consumer market represented by the majority?

If so, follow the dangerous practice of building a program that belongs to the teachers; disregard the pupils. As long as music belongs to everyone—and this is increasingly true because of mass media—there will be all kinds of music for all kinds of people. Take a long look at your high school youth, then build *their* program as well as *yours*.

After all, it's for them.

• FOOD FOR THOUGHT

1. Who should be responsible for helping music teachers in a secondary-school system plan together for an effective music curriculum?
2. Why is it important that such planning be encouraged?
3. In what ways is the work of elementary music teachers different from that of secondary music teachers? In what ways is it similar? Do the two factors of music and children furnish sufficient common ground for interest in planning together?
4. Why is it important that vocal and instrumental teachers plan together?
5. Does a heavy schedule of teaching assignments sometimes interfere with effective teacher-teacher relations? How?
6. Give some reasons why there is too often a dividing line between interest in elementary music and interest in secondary-school music. How can this be avoided?

# 9 · Secondary-school music: Program and philosophy

## *A Balanced Program*

Turn back to the discussion of basic concepts for the elementary program. Can you find any statement that does not apply in principle to the secondary school?

Again, it appears that the secondary-school music program has its roots in the elementary school.

If it does not, we find a situation such as that in Albert School District, where the marching band dominates the music program—a marching band of seventy members and eighty flag wavers, majorettes, and rifle twirlers. Yes, they look mighty good marching down the field on a bright October afternoon.

Trouble is, while they represent only eight per cent of the school population, they receive approximately fifty per cent of all the money that is expended on the school music program. This town doesn't know what the other children are missing. And frankly, there is little appreciative value to be had in listening to this band. It takes so long to teach marching and formations every September that there isn't much time left to spend on the music. The spectators applaud a show, not music. Here is a music director who has given up music education and gone into show business.

When the planning committee, which was last seen leaving the superintendent's office, came up with a recommended program for the secondary school, it included the following:

1. A broad-based general music program, requiring some participation in music through the ninth grade, also providing varied opportunities for participation on an elective basis through twelfth grade. General music classes in junior high school include many musical activities, some of which will be *true* musical experiences for boys and girls. (Remember: an activity is not necessarily an experience.)

Consumer courses on the senior high level are needed for pupils whose musical education terminates with graduation. Aside from the listening and singing, these youths need to know how to choose a phonograph, a television set, a record library. They need to know, too, how to care for these expensive objects once they are acquired. They should find out what a community needs in the way of a concert series, and how their particular community may have different needs from others. And although they may live in several different communities during their lives, they will be prepared to help build music in any town or city, having become acquainted with the process of supplying it adequately in one.

2. Courses—or at least one course—are recommended for the pupil who is and will be concerned with music in a more intensive way. Theory, history of music, sight-reading—these are not requisites to the living of most people, but they are to the pupils who are going on in music or music education, or who will become elementary classroom teachers.

3. Since the teenage and pre-teenage years are a period when boys and girls derive satisfaction and prestige from belonging to a group, musical organizations of many kinds are needed. These range from large, rather non-select groups to highly select bands, orchestras, choirs, and small ensembles.

Extensive opportunity for the musically talented and educated pupil to perform individually is desirable. Opportunity, not exploitation, is the key word here; opportunity for making music an outgoing facet of the personality, for contributing to the pleasure of the school and community, opportunity for achieving the self-expression of the individual that leads to realization of worth. For some, these solo-type experiences will be the high points of their school music. For many others, however, the times when they are involved with a group of their fellow-students in the making of ensemble music—in choirs, bands, and orchestras, for example—will be the high points. For such pupils the experiences of losing individual fears and anxieties, the feeling of being borne successfully on the waves of music pouring from the hearts and minds of an organization, will mean the most.

## *A Working Philosophy*

During recent years teachers have been confused at times by the perfectly acceptable philosophy that music should be an enjoyable experience for all. The statement that we should have fun with music is one most of us have heard many times.

In itself, there is nothing wrong with the statement. The substance of the idea is that learning can be a stimulating and rewarding experience, that we can assess children's interests and readiness, then help them learn through providing acceptable musical activities that accomplish the great feat of helping children want to learn about music. Music can be fun, but still accomplish this.

Now comes the conflict in interpretation of the "fun" idea —some individuals have come to believe that by "fun" is meant entertainment, random activity, undirected participation in any musical project that comes to mind.

This "musical chairs" viewpoint is vicious. Take Mr. Wilson, a school principal. He walks into a music class and gets the impression that he has entered Grand Central Station at rush hour without the trains. The teacher, at her desk, is knitting a sweater, presumably for a close relative; it can't wait. Four boys appear to be playing kick-the-can in the rear of the room. Eight girls are jitterbugging to a current hit tune. Five boys are huddled around a terror comic book. Two boys are attempting to shove a third out of the window; two more are firing paper wads into the lighting fixtures. The teacher says brightly, "This is the children's day to do what they want. I don't want to spoil their fun."

You think the picture is overdrawn? Travel around a bit! It happens.

In the superficial reasoning of this teacher, the only major premise is that, as somebody once told her, music should be an enjoyable experience, that children should have fun with music. Trouble is, the enjoyable experience may deteriorate to a point where all relationship to music and learning will vanish.

We can't predict that all children will learn from our teaching, but we can control the situation so they have a reasonable opportunity to learn something. We can set out to make music enjoyable for children, so enjoyable that they will learn about it and want to learn more about it, so enjoyable that it fuses with their lives.

Assuming that American children are alert, intelligent, and eager to learn—and if you have ever watched a child explore something in which he is interested, you can't doubt this assumption—we are shortchanging them badly when we do not assume the responsibilities of being teachers who have the treasures of a subject field charged to our accounts. Do we pay our bills? There are other kinds than those at the stores. There is the kind we owe our pupils.

The fact is that teachers are as badly confused as parents, caught between theories of permissive upbringing of children and a more traditional viewpoint. Boys and girls expect adults to guide and control their lives. This gives them a basis of security from which to operate. They also expect to be considered as human beings with ideas, viewpoints, and experiences. They expect to learn from their teachers. The expert teacher will see that they learn both from the experiences made available through her teaching, and from each other.

We have no wish to return to the days of key signatures and music symbols taken out of a musical context and placed on the chalkboard for memorization without any musical association. This effectively killed any budding interest in music for many, many children. But let's acknowledge that sometimes learning is fun, and sometimes it requires challenging work on the part of the pupil.

Help your pupils set up their learning goals, find appropriate musical materials, and help them work toward those goals. Evaluate with them, then, what they have learned. When they have mastered and can use certain knowledge, skills, developed certain appreciations, they will want to continue. *Awareness of mastery is a fundamental need in all of us.* Don't confuse fun and enjoyment; your pupils don't!

On the other hand, do plan classroom experiences in terms of child development characteristics. Knowledge of pupils is the most important key to effective teaching. Consider the following statement with regard to teaching methods:

> Teachers who have absorbed the child development viewpoint find that it profoundly affects their teaching. It makes traditional practices in many cases appear as what they are—dry and not necessarily interesting to all pupils. For example, the memorization of key signatures may be useful to some pupils —somewhere—sometime. But Johnny in the fourth grade can sing happily—day after day—without knowing even *one* signature. How is such information functional in his life? How can we help him realize the significance of the F# in "America" written in the key of G? An astute teacher might try playing the tune on the piano or tuned bells, and omitting the F#. Immediately the class realizes that this does not sound "right." "Why," asks the teacher. "Will someone try 'picking it out' on the bells so it *does* sound right?" Out of such an approach the child is asked to experiment, to notice, to discover, to perceive relationships, to make judgments; all this without being put in jeopardy of the "Quick, now, give me an answer!"

type of classroom procedure. When Johnny finds that F# in a song serves a musical purpose, he may move naturally to a knowledge of the G major scale, its position on the keyboard, a recognition of the tonal relations involved, and finally, he may look to see how the composer indicates in the musical score that he wants the sound of the G major scale in his music. Johnny may look for other songs in this key, too. If he has a teacher with wide comprehension of the ways children learn, he may watch Helen, a sixth grade violinist, show the class how she makes the sound of F and F#. Johnny will very likely be interested in all of this, because it involves the making of musical sound. Isn't it tedious to spend most of one's time learning about something if we never get right down to the something itself?

Thus the teacher who is thinking in terms of child development, and how children learn, is forced to use this knowledge in thoughtful, creative ways.

This is not an easy way to teach. It means that the teacher must be patient in biding his time so that learning opportunities are developed as they present themselves, resourceful in providing experiences that will stimulate children to grasp such learning opportunities, and persistent in pointing out relationships and leading children to perceive such relationships independently. It means "custom-made planning" on a day-to-day basis. Many teachers are discouraged by the challenge of such teaching and long for the "good old days" when knowledge of subject matter was enough, and an efficient lesson plan could be used from year to year, like the hand-me-down clothes of a large family (and received in much the same spirit). But other teachers have found that the reward is this: they grow with their pupils, and every year's teaching reveals new insight into the way children learn. This, for the real teacher, is sufficient reward.*

## *Is Instrumental Music Different?*

Is there one way to teach instrumental music and another way to teach general music? Are the goals different? Are the

* Maryland State Department of Education, *Planning for Effective Learning: MUSIC. 1956.* Bulletin issued for the Superintendent's Committee on Curriculum and Supervision. (Music Consultant: Frances M. Andrews)

pupils different? Let's look in on a group of teachers discussing this in a summer sessions class:

*Instrumental teachers:* "Who reads music better? Instrumental pupils!"

*Choral teachers:* "Oh, yes? Most of them just push down the valves and blow. Do they have any idea what pitch is going to come out?"

*Instrumental teachers:* "If you general music people would do something about teaching them to read music before we get them, we'd have time to teach something besides fingering."

*General music teachers:* "Look here, you're forgetting that we get *all* the pupils. Some of them don't know which end of a clef is up. *You* just take the kids who are interested and talented. Anyhow, the best time to teach a child to read music is when he has an instrument in his hands. He has a real reason for learning, then."

*Choral teachers:* "Why can't they learn a few music terms before they get into choir? Here's a 'crescendo' clearly marked on the second page of this music, and not one of my choir members paid any attention to it when we sang through the number."

*Class instructor:* "Let's sing through this choral number. (Puts up a piece of music on ninth grade choral level. Class sings through, misses notes, disregards dynamic and tempo markings unless stopped and corrected by instructor, manages to finish, dragged through by some stalwart members of the class and the piano, if any.) "Did you notice that you made some of the same mistakes and exhibited some of the very weaknesses you are complaining about in your pupils?"

*Instrumentalists:* "Our voices are not good—we don't sing much."

*Instructor:* "I wasn't referring to that. Isn't it true that if you can read music, really read it, you hear the sound represented by the note before you play it?" (SILENCE)

*Choral teachers and general teachers:* "Yes, how about that?"

*Instructor:* "And how is it *no one* read the dynamic and tempo indications? If we really read music, shouldn't we read all markings in the score?"

*Any one of the teachers:* "That's too much to expect."

It may be unfair to present such a simplified and abbreviated version of viewpoints. But it does raise several interesting points. They are worthy of some consideration. First, although it may not appear to be so, this is a constructive discussion. Teachers are freely engaged in a good-natured discussion. If the instructor is competent, no one's feelings will be injured, no one will go away hurt. Instrumental, choral, and general music teachers, through this discussion, are asking themselves and asking each other, "How can we do a better job teaching? What can I do? What can you do? How can we help each other?"

Notice that someone said, "That's too much to expect!" when it was suggested that the music reading process should include a total interpretation of the score. But the objective of reading music is to make music, and the signs and symbols disregarded in the little experiment are a large part of music. The individual note has no musical significance unless it is related to the whole musical composition. Bill in the ninth grade—or any other grade, for that matter—likes music, but when his teacher says, "Let's do some music reading," he takes out his pocket puzzle, carried for just such occasions. "Old Do-Re-Mi," he calls his music teacher. For Bill, who likes music but has an I.Q. of 80, the complex business of interpreting the musical score is overwhelming; it's "too much to expect." If we push him where reading is concerned, he may develop a negative attitude toward school music.

Out of this discussion emerges the familiar principle that we must know what to expect of children in terms of their ability to achieve. Forcing everyone to attempt to master the musical score is foolish. But all children should have an opportunity to do so, if they can.

Another point is that children sometimes know more about music reading than is apparent when they begin instrumental study. Attention is divided between the demands of an unfamiliar instrument (in terms of mechanics and producing musical tone) and between the music itself. Children who have been required to memorize key signatures without using them —a useless process in itself—may not be able to remember the names of keys, sharps, or flats.

With a solid background of *musical* experiences, however, a pupil will know *by the sound* when he plays a wrong note. This is the time to drive home the significance of the key signature, the meaning of sharp, flat, natural, accidental. A key signature is only intended to help the musician reproduce faithfully what the composer intended. The world has many people who have made music all their lives without knowing one key signature from another or "which end of a clef is up." Which is more important—the mechanics or the music?

The majority of children who study instrumental music in the schools receive class instruction with a necessarily limited amount of individual instruction. During class instruction— and the time available for this is limited, too—attention may be focused on mastering the instrument to a much greater extent than on mastering the music. Although a competent instrumental teacher would not do so, the fingering for each note is sometimes marked under the note on instrumental practice material. In such circumstances the pupil may ignore the note itself and concentrate his attention on the fingering.

Instrumental teachers might well ask themselves, "Where's the fire? What's the rush?" By drawing attention more often to the *sound* of the music in connection with the *picture* (score) of the music, we might help children read music with greater facility—read the *sound* of music.

Since music is sound, this is the important thing. It may take Nell a year longer to get into band or orchestra, but she'll be better prepared to be a contributing member of the group if we let her grow musically at her individual pace.

## *Readiness*

The question of readiness for instrumental instruction was not brought out in the preceding discussion, but the class might well have included it: we can allow or encourage a child to begin the study of an instrument in third or fourth grade, but in many cases he will learn faster and with more understanding of both instrument and music if we delay this until the fifth grade. Some children undoubtedly become discouraged because of their slow progress in making music when they begin at too early an age, so back goes the instrument to the store.

Did you ever see an ad such as this in your daily paper?

> FOR SALE: one clarinet, almost new, used four months. Call Headstone 4-6772.

This clarinet belonged to Pete. The night before he got the instrument he couldn't go to sleep. Excited? Eight-year-old Pete was, in his own words, "Flipping!" Four months later the ad appears—it's Pete's clarinet for sale.

What happened? Pete wanted to be in the band. But he didn't know learning to play a clarinet involved practice that would conflict with other interests. His motivation was extrinsic. It wasn't love of music, particularly, that pushed him toward the instrument. He wanted to make music, though, and he had an idea that this would be possible right from the start. Instead, he found that playing exercises involving long notes that didn't go anywhere, and not many different notes at that, was the procedure day after day. He tried to pick out some familiar tunes on his clarinet, but was thwarted when he couldn't find the right fingering to produce them. After four months of this he decided to help his brother on the paper route instead.

His cousin Mike also began clarinet, but with a different teacher. Mike was encouraged to play simple tunes "by ear" as soon as he was able to produce a tone. After he played the tune, his instructor wrote out the notation for it, sometimes on the chalkboard, sometimes on individual papers. The result? In a month, Mike went through the "break" and is still playing happily on his instrument.

How did he progress so fast? Well, he kept looking for more

notes so he could play more tunes, and when he was "stuck," the teacher helped him. After a few weeks of this he began using a book of exercises and tunes. The transition from playing by ear to playing from notation was gradual and painless.

Of course, you may say, these were two different boys. Of course. But the advertisement might never have appeared if Pete had been encouraged to *make music* from the beginning. The impulse of children with regard to any musical activity is, "Let's sing!" or, "Let's play!" In other words, they want to make music, not talk about it.

The preceding discussion may be summarized thus: it is best to make sure a child is physically, mentally, and emotionally mature enough to begin study of an instrument. It is best to determine whether or not his motivation is truly musical. And in all cases it is best to teach so that the mastery of reading skills develops from the making of music.

## *Developing Reading Skills*

In musical organizations pupils have—or should have—abundant opportunity to develop reading skill by playing or singing through much music. As they play through this music, the instructor has an excellent opportunity to assist them in developing skill. Mrs. Cane, the band director at Speak's High, tells her band to look through the score of a new number before they play it. "Think through it," she advises them. Often they hear a recording of the number before they play it. Regarding this, Mrs. Cane says, "Get an idea of the whole composition. Check the tempo, the dynamics, look for difficult passages, decide whether you like the recorded performance." As the band looks and listens, they are having a *hearing-reading* activity; they are forming a concept of the total sound of the music.

"It is regrettable but true," says their director, "that some bands play number after number without having much idea what the composition as a whole sounds like." Joe, a third trumpet player in a band 200 miles away, gets so tired of playing submerged parts that go "ta-ta" he says he'd quit if it weren't for the uniform. He isn't alone in this feeling.

Mrs. Cane also uses the tape recorder. She keeps it running throughout a rehearsal, sometimes, then studies it to spot difficulties various band members are having. She also spots her own difficulties. She sometimes records at the time the band is fairly familiar with a number, then encourages them to make their individual criticisms of the performance. This leads to the development of understanding and values.

Mrs. Cane knows, too, that total dependence on the director may discourage musical intelligence. If a crescendo is indicated in the music, the band members know they should read this; Mrs. Cane indicates and controls it rather than drags it forth by brute force. And she tries to help musical learning develop cumulatively and with continuity. "Remember the crescendo we played in *X Overture?* Look at this one; will it be as big?" Yes, she's limited for rehearsal time, like most of us, but she feels that her responsibility is music education, not simply beating time and calling out an alternate fingering for G-flat.

The same kind of teaching should prevail throughout the music program. Musical skill develops as we relate it to and associate it with the making of music—music made or listened to by any group of children or any individual anywhere.

Each music teacher has literally hundreds of opportunities for doing this every week. No time? Then we say that we have no time to help a child understand music. Too difficult? Then our materials are over the heads of our students. Too much trouble? Then we should be working with musicians who have already mastered their art.

Think it over, educators!

## *Senior High School Music: Special Needs*

The break between elementary and junior high music is often too sharp, too sudden. This is due to a change from music as part of the self-contained classroom to music as part of the specialized secondary program; specialized in terms of being solely taught by a music teacher.

The difference between junior high and senior high music? This is another story.

Senior high school music at present is, by and large, a program for instrumentalists and vocalists. It appears that in senior high school, music teachers are teaching the pupils who are music "specialists." Most of the music courses and activities planned are for these "specialist" pupils . . . a small per cent, indeed, of the total school population.

What has happened to all the children who liked and enjoyed music in first grade? Where are all the eager youngsters who began to take lessons on instruments? What happened to all the classes who blew on melody instruments (for a time)?

Since music on the senior high school level is largely elective in the schools of our country, all the missing students either must have decided music was not for them or have been unable to schedule it.

Yet no one is so rash as to believe all senior high school students would be happy in required music classes. We simply cannot force all students to take all subjects, no matter how much we believe in their value. It's obvious to any thinking adult that the roar of a well-tuned motor is going to make much more beautiful music to Ron, a member of the hot rod club, than is the sound of a symphony—at this stage of his life. If there isn't room for both in his life, he must have some say in deciding on one or the other.

Nevertheless, it is also obvious that our methods of building the music curriculum have put off many pupils. Speaking plainly, too often we have offered courses for those who were already deeply interested in music; we have given up thinking of ways in which school music might add to the lives of the disinterested majority. Some high schools, of course, have tried to provide for the consumers of music as well as the performers. These courses, however, pale by comparison with such offerings as band, orchestra, or chorus. They can't be put in the musical showcase, so they are likely to be undernourished in teacher time and materials, even where they have been included.

We have said that consumer courses are needed. Offer them on an elective basis. Call them Music I and II, Music for Consumers, or whatever you wish—but offer them. Build them on the basis of the musical interests and tastes of the majority of pupils in your high school. Begin, if you must, with Dixieland, hillbilly, or Rodgers-Hammerstein—but begin where you can get a good musical foothold in terms of your pupils' interests. Go from there. Build in terms of listening to music, discussing what makes it attractive to its devotees (whether they are Bach, bop, or cool jazz). Analyze it—your students will be learning about music. All the elements of music are in all kinds of music. Take it from there.

On the other end of the scale, we need a course for the students who are ready to synthesize their musical experiences, the boys and girls who have been in band, orchestra, choir, small ensembles. Amazing as it may seem to the layman, some of these youngsters have not yet figured out the why and how of musical mechanics.

How many performing organizations should a high school have? If you want an answer, ask these questions: How big is the high school? How much money is available for instruction and equipment? How much does the town want music in its high school?

The answers will have to be worked out by the administration and the faculty. There should be opportunities for the small per cent of highly talented and skilled pupil-musicians to participate on a level that will be rewarding—probably in small ensembles. There should be opportunity for the musically interested with average talent to participate—probably in larger organizations. And there should be room enough for every pupil to feel that, if he honestly wants the experience of singing or playing, he can have it. This means some beginning groups on senior high level. Probably the members of these groups will never hold first chair in chorus or orchestra; they won't bring home honors from contests. But this isn't the purpose of public school music.

## • FOOD FOR THOUGHT

1. Discuss ways in which music can be both enjoyable and a learning experience for children.
2. How can the idea of having fun with music be misinterpreted?
3. List five ways in which child development characteristics can serve as a guide to music teachers.
4. What is the difference between reading notes and reading music?
5. Can all children learn to read music? Should all children have the opportunity to learn to read music?

6. Analyze the way *you* learned to read music. Do you consider your experience to have been a good one? How might it have been improved?
7. Why do many children lose interest in piano or other instrumental study?
8. List ten ways in which band, orchestra, and choir directors can help their pupils improve music reading skills.

# 10 · General music classes in secondary schools

## *Common Problems*

The area of greatest difficulty and least security for teachers is certainly the general music program in the secondary school. As teachers discuss and write of their problems here, the same questions arise again and again. For example:

1. "The children don't seem to know much when they come to us from the elementary schools. What do those teachers teach them? I don't know where to begin working with them!"

Listening to this, it is always a temptation to inquire, "Have you talked this over with the elementary teachers? Do you know their total program? Isn't it true that children forget a great deal of what they learn in every subject? Are you thinking in terms of factual information acquired when you say, 'They don't know much . . . ' If so, have you considered thinking in terms of the broader music experience—listening to music, singing many songs, participating in rhythmic activities, going on field trips, creating music that develops from in-school or out-of-school activities? Do you know what the total load of the classroom teacher is, how much is expected of her in carrying on the music program in her room, how much time the music specialist can give to helping her, whether or not she has had adequate preparation for her work with the children's music?"

Investigation of such questions is an eye-opener for secondary-school music teachers. The elementary classroom teacher is responsible for teaching many subjects—the music specialist usually has only one major responsibility. The elementary classroom teacher tends to think in terms of the children and the total classroom program; the music specialist tends to think (more or less naturally) in terms of children and music. Understanding each other's work and viewpoint is much too limited.

We may as well say at once that the "sudden death" approach —complaining about the results of the elementary music program—is the best way to cut off understanding of the situation. The elementary teacher who is doing the best she can, then hears complaints about her work, usually becomes defensive, tense, or unhappy about further efforts in the area concerned. A better approach is to try to discuss with elementary teachers what they are doing in music. Try a positive viewpoint: "I will be better able to continue your work successfully if I know what you have given the children before they came into my class." Such questions as the following may develop useful information:

(a) What musical experiences did the children find most interesting?

(b) What songs and records were favorites?

(c) Which children seem to have unusual musical talent? How was this evidenced?

(d) Are there areas in which you feel the children need particular help?

(e) In what musical skills are the children strong? What skills did they find difficult to master? What approaches did you find effective in developing skills?

In discussing these questions with elementary teachers, remember to discuss, not criticize. Remember, too, that having asked a question, it's a good idea to listen rather than expound. You may be tempted to answer your own question by giving advice on what should have been done. Don't! This will certainly put your colleague on the defensive; it may shut off communication between you. Eventually your colleague will be convinced that you are interested in what she is doing; you may be asked what your ideas are, what suggestions you have for more effective methods and materials, and your ideas will fall on receptive ears. This approach takes time; be patient.

It is also important to remember that, having consulted the elementary teacher about her program, and having received information, it is wise to keep in touch now and then. Let her know how you have used the information in your teaching. Knowing, for example, that Benny is a slow reader should be a real help in understanding why he may not join in with the class at once in singing a new song. A seventh grade teacher who learns, from talking with the sixth grade teacher, what songs her class liked best during the preceding year has a positive basis on which to build this year's song repertoire.

Generalizing, it is safe to say that secondary-school music teachers can learn much from elementary classroom teachers, and vice versa, as long as the lines of communication are open. Some of us never bother to pick up the receiver and dial the number; we have no right to complain, then. By and large, the biggest complainers are the least effective teachers.

2. We have been told many times that effective learning is related to a goal. This may be the answer to a problem music teachers sometimes face—the attitude, "Music isn't important. We only have class twice a week, so it's a minor subject." If pupils display this attitude, they are saying, "We don't see any reason for coming to music class." This may be failure to recognize the goal of their efforts. Why not discuss it with them?

One teacher asked his class, "What would the world be like without music? What would you substitute for music?" In the course of the discussion that followed, class members talked about the ways in which music is made, the people who compose music, the differences in various types of music, what they liked best in music and the reasons why. In discussing this they were establishing a background for setting up goals within their understanding. The teacher then built his classes around musical goals the class set up with his guidance. Each class began with a discussion of what was to be achieved during the class and what had been achieved during the last class (thus establishing continuity), and so had a positive basis for action. At the end of the class a short summarizing session took place. This was a review in discussion form, a series of questions, or even a series of answers with the class framing questions to fit the answer. The last procedure, a reverse twist, stimulated some thinking on the part of pupils who might otherwise have been disinterested.

For example, after playing a portion of a song with which the class was familiar, the teacher placed on the board several words or phrases pertaining to it; for example, "folksong, minor, two-part, major." A student might then ask another class member, "Is (song title) a two-part folk song ending in minor and beginning in major?" The answer might be, "No, it's a two-part folksong beginning in minor and ending in major." Of course all points of information used in such a procedure had been stressed as the students learned the song. The procedure is a summarizing one; it helps pupils become more aware of what they have learned through music, and assists them in relating it to the musical experience, which, of course, is primary in importance.

3. "What shall I teach in junior high general music?" First, look at the pupils who make up these classes. You will find that in many schools everyone takes general music. This means classes of "captive audiences," not all of whom are willing "captives." Some, though, already have established a lively interest in playing an instrument, or in a particular type of music. Analyze the classes you teach; offer them a program of

experiences geared to their maturity, interests, background, knowledge, and skills.

## *Planning General Music Classes*

If your school has not thought through the basic philosophy of what and why you are to teach children music, you may have to do this on your own, or with a small group of interested teachers. Whether you are working alone or with others in this process, however, the same planning principle will hold true. This principle has to do with the use children will make of music both in their present lives and in their adult lives. In the general music class we have all the pupils; most of them are and will continue to be consumers of music. Some already are performers in bands, orchestras, and choruses; a few are experienced soloists. Not many, though, will become professional musicians. How will the majority use music in their lives? All of us listen to music; we can't escape it. Some of us sing as members of the congregation in church, some as members of service clubs. A small number play or sing in amateur instrumental or choral groups. An increasing number are becoming hi-fi enthusiasts and record collectors. Some adults become music hobbyists; some go further and regard music as an avocation.

A conclusion is evident from this brief discussion of the way people use music in their lives. Emphasis in general music classes should be more on developing the intelligent consumer and less on forcing *everyone* to reach a performing level. In attempting the latter teachers and pupils alike develop severe cases of frustration; it is an artificial and false goal. If everyone tried to play on the baseball team, the bleachers would be empty.

Why do you suppose the cereal manufacturers combine a variety of cereals in one big package? They evidently know that their consumers like a change of taste, that wherever a housewife has to buy for her family there will be different preferences within that family, and that the more popular cereals will help sell the less popular when they are packaged together.

The secondary teacher can take a cue from this for her general music class. Here we need a variety of different musical activities because our pupils are different in their musical abilities, interests, and tastes; because the teacher must plan to feed these differences with varied experiences; because some of the more popular aspects of the program—but still necessary and useful—will help sell the less popular, will even make them more easily understood.

John and Susie, American children, are growing up in an American home where they see many choices open to their parents, many manufacturers and producers of products varying from breakfast cereals to TV programs bidding for their favor. "Are you going to buy a car? Buy our Super Leaper, the best built car on the road!" "Do you want to keep your gums forever free from erosion? Use our Perma-Pleasant Toothpaste—absolutely frees you from gum gook forever!"

Susie and John come into eighth grade music class the same year Miss Allen, fresh from college, arrives to become their new music teacher.

"Boys and girls, today we are going to hear a 'cello concerto by a great composer who lived from 1810 to 1856. This is beautiful music, and I hope you will listen attentively." Miss Allen turns her back to adjust the record player and several things happen immediately—John signals "SQUARE" to the boy next to him, Herman in the back row opens a comic book and begins to read it under the desk, Red Smith aims a firm kick at the fellow in front of him, Miss Allen is hit by a spitball, and Susie says, "Why can't we hear something good, like 'Don't Stop Your Moanin' by Willie, the Squealer?" Chaos reigns. The next year Miss Allen gets another job.

Does she know what happened, though? It seems that she forgot junior high youngsters have their own ideas about music; that, being members of families who make free choices (subject, of course, to all kinds of advertising pressures), they expect to have something to say about their music. She forgot to look at them as people accustomed to expressing ideas; she assumed they would accept her own acquired and highly trained values. If Susie plays the musical saw, if Melvin plays the harmonica, they do so because they like it, and it has, to them, just as much prestige as the 'cello. Willie the Squealer, their current singing idol, grosses a million dollars a year, and they know it, so why not listen to him? Besides, his band has a real gone beat.

Now there is nothing wrong with Miss Allen's desire to share her own musical enthusiasm with her pupils. But she should have built, with their help, a variety package of musical experiences. And she should have remembered that it took her many years and much training to develop an appreciation for the 'cello concerto.

The goal that emerges from this? MAKE A MUSIC PROGRAM THAT IS FUNCTIONAL IN CHILDREN'S LIVES. In large cities where children have many opportunities to hear good music, we may begin on a higher plane and progress more rapidly, perhaps; in schools where children come from isolated rural communities with a marginal level of good musical experiences available, the situation is vastly different. Remember this, Miss Allen, in your next job!

In Mr. Carey's seventh grade music class Tim and Ned, both over-age for seventh grade, have rushed into the room carrying a large nailkeg drum. "Look, we've finished it!" Classmates gather round to admire and examine their handiwork. "It sounds cool," says Johnny after administering a satisfactory thump. Mr. Carey suggests, "How about using it for an accompaniment? Who wants to find a song that needs a good, solid drumbeat in the background?" During this class period a song is reviewed, drum accompaniment worked out, notation for accompaniment placed on chalkboard by Helen and her pal Mary, and five or six children take turns playing it. Things are not silent in this classroom—there's a busy hum of activity. But who would have known, viewing the scene, that Tim and Ned had been chronic offenders with regard to acceptable classroom behavior? That is, until Mr. Carey found a project that interested them, and provided plenty of encouragement plus liberal praise for their efforts.

"This isn't education," sniffs Miss Thistlethorne, who teaches in the next-door room. "It's just keeping them busy. What could they learn from making that awful-looking drum? I think this is selling children short—none of this will go on in my class, believe me."

Miss Thistlethorne, we believe you. And we have news for you, particularly in view of the fact that you ejected Tim and Ned from your class ten times last year, then requested that they be assigned to another teacher this year. Tim and Ned are learning quite a few things from their drum. They read the instructions for making it, and this was all to the good; both boys are retarded in reading. They located materials. They put three different heads on the drum before they were satisfied with the tone; this was developing listening skill. They helped make the drum accompaniment for the song; they were interested, even, when the notation was worked out on the chalkboard. And for a change, they were praised by the teacher for their work; they had a chance to bask in their classmates' admiration. They became a wanted part of the group—they had prestige. Tim and Ned will never write a "Toccata for Percussion." But they are beginning to think they have a place in music class, perhaps in school, too.

We hope Miss Allen and Mr. Carey meet sometime, somewhere, and exchange ideas on their teaching. It seems that Mr. Carey knows quite a bit about boys and girls as well as about music. And it would seem that Miss Allen knows quite a bit about music, but not enough about boys and girls. To teach successfully, she needs both.

By the way, did you assume that Miss Thistlethorne was a music teacher? She teaches another subject. And she is under the impression that music teachers cause a lot of noise plus waste motion on the part of the children. "Waste motion" includes square dancing. It will take a long time for Miss Thistlethorne to understand Mr. Carey and the way he teaches. But she's beginning to wonder . . . and envy him a little. The children seem so anxious to get to music class.

## *Scope of Program*

Everyone, then, who plans the content of general music classes should remember that word "variety." There are still classes where the pupils do nothing but sing, still classes where they just listen. *This,* we think, is selling the children short. Music is a wonderful big variety package in itself, full of excitement and surprises—so are children. Together they make a fine combination for the understanding teacher.

If you are planning for general music classes, try to include:

1. Songs of many countries and many moods. Work songs, play songs, love songs, ballads, and many other expressions of man's feelings about the world in which he lives, all serve as a lively means of emotional expression. Help your pupils discover how these differ in their musical construction, how the composer uses the same medium, music, to express many different attitudes and emotions. Ask them why they sing the "Caisson Song" with one spirit and "Tell Me Why" in a very different way. Analyze this. *How?* Is it through dynamics, tempo, voice quality? Is it because the two songs are written in different meter signatures? Is the form of one of the songs different from the other? In what way do the accompaniments differ? Such points, and many others that will occur to the teacher, have in them the seeds of the learning experience. They also have inherent in them the basis of developing musicianship, for a class cannot possibly sing these two songs in the same manner without being conscious that something is wrong. In tracking down this "something" (which may exist in children's consciousness only as a vague difference) children develop an

interest in the reasons why and how one song effectively expresses one idea and spirit, another song a different idea and spirit. And in doing so they are building a knowledge of the materials of music and its techniques; they are building skills. Encourage them to learn through discovering for themselves. Set up, through your teaching, a situation in which they may do so. Obviously this is a far cry from placing on the chalkboard some information about the song and requiring that they memorize it. The latter process requires no thought. The former does.

2. Correlate with other subjects, interests, and activities. Ginny Craig, a music teacher, has always said she would like to know more about how to correlate music with other subjects. She feels there is a great, unrevealed mystery about this somewhere, and that no one has taken the trouble to divulge it. Yet day after day she goes on teaching songs, playing records for her classes. Will Kent, another music teacher, knows that correlating music with other subjects and interests is a good procedure. When his class sings the "Caisson Song" or the "Marines' Hymn" he may ask, "Why do people march? When? Where?" As soon as hands go up, he is on the way to correlation. Perhaps this is part of a planned unit, perhaps it is spontaneous. In either case, Will teaches this way.

He makes sure that his class understands the words of the song they are singing, too. The first year he taught and the class gleefully sang "corpse" instead of "corps," Will took a few minutes and discussed the two words with them. " 'Corps' is a much stronger word than 'corpse'," he told them. "It packs more wallop. Now, tell me what each word means, Linda." The next question was, "If you were writing the words of this song, would you use 'corpse' or 'corps'?" By this time both words were on the chalkboard. It took a few minutes, but the class enjoyed the discussion. The next time someone tried to be funny by singing "corpse" the class ignored him. That was the answer to the problem.

Lines of correlation are far-flung, but one thing is sure; we can't plan to correlate on rainy Tuesdays and dry Fridays only. It is an integral part of teaching, and its effective use depends on the teacher's understanding of music in its relationship to the people who make it and hear it, past or present. This understanding appears to be a product of the teacher's education; it is also inherent in a viewpoint that looks at a subject from many angles in terms of many relationships. Correlation *is* relationships.

3. Include many listening experiences. See that these are related in some real way to the songs your class is singing. This may be either through singing a marching song, for example, and analyzing a band recording of a march, or listening to the Vaughn Williams "English Folk Song Suite" after studying and singing English folk songs. The lesson may point up a musical relationship in which your pupils investigate the musical characteristics prominent both in a recorded composition and the songs they are singing.

4. Use materials of current interest. If a popular song in which your pupils are interested has effective harmonization, rhythmic background, or modulation, for example, don't hesitate to bring it into the classroom and use it to help develop a singing or listening skill. Interest in a "pop" baritone singer today may facilitate understanding an operatic baritone, may even lead to a lasting interest in opera if you help open the door. Your objective is to help your pupils understand and appreciate music.

Mr. Low in Hughes School has an accelerated ninth grade class. They are interested, even excited, about investigating overtures of different types. They plunge into the music, listen, discuss, take notes, analyze like seasoned veterans. When themes are placed on the chalkboard they immediately copy them in notebooks. No one tells them to; they just go ahead.

It would be very foolish for Mr. Low, in this class, to introduce a symphony by playing a popular song that incorporates a melody from it—foolish, and a waste of time. This class needs no "stimulator." But Mr. Low also has a ninth grade class of slow-learning boys and girls. He can help them in listening to music by using, at times, the story approach, and he does not hesitate to do so. They became interested in listening to, and discussing, opera when he wrote short, dramatized, modern language versions of the libretto and, passing out copies to each pupil, called for volunteers to read the lines of various characters. "What kind of a voice would the Count have?" And "Let's see, this fellow is a lively person, and he's quite angry at this point in the opera. Listen to him sing, and then describe the kind of song the composer wrote for him."

Mr. Low has average classes, too, but whatever class he is teaching, he takes a long look at its members and then picks up wherever they are in terms of interests, background, and abilities. Mr. Low's principal says he's a good teacher. It isn't difficult to understand why, is it?

5. Include rhythmic activities in the music class. Play a march. Any drummers in your class? Invite them to bring in the drums; ask them to demonstrate various rhythmic patterns they play in familiar marches. This is particularly interesting to many classes when the patterns are notated on the chalkboard. Junior high is a good time to use square dancing, play party and singing games, too—good for several reasons, one of which is that boys and girls now are conscious of each other in a social sense, and need to acquire ease in group activities. Another is that for the boys, these activities are a natural—on the frontier, dancing was a part of the masculine role; it was recreation after a day of helping a neighbor raise a barn or cut a stand of timber. It was an expression of robust youth. And be sure to use rhythm instruments. Junior high pupils are greatly interested in them.

Suppose you have no instruments, no records. What then in rhythmic activities? Try the different varieties of clapping hands, snapping fingers, tapping with pencil (eraser end) on book.

Whatever your class may do with this aspect of the program, make sure it relates, in their thinking, to the musical framework out of which it developed in the first place. Extraneous snapping, clapping, or thumping is certainly no musical activity. In addition, you may find yourself in the unhappy situation of Miss Haden, whose class ends up in a free-for-all, slapping and punching after the preliminary snapping and clapping. This has a greatly disturbing effect on the principal and nearby teachers. Miss Haden includes these activities because she read somewhere, or heard, that they were desirable. Does she have a true understanding of their purpose?

Miss Burton, not too many miles away, also uses them, but she and her class together decide where they are appropriate, and from what musical basis they evolve. For instance, there isn't enough room for everyone in Miss Burton's class to square dance at the same time. They discovered through reading and possibly movies or TV that the onlookers participated by stamping and clapping, becoming part of the accompaniment. So the stamping and clapping is part of the music, and Miss Burton does not have to scream, "Children, children, that's enough of that!" Neither does the principal have to arrive with a copy of the Riot Act. Miss Burton, too, is likely to use portions of Copland's "Appalachian Suite," or Siegmeister's "Ozark Set," to show how a composer uses "dance" music in his work. The class may also locate and sing folk songs in the dance spirit; from all these they will find the musical characteristics of American frontier music.

6. Whether teaching is done in units, single complete lessons, or any other way, establish a unifying thread. One class investigated "Pioneers in Music Making." Beethoven was a pioneer, you see; so was George Gershwin. Remember his "Porgy and Bess?" The class decided he was eligible because this was a folk opera—a first in American music.

Another class became so interested in the musical characterization of great men that they chose several musical compositions for study—Copland's "Lincoln Portrait" was one. The emphasis seemed to fall naturally on how the *music* added to the historical fact, figure, or legend. The brooding mood of the "Lincoln Portrait" in its opening passages revealed the sombre side of Lincoln's nature; but they listened to Robinson's "Lonesome Train," comparing how he portrayed the robust, fun-loving facets of this great man's personality as well as a more serious side. When pupils learn in such a way, the unifying thread of their investigations never disappears, for this thread lies in the very stuff of the music itself. What is the spirit—the mood—of this music? How did the composer achieve it; through use of mode, instrumentation, form, dynamics?

As pupils search for the answers, the skills begin to emerge. They hear crescendos and diminuendos, fortissimos and pianissimos. Why are they there? How did the composer indicate that he wanted them there? Keep cumulative charts with these musical symbols on them, pulling them from the music as they seem significant, and as they are part of a musical experience. Encourage pupils to describe them in their own words. One class listened to a coloratura soprano—she was singing on TV that week. "How would you describe a coloratura soprano?" was the question. One boy who seldom participated promptly said, "It's a voice that's all over the place!"

Crudely stated? Yes—but what a wonderfully spontaneous answer. "Say, that's good!" said the teacher before he went on to other answers. "I like the way you put that, Sam." And because praise and recognition are keys to self-motivation, Sam began to participate more regularly. In addition to the motivation, however, music seems to *make sense to pupils when it has a unifying center of interest*. This is a big objective.

7. To learn about many technical matters relating to music, use visual materials and aids. "What is the difference between the sound of a cornet and a trumpet?" a class once asked. To answer this question, one teacher had a trumpet player come

in with both trumpet and cornet. The class was fascinated when he announced that he would retire into a small closet just off the classroom and play the same melody six times, changing at will from trumpet to cornet. The class was instructed to listen and try to decide whether the melody was played on trumpet or cornet the first time, the second time, and so on. They were asked to indicate this on a piece of paper. A wonderful silence fell over the room, the silence that tells a teacher his pupils are engrossed in a challenging and interesting task. What were the visual aids? The trumpet and cornet; not pictures of these, but the real thing.

Another time the class hit the same interest peak when they worked with a metronome to determine the tempo at which certain marches were played on recordings by two different bands. A fuzzy concept of the meaning of "tempo" was clarified in this class.

Still again, the use of tuned bottles in developing a simple accompaniment revealed in specific terms much about pitch. Furthermore, it "activated" two of the over-age boys in the class, boys who had been "sitters" rather than "doers." "Make a tone on a pop bottle? Sure—it's easy!" When the tones were put together and turned out to be a song accompaniment, their expressions of surprise, pleasure, and achievement were sufficient reward for the teacher's extra hours in planning the lesson; particularly when the boys figured out the pitch of each bottle, located it on the staff, and worked out the notation for their accompaniment.

Yes, they had help. Isn't that what a teacher is for?

### *Stop! Don't Use Those Books!*

The silence in Room 33 is ominous. Forty pupils in music class bend over forty books, copying something on forty pieces of paper. Miss Wood stands in the front of the room. She's the teacher? This is music class? Where's the music?

Step closer to the desk of Willie, who has some difficulty reading. Let's see what he's writing. Isn't that . . . yes, he's trying to write "Tchaikovsky." Letter by letter, he copies it laboriously. In five minutes Willie manages to copy one sentence. But don't ask him what it means. Willie is doing what he was told to do; he's copying. This is music class?

Miss Wood, wherever you are, please don't use those books, don't use those teaching methods. The copyright date is 1920 or thereabouts; we can't be sure, because Willie's copy is so faded. The books are three times Willie's age, and they couldn't bore him more if they were a hundred times his age. They are not great classics. They were written for the use of youngsters who sat in schools more than 35 years ago, and even Willie's mother didn't like them.

But wait; Harold, second seat in the third row, rebel and free spirit, has raised his head and laid aside his pencil. "Let's sing!" says Harold.

Bravo, boy! You think music class is for making music. You can copy forever and never know what Tchaikovsky's music says and means.

And you, Miss Wood. Some night you should get the custodian and clean out those music closets. Throw away the stale, battered books that are not for today's boys and girls. Better throw away some of your methods, too. Your pupils want to make music, and they're right.

## *Listen to What Your Pupils Say*

It sometimes seems that we teachers become so busy with our teaching that we fail to listen to our pupils. This is particularly true of beginning teachers, of course, for they must learn to understand the language of children, learn that their answers may be correct even though clothed in somewhat unusual verbiage.

One example has been given in previous pages—the child's

description of a coloratura. Two more may help to impress this on the reader:

One teacher was doing an excellent piece of work helping a class understand the various rhythmic effects of certain patterns. After they had encountered a particular rhythmic pattern in a song ($\frac{6}{8}$ ♩♪♩♪) she asked them to describe the way

it made them feel in terms of motion. One boy said, "It's like riding on the rumble seat of a horse!" His friend added, "The 'rumble seat' is riding back of the person who's in the saddle. It's bumpy, you know!"

This is the kind of answer that might mistakenly be passed over as frivolous. But it describes in the child's reactions and language what this particular rhythmic pattern means to him in movement. It has an authentic quality.

Another child said, comparing the tone of a cornet to that of a horn, "It's more gathered up!" We don't need to paraphrase her answer—you know what she meant, and so do her classmates. This answer shows a child is having a musical experience, is thinking about it, is translating it into words.

Let's listen to children's responses; let's encourage them to put these responses in their own words.

## • FOOD FOR THOUGHT

1. How can secondary music teachers work with elementary teachers to develop an effective transition from elementary to secondary music?
2. Why is a planned variety of musical experiences important in general music classes?
3. Make a list of the ways in which several of your friends (not musicians) use music in their everyday lives. Are these ways related to the music learning experiences they had in high school? Was high school music a help in developing their musical tastes and interests?
4. Ask several of your friends (not musicians) what they most enjoyed about music classes in high school. Inquire as to their ideas concerning improving general music classes.
5. What is meant by "consumer" education in general music classes?
6. How can slow-learning children make a real contribution to music classes?
7. How can teachers hold the attention of accelerated pupils in heterogeneous classes?
8. Examine a song textbook used in an eighth grade music class. List ten songs the class would enjoy singing. Make a large chart on which you list ten musical terms or symbols the class might learn to use from singing these songs.
9. Make a song accompaniment for a Latin-American song using rhythm instruments such as conga and bongo drums, maracas, castanets and claves. Examine the piano accompaniment for suggested rhythmic patterns.

# 11 · Instrumental and choral problems

## *Instrumental Specialists*

Ever since man discovered that he could make music on other instruments than his voice, he has been intrigued with the idea and its implementation. The making of such music is a means of self-expression, of artistic and social communication—a wordless projection of the individual's thinking and feeling.

These same reasons continue to interest today's children in making instrumental music. To assess the position of the instrumental music program in modern education, we need to know why it has a place in the curriculum. One reason is that the self-expression of the individual is important. A second reason is that, because the school can reach a large group of children, instrumental instruction is economical and efficient. A third reason is that, since public school teachers are certified and must meet required standards, it is possible to upgrade the quality of instruction through selection of the type of person who teaches our children.

But all these reasons may be reduced to a basic one: *the instrumental program exists for the benefit of the children*—not the school, not the community.

Certain interesting problems arise out of this situation. Some of the major problems that deal with organizations will be discussed in a later chapter; aspects of these that have most to do with pupils we will discuss here.

1. It is difficult, often, to schedule the instrumental program. In some ways it seems to be a stepchild of the school, an extra. If it is worthy of its place, however, it should be scheduled on school time. Children should not have to come before or stay after school for this purpose.

Sandra is in eighth grade. She is studying flute, and making rapid progress. In order to receive instruction from her high school instrumental teacher, though, Sandra has to come to school forty-five minutes early every Tuesday morning. This means a long day in school, a long time between breakfast and lunch. And since she lives two miles from the school, her mother has to drive her to school. The family has only one car; Dad has to take the bus or ride to work with a neighbor on Tuesdays.

Now multiply Sandra by thousands of children over the country who are in the same situation. Shouldn't music be scheduled on school time? It looks that way.

2. Who shall participate in the instrumental music program? The schools are for all the children, supported by public funds. Weber Township Schools have had an instrumental director for three years. But he has to raise all the money for the instrumental program, materials and instruments both, any way he can. He has a feeling that all the children who want to play an instrument should be given the opportunity to do so; he knows, however, that there are many who simply can't afford to buy or rent one.

He also feels that having been educated and employed as an instrumental teacher, it is somewhat of a waste of time when, instead of teaching children, he has to supervise the sale of magazines and chicken dinners, and ten other varieties of money raising plans, in order to buy new music for the spring concert.

If the instrumental program is worthy of its place in the schools, it should be financed by the schools.

3. A third point involves both philosophy and teaching methods. If the instrumental program is part of the total school curriculum, its basic philosophy and methods should be consistent with those in other subject areas. By this we mean that there should be instrumental education, not instrumental training.

Most of us have heard the distinction put something like this: we train a dog, cat, or parrot; we educate children. This may be a fine distinction, but its essence is that *children* think. When they relate their thinking—as well as their feeling—to the making of music, we help develop the individual potential of each child. If, on the other hand, we enlist them in the instrumental program mainly for the purpose of training band and orchestra replacements, we may unconsciously slip into the training business instead of the educating business.

To make this discussion even more pertinent, if you are an instrumental instructor, ask yourself how many of your students can and do play solos, either for their own enjoyment or for that of others?

No one will question the value of playing in an instrumental organization. But group expression is one thing, individual another. This is a matter of personal teaching philosophy; it is also a matter for the school to think through.

4. A fourth question that arises in the instrumental program is who shall be in the band or orchestra, and how the selection shall be made.

Here we find two very different schools of thought, although some teachers strike a compromise. Certain directors feel that the school band, for example, exists only for the most talented and able pupils. Band members are rigorously screened, and no matter how much Jimmy wants to be in the band, no matter how much his homeroom teacher or guidance official says he *needs* to be in band, he is not accepted if his ability to play an instrument falls below a certain level. Mr. Barrett, the band director, says "the band won't sound good" unless its members are selected on such a basis. Their standards are high; their concerts are beautiful. They march with precision. They are greatly in demand for public performances. Jimmy sits in the audience or stands on the street watching and dreaming—"if only I could play with them."

Chances are he never will, because he is neither very bright nor very talented. His real need is a social one. Mr. Barrett believes this is not part of his responsibility as a band director.

If Jimmy moved to Lockport, he would be accepted as a member of Dick Herbert's band. Dick thinks that if a boy or girl needs to be in the band, and if he can play even reasonably well, he should be accepted. Dick's band doesn't sound quite as well as Mr. Barrett's—you hear a "clinker" now and then as they play. And occasionally someone gets out of step during a parade. On the whole, though, it's a good organization; both members and townspeople enjoy it.

We have no intention of criticizing either one of the two band directors in this discussion. The truth is that each one of them does an effective job, and each is well accepted by the school and community he serves. The chief question arising from the comparison is this; does the organization exist to serve the pupil, or does the pupil exist to serve the organization?

Mr. Barrett will tell you, if asked, that boys and girls learn a great deal from being part of a band where they have to meet rigid standards. This is true, if they understand and have a voice in setting these standards, and if the standards are reasonable to a degree that the majority of instrumental pupils can meet them. Mr. Barrett says, "The football coach fields only the best—so do I."

Is music competitive? Should it operate on the same philosophy as competitive sports? Each school must work out its own answer to such a question, but certainly on the basis of determining what is best for the children involved. The children *are* the school.

### *Choral Specialists*

Instrumental teachers are sometimes heard to remark that choral teachers have a comparatively easy time since the pupil always has his voice with him; the most he has to lug around is music, and sometimes a choir robe. Some choral teachers, on the other hand, feel that the instrumentalists have an advantage, since a pupil who is shy or otherwise inhibited as to singing can get behind his instrument as a shield and make music through it.

We suspect that each has advantages, and that both face

fairly similar problems. Much of what has been said about the instrumental program applies to the choral program:

1. Scheduling should be during the school day.
2. The program should be financed by school funds.
3. The teaching philosophy should be in keeping with that of other subject areas.
4. The selection of choir members should be to the best advantage of the individuals involved.
5. Neither choirs nor bands should be exploited for the glorification of the director or the community.

Performance levels should be in keeping with the ability of the majority of children—otherwise, how can the music program function in their interests? In large high schools it is sometimes possible to have a select group limited to the most capable pupils, and an elective group open to all comers, barring only those who for specific reasons cannot sing. This second group, while serving as a feeder for the first, should be a musical organization in its own right, developing satisfying experiences for its members.

Some choral directors make the mistake of being overly ambitious for their groups. Nothing is more frustrating to a group than struggling with music too difficult to sing satisfactorily. This is where the musical standards of the director must adjust to the musical standards of the group and their ability.

The Porterville High School Glee Club, when Helen Runner became its musical director, was suffering from a severe inferiority complex. This was a "second" organization; the school choir was the showpiece of the school. Most of the Glee Club members had tried out for the Choir but had failed to make it.

For several years they had struggled along, often spending weeks rehearsing material too difficult, singing flat, looking and sounding dispirited in spite of the well-meaning intentions of the director. "The first thing this group needs," decided Mrs. Runner, "is a booster shot of self-confidence." Investigating the musical activities of the school for a number of years back, she found that no musical group had given a talent show. In a meeting with the officers of the Glee Club she suggested the possibility of giving a concert. The reaction was, "No, we can't sing as well as the Choir; it would be a flop."

Mrs. Runner then asked whether the group would consider a talent show. Faces brightened—now the reaction was, "This would be something we could do as well as any other group." The talent show involved much committee work, much searching for talent and many tryouts. But now the group had a unifying project underway, something obtainable in the way of objectives. The talent show played to a packed auditorium, the Glee Club displayed an enthusiasm and spirit that fired the audience to satisfying applause, the venture was a success.

Would you condemn Mrs. Runner for lowering her musical standards? Or would you praise her understanding of the situation? The members of the Glee Club gained prestige and self-confidence through an experience geared to their level. If this group had continued to give talent show after talent show, we would have reason for considering it a limiting experience. The fact is that the group went on to reach a higher level of musical experiences and performances; the talent show, as a kick-off project, served its purpose. It was not a conclusive end in itself, but rather the means to an end.

Both choral and instrumental specialists are in a unique position, vulnerable because of the public nature of their work in terms of performance, walking a slippery road because their teaching programs often involve a large proportion of the school population, both as audiences and performers. They are subject to pressure through requests for both school and community performances. Few of these teachers use their positions as a means of personal glory. Few work for the limelight of public appearance. It would be safer to say that they accept these responsibilities as part of the position.

For every public appearance a director makes, he works many, many times with his group in the equivalent of a classroom situation. What brings the most pleasure and satisfaction in his work is the enjoyment and pride the members of a musical organization take in growing to a point where they understand the music they are performing, where they can express this understanding through their skills in bringing it to an audience.

Perhaps there are a few directors who isolate their efforts to such an extent that they end up with a miniature conservatory attached to the rest of the school. This is unfortunate. But the vast majority of music educators who direct bands, orchestras, choruses, and glee clubs are working to make music a part of the total school program. As they succeed in doing so, more and more pupils will become involved in the musical organizations of the school.

## • FOOD FOR THOUGHT

1. Give three reasons why instrumental music should be included in the school curriculum.
2. Should all students be permitted to have instrumental instruction free of charge?
3. Approximately what percentage of pupils should be in the instrumental program, secondary level? Why does this percentage vary radically from school to school? Is it really possible to say that a definite percentage of any particular school's population should be in the instrumental program?
4. List four criteria for accepting students into a musical organization.
5. Give examples of what may happen when a choir director encourages a choir to attempt performing music that is too difficult for them.

# 12 · The administrator looks at the secondary-school music program

## *Relationships Within the Secondary-School Music Program*

The problems of the music specialist in the secondary school are many and varied. Chief among them is the establishing of good working relations with the other teachers on the staff. On his success in establishing those relationships depends the ultimate success of his music program and the degree to which he will find personal satisfaction in his own professional life. What are the situations from which arise the misunderstandings that cause friction? How are these situations viewed by the music teachers and by some of the other faculty members?

## *Music Activities Are Popular with High School Pupils*

A music teacher's viewpoint: "Our music program is attractive to the boys and girls. It is varied and has an appeal to a large segment of the school population. More pupils want to be in the choruses than we can possibly take. Our orchestra and band are large and we have a junior band and orchestra. The boys and girls believe that the music program fills a need in their school life. Because they feel that way, we music teachers believe that we have a wonderful opportunity to guide and counsel the students."

Another view: "The students flock into the music activities because it gives them a chance to show off. They fill their programs with subjects that require no homework and no study. They resent the academic subjects that require reading, library work, and home study. They feel that being members of the chorus and orchestra is like being members of an exclusive club. The music teachers are always championing their talented performers."

### *Music Activities Have the Support of the Pupils' Parents*

A music teacher's viewpoint: "You can't have a band without uniforms. Someone has to help chaperon the chorus when we give concerts out of town. We have to have cars to transport the pupils to district music affairs. The instruments the pupils own and the few provided by the school board are not enough. The parents are interested in the music activities of the school. Some have paid for private music lessons for their children; they have bought instruments. They want to help. That's why I have organized my band parents into a group. It is an actively interested group. It is good for the school and community."

Another view: "The Band Parents group is a pressure group that the music teachers have organized to get them the things that they want. We need things for our classes, too. Can we organize Mathematics Parents Clubs—English Parents Societies—Chemistry Boosters? The Band Parents are interested in seeing their children perform. They aren't interested in the school. Why should one group of teachers be permitted to organize the parents of their pupils?

### *Music Programs Reach Beyond the Music Classrooms*

A music teacher's viewpoint: "One of the wonderful things about the music program is that it reaches beyond the classroom. It touches and enriches every part of the school. Some people think that the parade before the game and the band show between halves is the best part of a high school football game. The dramatics department depends on music for the Christmas pageant. The orchestra always plays for our assemblies. The city, county, and district music activities help our pupils to adjust to many different people and many new situations. The public performances help the students develop poise. Without our music program the other departments would be poorer. Of course, any program that reaches beyond the music classroom will have to reach into the other classrooms. We have to get ready for programs. Soloists need special help. When we ask to have pupils excused from other classes to rehearse for music it is because we believe that what they will get from and give in the music activity will justify the time taken from another class."

Another view: "The music teacher wants the pupils who are in the music activities to be privileged characters. When he is getting ready for a concert, he thinks nothing of asking to have individuals and groups excused for special lessons or rehearsals. If we refuse to let the pupils go, the pupils are resentful of us and the parents don't like it. Yet the parents are the first to criticize us when the students do not have high academic achievement. If we aren't willing for music people to miss our classes we are accused of being uncooperative. Yet we can't get the music teacher to excuse a pupil from orchestra or chorus to do special work for us. The music teachers say, 'If you aren't at practice you can't play.' "

## *Music Is a Part of the School's Public Relations Program*

A music teacher's viewpoint: "When our pupils provide entertainment for the noon luncheon of the service clubs or for the women's civic clubs, it is good public relations. When I lead group singing or accompany soloists, it is a service from the school to the community."

Another view: "The music teachers can go anywhere they please during school hours. None of the rest of the faculty can take two hours off at noon for lunch. We are expected to be with our classes. Why do they have privileges that we don't have?"

Is this an exaggerated presentation of the situations that exist in secondary schools? Conversation with teachers will soon reveal that what has been written is only a sketch of the deep

feelings of dissatisfaction that lie close to the surface in the relationship of the music teachers to the faculty in many schools. What can be done about them? Who is to do it?

*First, let us recognize that these feelings are not directed against a person.* Paul Ross and Emmett George play golf together, their families are friends and they frequently visit in each other's homes. But when Emmett George, *mathematics teacher,* looks out of his classroom window and sees Paul Ross, *music teacher,* get into his car at noon, five minutes later in the cafeteria he may be heard to say, "Those music fellows sure have it soft. I wish I were free to go to the hotel on Tuesdays to luncheon."

Helen Correll and Belle Wolf have been lifelong friends. They went to college together and have taught for ten years in the same high school. On the day when a pretty young junior comes to Miss Wolf's desk and says, "I can't come to Latin class tomorrow, our quartet is to sing for Tuesday Afternoon Music Club," Miss Wolf's opening remark in the teachers' room is, "Well, it's started again; who do those music teachers think they are?"

Frank Roberts is a member of the Faculty Men's Bowling Team. He is well liked by his co-workers, except on the days when he and eight pupils are away from school attending a state choral festival. On those days his team members, gathered in the smoking room, decide that "It sure pays to be a music director—who else gets to go away three or four times a year?"

All music teachers know that taking pupils to participate in music programs is not a day or an hour "off." It is work, frequently under the most trying conditions. They know that only very important reasons force them to request that pupils be excused from classes. They know that demands for services are made upon the music department in ways that make it almost impossible to refuse.

How can this knowledge be communicated to the rest of

the faculty? How can two different views of a problem be fused into one view?

### *Inter-Faculty Councils*

The inter-faculty council is one of the most effective ways of reaching the goal of a united faculty. Within these councils the various department representatives have the opportunity to hear their problems discussed by the entire group as well as the opportunity to present the department point of view. The groups are small enough and have time enough to work for a consensus when solutions to school problems are sought. How did such a council operate in Stone City as the expanded music program was being planned?

The Superintendent of Schools, George Fredrick, was an ex-officio member. Henry Fisher, representative of the language arts teachers, was elected chairman at the first meeting following the invitation of the high school principal to the teachers to choose a representative from each department to form a council. Art, music, mathematics, science, guidance, vocational education, social studies, physical education, and health were each represented on the council. The elementary supervisor was invited to join the council as a liaison member. The council met regularly the first period on the fourth Monday of each month. Senior members of the Future Teachers of America Club took charge of the representatives' classes that met during that period. At the meeting in September the group had agreed to make a yearly schedule of activities which would require the pupils to be away from the school or from any classes. In October the representatives returned with the lists which the departments had prepared. (A master list was later compiled, mimeographed, and distributed to each teacher.) When the music department presented its list in October, Jane Moore of the science department raised a question. "Is participation in all these regional music programs contributing to our boys' and girls' growth? They seem out of proportion to the number of things in the other departments. The rest of us have two or three activities—a science fair, a trip to a museum, a student government conference, and things like that, but the music department has nine separate events."

"I wonder about that, too," added the guidance counselor. "It adds up to a lot of time."

Frank Roberts, Director of Music, said, "May we spend the November meeting in a careful consideration of this matter? I'd like to bring all our music staff in to hear your questions and comments, and I would like you to hear their opinions as well as mine. Maybe we do need to re-think our participation in these activities."

The dissemination of accurate information, the sharing of opinions, the questioning, the discussion which takes place in a faculty council can be the means of establishing within a school a unity of philosophy and viewpoint which is basic to harmonious staff relationships.

### *Advisory Committee*

The nature of an inter-faculty council is such that its formation is the responsibility of a person in an administrative capacity. However, a music director or teacher who works in a school system where the administration has not begun to use the council as a clearing house for school problems can achieve some of the same results by inviting members of different departments to serve in an advisory capacity to the music department.

The problem was approached this way by Nita Caden, head of the music department of a high school, as she talked to the high school principal. "At times our music program causes us to ask the cooperation of other teachers. Sometimes pupils miss classes; sometimes we ask to have them excused early. Last year I felt that some of the teachers resented our requests. The other two music teachers and I would like to invite several teachers from other departments to meet with us in an advisory capacity when we begin to plan for our concerts and shows and for our general activities. I'd like to invite Gene Ives, the art teacher, Neva Milan of social studies, Tom Berg from guidance, and one other you may wish to suggest. Do we have your permission?"

An advisory committee such as has been described by Nita Caden could render very valuable service to the teachers in the music department. They could bring a total school point of view to the music department view and together the best ways of procedure could be sought. The members of the advisory committee would become channels through which the music program would be understood by the whole school. The music teachers could benefit from the varied experiences of the advisors.

### *Written Bulletins*

In some schools teachers receive so many bulletins on so many subjects that it is doubtful if they give any of them careful consideration. Yet the written bulletin is still a quick and effective means of communication if it is well written and attractively reproduced. An administrator's written communication to teachers can be the means of bringing about better understanding of the various departments and the activities of the teachers. Consider the effective way in which a common cause of irritation was handled in the bulletin of the Superintendent of Schools of Boroville (see page 153).

With a few words the Superintendent has given recognition to a group of teachers. With no preaching he has shown that leading songs for a civic group is a responsibility.

At the same time he has shown that music teachers are not the only people in a school who have time "off" for activities with local groups.

A type of written bulletin which could be initiated by the music department and used by that department to help build

*November Bulletin of Boroville School*

Boroville Teachers Serve their Community

Sue Doe—Member of Board of Directors of Red Cross Chapter. Sue will attend the State Board Meeting on Dec. 7, 8 and 9.

Richard Ron—Scout Leader of Explorer Scout Troop. Dick will leave Thursday of next week to attend a week-end encampment on Birch Lake.

Agnes Mees—President of Local Quota Club. As president of local group Agnes will meet with the inter-service club council on the 2nd and 4th Wednesdays for noon luncheon.

Clair Rigel—Song leader for kick-off luncheon of volunteer workers for this year's Red Feather Drive.

understanding is illustrated by the "flyer" which was used by Vivian Musser, the only music teacher in a small village school system (see page 154).

In a light manner Vivian Musser has made the whole faculty a part of the Christmas music program. In one paragraph she has made the concert a concert by the school pupils rather than by the music pupils. By giving advance notice of group rehearsals she has made it easy for teachers to cooperate. The results that informal bulletins achieve are worth the professional time that goes into their writing and the secretarial time that goes into the duplicating and distribution.

Good relationships between the music teachers and all the other members of a faculty are worth planning and working for. Where there is dissatisfaction, there is usually a lack of definite information which has resulted in misunderstanding. Administrators and music teachers will need to use all the channels of communication that are available to them to promote understanding and acceptance of the music program in all its varied aspects.

*From* That Music Teacher
Vivian Musser

*To* All My Colleagues in Unionville School

*You Asked For It*

Christmas Carol Sings around the trees in the school halls the day before vacation.

*I'm Asking For It*

Your cooperation in making it possible for us to have a rehearsal on:

Dec. 21st at 9:30 A.M. High School
1:00 P.M. Elementary Building

*Are You Coming*

To hear the Orchestra-Chorus Candle Light Musicale on Sunday at 4:00 P.M.? Your pupils would like to have you hear the concert.

A second problem area in music education in the secondary schools is one that is concerned with the several relationships among students, music teacher, and other teachers. In one sense it is a part of the question discussed in the beginning of this chapter, but because of its importance in the whole school picture it is discussed here as a separate relationship.

## *The Music Student and the Music Teacher*

Many high school students are enthusiastic about the music program of the school. It is their chief interest. They like it because they are active participants, because they have had success in it and recognition because of music. They have formed an attachment for the music department, the other pupils in it, and often for the teacher. All of this is good, except that in characteristic adolescent fashion these same pupils often show their interest in what are undesirable ways. One of these is using the music room as a hangout. Pupils who are assigned to be in the library are discovered in the music room, "waiting to ask Mr. X about my oboe." Little groups of girls cluster in the room, to "see what time the bus is leaving for the concert." A horn is tooted, or a drum is thumped by an idler who is "waiting around for practice."

While each music teacher must feel some inner glow of satisfaction that the students want to be around the music room, he should also feel some sense of responsibility to the discipline pattern of the school. Most teachers feel that the casual use of the music room and music room facilities is detrimental to general school discipline. In this area, the music teacher may need to sacrifice some of the informality that he likes in order to have his program well accepted by other faculty members. At least he needs to examine the situation and try to find an honest answer to the questions, "Is the pupil use of the music room legitimate? Is it necessary? Or have I allowed the music room to become an in-school hangout?"*

Another unacceptable way of showing interest in the school music program is in the pupils' assumption that the chorus, band, orchestra or other group is a select club, a sort of "400" of the high school set. Some groups are picked groups, and talented groups, but they require wise guidance from a good music teacher to keep them on an even keel. When a popular music group within a school begins to set itself apart from the school, it begins at the same time to build antagonism toward the music department. When the town begins to say "the best *pupils* are in the choir" instead of "the best *singers* are in the choir," trouble is not far away.

A third undesirable way that adolescents show their interest in music is in an overemphasized attachment for the teacher—and not only for the young and pretty teacher just out of college. The feeling that was expressed by Charles when he said, "When Miss Green told me I had to come in during my vacant period to rewrite my paper I knew I could get Miss Verden to

*This problem is developed further in Chapter 17.

tell her she wanted me to be at quartet practice during that period," is not a wholesome one for a school. The knowledge that the music teacher is interested in the individual is good for a student to have; use of that interest to circumvent other teachers is not good. High school students are past masters of the technique. The music teacher needs to be alert to motives behind what seems to be a burning thirst for more practice or more help in music. To be a confidante of youth, a real counselor, requires foresight and insight.

The music teacher-music student relationship can be one of the most satisfying of professional relationships, but it dare not destroy the adult co-worker relationship which is essential for faculty unity and the well-being of the school.

## • FOOD FOR THOUGHT

1. What situations have you observed in secondary schools that have caused poor relationships among faculty members?
2. How can a teacher be friendly with high school pupils without having the students become too familiar?
3. In the school that you know best how well do the various departments understand the work of the other departments?
4. Write a bulletin to tell the other teachers about your planned Christmas music activities.
5. Conduct an inter-faculty council meeting, with class members assuming faculty member roles. Discuss the participation of the school in regional and state music activities. Try for a consensus of the faculty in forming a statement of policy.

# 13 • Performing organizations

## *Their Purpose*

Walk down the street of any town and ask the first person you meet, "How's the school music program here?" Odds are that he'll begin telling you about the school band, the orchestra, the chorus. Odds are against his telling you about elementary music, general music classes, or the high school theory class. Yet these submerged areas are the largest part of the music program, the part that involves all the children somewhere along the way.

Now, why is this? The answer—we *know* what we *see*. We see performing organizations the most. They get around the most. They meet the public. They have prestige. Their members talk about them, the parents of their members talk about them. "Johnny's in the band this year!" means that Johnny has lifted himself out of the ranks. He's a member of a musical organization. We're all proud of Johnny, and we should be. Every town is proud of its performing organizations. They glitter. But all that glitters . . . .

These performing organizations are made up of children. Or, call them youth. Anyhow, they can be anywhere from eleven years (but sometimes younger) to eighteen (or sometimes older). And the purpose of the bands, orchestras, and choirs is just the same as that of the entire school; making possible the best of educational experiences, whereby the pupils learn and grow.

Trouble is, sometimes community pride becomes community possession. Then the educational experience becomes exploitation.

"Does this town back music?" asks Peter Hunding. Peter has applied for the instrumental position in Wells Springs High School. "I should say we do," replies Will Strong, President of the Board of Education. "Just last year we raised five thousand dollars for new band uniforms. My company gave three hundred. Did we ever make Dark River's band look sick when we marched against them in the Tuterville Parade . . . ."

Watch it, Peter! Mr. Strong, in one sentence, has dropped some clues that should make you wonder. Or are you a music educator?

To begin with, it looks as though band has gone to the heads of the town citizenry. They don't think music; they think band. This means all kinds of pressure on the director. The five thousand dollars given by this generous community looks good. Do you know, though, how many large sums were given, and what is expected in return? And did you notice that Mr. Strong said, ". . . when we marched *against* them." Is he thinking of boys and girls, or of Wells Springs showing up Dark River?

We can't help liking Mr. Strong. We enjoy his pride in his town. He's a good citizen. But he is not a music educator. The band belongs to the school, the school to the community—in that order. Mr. Strong has by-passed one big step in this order. In his book it reads, the band . . . belongs to the community.

A thousand miles away from Wells Springs, Mike White, band director, calls a friend of his who teaches music. "Let me know if you hear of any good openings for next year," he says. "I marched my band so much the first two months of the school year that we didn't have any time to learn new music. I see marching feet in my sleep. My own feet are getting flat. Through rain, snow, sleet, hail . . . that's us."

Well, you get the idea. We began with bands. Fortunately,

orchestras and choruses don't march. They feel pressure, too, but not as much.

In the preceding paragraphs, how many times do you find the word "hear" used in connection with the marching band? Let alone "listen." The accent isn't on music. This troubles some fine instrumental teachers. They believe in performance, but in the performance of music. Music, it seems, sometimes has been lost in the shuffle; or, if you will, read "cadence" for "shuffle."

## *Their Origin*

How did we get so far from the original purposes of performing groups, so far from an accent on music?

It all began with Lowell Mason, the Father of Public School Music. One way Mr. Mason astutely helped entrench music in the public schools was through training children's choruses and presenting them in public. This "shoe-horn technique" worked; music became part of the curriculum. This is not meant to belittle Lowell Mason. He was intelligent enough to know how he could get music to more children—through public schools. But he had to persuade the public, and the only way at that time was to show them children performing.

Although we hear more about Lowell than Luther Mason in connection with school music, the latter developed a series of music books to help children learn music. His books were used both in the United States and abroad.

We have a feeling that Lowell and Luther Mason both would be rather surprised to see what their efforts had wrought should they return and chance upon an eighty-piece band with its sixty-piece flying wedge of majorettes, twirlers, and flag wavers proceeding down the street on a Saturday afternoon. Nevertheless, should they explore the relatively hidden aspects of school music, they would find that a fairly good job has been done in balancing the program. Music in our schools is, by and large, available to all children, whether or not they are in performing groups. And a child does not have to be a musical prodigy to be a member of such groups, as you can see from their size and number. There just aren't that many prodigies.

Although a battle continues between certain music educators who feel that quality of performance is more important than quantity of children who have the musical experience of belonging to performing groups, many teachers of music find places in their organizations for practically all pupils who seek membership. The wonder is that we have so much of both quality and quantity. The battle lines, where they can be distinguished, seem to be drawn between those teachers who *screen out* and those who *screen in.*

### *Will Mary Make the Choir?*

If you really believe that teachers are responsible for the welfare of children, Mary will make the choir if she *wants to,* if she *needs to.* Larger schools will accomplish this through scheduling rather selective groups and also elective groups. There will be a place for Mary in one or the other. If she can't make the top group, she can make the alternate group and gain the experience and skill needed to try again. Smaller schools can't afford to be as selective; the materials are not there to choose from. So Mary has a good chance here.

But Mary's chances of making it may have been determined long before she tried out. They may have been influenced in first, second, or third grade when she began to develop an attitude toward, a receptivity of, music. Perhaps she decided that she liked it and counted herself in. Or she may have been made to feel she was an outsider, that music was for a few special individuals.

So again we see that the program must develop as a whole if it is to stay in focus. The stage lights will always shine on the performing organizations, but these have their roots in the elementary school where we can either create musical situations that help children count themselves in, or ones that result in a proportion of pupils saying, "It's not for me." Teachers decide this, when they plan and work together.

### *It's the School's Choir*

Walter Babcock has a good high school choir. It includes about a quarter of the school population. Every spring Walter sits down with the school official who schedules the activities calendar and plans all choir appearances and a limited number of necessary out-of-school rehearsals.

Walter knows that the families of his choir members have to plan for trips, for shopping excursions, for dental and medical needs. He knows that choir members are involved in football, basketball, track, soccer, baby-sitting, church choirs, band, orchestra . . . ad infinitum. Walter and the athletic director make sure that the choir doesn't schedule its spring concert on a date when the track team travels seventy miles for a meet, leaving after school. The activities scheduling officer does a superlative job in clearing all extracurricular events. Things run smoothly here.

Before a student comes into this performing organization, he knows what is expected of him. His family receives a copy of the choir calendar; they know what cooperation is expected of them. They know, too, what choir membership may do for their son or daughter; Walter invites them to a meeting where these things are discussed. They become aware of the extra-musical values of membership—learning to assume responsibility, to cooperate with others, to develop leadership. (Walter's choir members have worked out a student government for themselves.)

This large organization doesn't travel much over the community. Small ensembles assume such responsibilities; they try to keep their schedules open for this. Thus conflicts are avoided.

All conflicts? No. Once in a while another teacher may throw a monkey wrench in the works by thoughtlessly arranging a conflicting trip without the knowledge of the activities official —without consulting other teachers. Then the pupils are caught in the old tug-of-war. Walter feels that decisions in such situations should be made by the pupils who have already committed themselves when they become choir members. Making choices is part of growing up. Sometimes they decide one way, sometimes another.

Occasionally, however, decisions are squarely up to Walter, even unpopular decisions. The toughest ones usually involve saying, "Sorry, we just can't do it," to an influential individual or group. For example, let's say that such a group is host to a large convention. Long after the school calendar has been set up, Walter receives an invitation for his choir to sing at the opening session. Walter discusses the invitation with the choir officers; they discuss it with the group. It develops that most of the choir is planning to support the basketball team on the night involved. They don't want to change their plans, and they have a right to decide not to perform. (If this is really student government, that is.)

The decision squarely up to Walter is whether to okay the choir's decision or to pressure them into an acceptance. Yes, the choir's corresponding secretary will write a polite note declining the invitation, but Walter may be unpopular in certain community quarters for a while . . . Mr. X, who issued the invitation, doesn't know the system. He'll say Walter isn't cooperative. He thinks the town owns the performing organizations. He won't be satisfied with the choir's offer of a small ensemble. "Why do we pay taxes?" he'll grumble.

All this Walter will have to accept. You can't explain to everyone what goes into the workings of a group made up of one hundred high school pupils, although from time to time articles giving information about the organization and policies of choir, as well as other school information, appear in the local paper. Mr. X never misses the sports and financial pages. He skips the school articles. And his advance planning isn't so good, is it?

Well, Walter, even the major leaguers hit under .500!

## *Schools Are for the Pupils*

If you believe this, you'll agree that the principal responsibility of each performing organization is to its members, not to the community. Again, now, we have to knock on the principal's door. Where these organizations become more of a show-case for the school than a musical experience for the child, school policy is out of joint.

Public performance is certainly a definite part of "musical experiences." But it's not the main goal. We called them "performing organizations" to focus attention on what is often a problem: they *should* be called "musical organizations." They have a place in helping with good community-school relations, but they should not be saddled with this as a reason for their existence. For their members are not adults, not professionals, but young people learning about making music together. Performing for others is a goal, but not the chief goal. It is a by-product of the educational experience.

## *A School Policy*

Can you see what is needed to make and keep it this? If so, you'll know why we are knocking on the principal's door. He's the one who can help us develop a clear-cut school policy with regard to musical organizations. This can be worked out with the entire school faculty participating and understanding.

When we said "clear-cut" we meant it. Fuzzy generalizations won't help. Pick up a box of cake mix next time you shop at the supermarket. Notice: definite steps, clearly stated. If you have an electric mixer, you do thus and so, in this order. If you have only a spoon, you do this instead. You use certain size cake pans for certain size layers. Of if you want a loaf cake, you use another size. Your oven should be so hot, and you should bake your cake for so many minutes. In case you live at a high altitude, here's what you do . . . . If you want icing on your cake, the recipe is . . . .

Now *this* we call clear-cut. But notice that this one basic mix, to be used by many different people with mixers, spoons, different-sized cake pans, at this or that altitude, is adaptable. Notice, too, that you may have to furnish a few ingredients of your own.

Makers of cake mixes have to be explicit. If you make a mess of their mix, chances are you won't buy another, so they try to insure your success. Keeping the objective firmly in mind, they set about helping you achieve that luscious pecan frazzle cake. This is the kind of help we need to keep our musical organizations on the track. We can have it, too, if we are willing to work as hard as the makers of the mix worked.

Try these steps as a basis for formulating policy:

1. Consider your community, your school, its children. Decide what music program will best suit their needs.

2. State the objectives of the music program. Base them on your knowledge of children and music.

3. Outline your plans for music courses, experiences, activities. This will include the musical organizations.

4. Define the relationship of the music program to the school and the community.

5. Draw up a clearly-stated policy with regard to public performance. This should be in terms of what is best for your pupils. Subordinate your personal desires and community ambitions.

6. Publicize the policy and the reasons for it. Once won't do; this has to be a continuing campaign. Put it in the newspapers, the school paper, on the backs of programs, explain it to such organizations as the PTA, service clubs, and Home Room Mothers. Enlist their cooperation. See that your pupils understand it, too; they can help.

7. *At every step of the way, plan with others.* No decision can be yours alone; each must represent the thinking of the school staff, including administrators, teachers, custodians (par-

ticularly influential harbingers of good will), school board, community representatives.

8. Don't rush it. (Remember: Depending on the size and shape of the cake and the altitude, you have to bake it for different lengths of time!) It may take longer than you would like for this process to develop. The results will justify the time spent, the patience expended.

### *Contests*

"That man is contest-crazy!" Who's "that man?" We don't know; it doesn't matter. Some music teacher is being pressured and doesn't like it. Are musicians, as individuals or groups, competitive by nature? Is it good for them to go out and beat someone else? Do they thrive on the town's cries of welcome when they return from playing a round or two against other organizations? Do they have to engage in such activities to rouse community support? And is this a desirable type of support?

When Whitney Maxwell took a job at Super High, he was told by his principal that the school had taken top honors in state competition for three years straight. "The whole town's excited about this," Whitney was told. "Let's make it four straight this year."

Whitney was young and eager, and he rose to the bait. What he didn't know was that the whole business of cutting the pupils to a fine edge of performing ability was getting tougher. After three years of it, they were not quite as interested. They were not as eager to practice and practice on a limited group of numbers. He didn't know that his predecessor had sensed this and had decided enough was enough.

Whitney's career got off to a bad start. The "fourth straight" year did not materialize. Yet Whitney was a competent teacher. The winning streak ran out. Too bad. He learned, though.

The original business of contests may have had some value; it was undoubtedly intended to upgrade music by furnishing an incentive for practice, for improvement. Its present advocates are likely to say, too, that life is competitive, and therefore it's good for young people to have some practice in competition. Is it?

Individuals who judge such contests year after year differ in their attitudes toward the matter, but many of them soon tire of the whole affair and wash their hands of it. Why? Here are some reasons:

1. Judging is a tough business. Often the line between a first or second place is so thin as to be almost invisible.

2. Judging is often subjective. The basis of judgment may be indicated on a rating sheet, but the points listed on the sheet may be interpreted very differently. Split decisions may be a cause of difficulty—particularly if the contestants inquire about them.

3. Even competent judges are likely to be challenged by contestants—"Just why was so-and-so better than I was?" In cases where there wasn't much difference, this is a real head—and heart—ache.

4. Where rating sheets are given to the same individual or organization by several judges, disagreements are sometimes so pronounced that the contestant is confused.

There are other reasons, and there are also reasons why some judges stay with it year after year. They honestly believe that competing against others is a good way for youngsters to grow. Certainly they would not do it for the money involved—it doesn't amount to that much.

A fundamental objection to contests is that they are extrinsic in motivation. A contest is about as valid in its *musical* motivation as a pistol in the back would be in extending a polite invitation for a moonlight walk. Yes—it must be admitted that extrinsic motivation operates on many levels in our everyday life. It isn't difficult to spot the people who would stop work tomorrow if their paychecks failed to materialize. Extrinsic motivation isn't unusual. It's when we attach it to music that the question arises. Music is an art—it should bring enjoyment and happiness. Have you ever seen a happy music loser? Competition doesn't seem appropriate to this art.

Then there's the question of readiness for competition; the question of maturity. Competition is overwhelming to many boys and girls, sometimes resulting in tears, hysterics, nail-biting, nausea. It takes a long, long time to prepare for the strenuous business of pitting one's self or group against another. Most teachers do not have the time to devote to this, even if they wanted to do so. Competition is only one part of a teacher's job, whether he does it voluntarily or not.

Thus the combination of immaturity, lack of preparation, and previous experience may result in a fiasco for pupil and teacher alike. One student, in relating his experience in failing to secure a high rating said, "I came home and smashed my horn. I never played again."

If the objectives of a school and its music program are educationally sound, they do not need organized competition as a means of stimulus.

And certainly, competition should not be used as a means of gratifying the ambitions of an individual or group—school or community. Yet, sometimes it is. In your community?

### *Festivals*

This is a broad designation for music gatherings of instrumentalists, singers, or both. Festivals have taken the place of contests in many locales. They may be sponsored by several school districts, by the music educators of an area, or by one particular school.

The festival, of course, differs from the contest in that a number of organizations or representatives of organizations form a large festival group for making music. Although competition is sometimes a part of the festival, in the form of tryouts for rank assignment or solos, it is much less emphasized.

The advantages of the festival over the contest include the following:

1. The musical resources of many schools and individuals are pooled to produce good music.

2. Less tension is present, due to cooperation rather than competition.

3. More individuals participate.

4. The festival is better suited to the maturity of adolescent boys and girls.

5. Pupils who have participated in a musical event where they played with a hundred or more young musicians from other schools, under the direction of a well-prepared leader, often have the feeling of being an integral part of a significant event. Members of the audience, parents and teachers, share a feeling of pride and a musical thrill when several hundred youth produce excellent music together. Student friendships and self-confidence initiated at such events may last for many years; musical inspiration may be life-long.

6. The experience of making music with pupils of other schools, rather than *against* other schools, has positive musical and social values.

All in all, the festival seems better suited to music and to the needs of high school youth than does the contest. While the occasional highly talented pupil may respond well to contests, it may be that the response is largely other than a musical one for many pupils. The emphasis in public school music is on its value for everyone. Festivals come closer to a realization of this than do contests.

## *Preparing for Concerts and Trips*

The first step toward a public performance of any kind is clearing the date with the official responsible for the school calendar. This applies equally to excursions involving two, or two hundred, pupils. And teachers.

The reasons for such advance scheduling have already been given. In case you cannot turn in an advance date (in some cases host schools for various festivals are not obtained for some time) give your administrator an approximate date; let him know the nature of the event, and any details you can.

The school policy with regard to how many days teachers and pupils may be absent for festivals and other music trips should be the guide in asking for permission to attend such events. If a school does not have such a policy, teachers must be particularly careful to establish an understanding with administrators as to what each may expect.

With the large variety of meetings, musical and otherwise, that take place within a school year, it is necessary to choose those that seem to be of particular value and pass by others. In some states the music teacher could be absent from classes more than fifteen days a school year and have legitimate cause for the absences—educational conferences and music festivals would easily comprise the fifteen days.

The question is: what happens to hundreds of pupils while the music teacher is looking after the needs of a relatively small number?

To learn the answer, we'll look at two different situations.

In the rehearsal room of Solidd High, the orchestra president announces, as he taps on the director's stand, that Mr. Leed is absent, having accompanied five orchestra members to district orchestra. He reminds the group that the first chair violinist usually directs the rehearsal in the absence of Mr. Leed, but since he, too, is at the district event, the rehearsal will be directed by the orchestra president—and things will proceed as usual. They do. The work has been planned by the president in conference with Mr. Leed. He makes a tape recording of the rehearsal as the period continues. Before the bell rings, he reviews with the orchestra members what they have accomplished (for example, the bowing on one number is now correct, marked in all copies) and says, "Thanks for helping out."

In the rehearsal room at Rocky Road High, however, things are very different under the same set of circumstances. The principal, whose office is right above the rehearsal room, says to his assistant, "Better go down there and see what's going on, Hal. Sounds as though the boiler has broken." Hal appears in the door of the room and two 'cellists, who have been engaged in a mock duel with 'cello bows, freeze in their tracks. The second clarinet, who has been attempting to stuff the flutist into the tuba, skulks back to his seat. The pieces of a broken baton sail through the air and are retrieved by the assistant principal. Chaos is complete.

It isn't difficult to find the reason. Rocky Road's music director left word with the principal that he would be absent for district orchestra. He didn't remember to do this until the day before he left. The principal sent word to a teacher that he should substitute for the music director. The teacher somehow didn't get the message. Result? A state of total disorganization, forty pupil hours wasted, plus the time of the principal and his assistant.

Don't go to those festivals or meetings unless your pupils will have adequate supervision in your absence. You took the job at a specified salary. The salary meant you were to work with pupils at certain hours. If the hours have changed since you took the job, straighten out such affairs with your administrator. If they have not, keep your side of the bargain. A contract is a contract.

When you take pupils from the school, be sure the school and their parents are aware of this and have given their permission. Sometimes such permission is required in written form. Protect yourself, your school, and the host school by following all instructions concerning this—you will be protecting the pupils involved and their parents. And the fact that you follow such procedures doesn't mean you distrust your charges—it means that you are looking out for them in every possible way.

By the way, if a musical event is to be open to the public, get the publicity to the local papers, radio, and TV stations as early as possible. Use as many pupil names in the copy as you can . . . both parents and pupils like to see or hear these names. And don't restrict this to the names of soloists—you couldn't have a concert without the chorus, so Herbert, singing bass with never a thought of "soloing," is just as much entitled to his share of the limelight as anyone else. His parents think he is, too!

### *Would You Like to Buy a Ticket to . . . ?*

School concerts should be free to the taxpayers. Why? Because everything they represent should be paid for by tax money. Should be, but isn't. Well, let's see.

We charge admission because we are raising money for some part of the school music program. We need choir robes, an oboe, a new piano, more music. The administrators, the school board, say no. So off we go with the tickets. We'll get that equipment somehow.

It is a well-known principle that you can't be tried twice for the same offense. Or taxed twice on the same item by the same agency. Now think of the plight of the parents. Having made it possible for their children to participate in a music program, purchased new shoes and white shirts, seen to all the other details, and rushed them early to the school, they now have to pay to witness the performance. Furthermore, if the child has two, three, or more siblings who wish to witness the same performance, this is going to cost several dollars. If parents were not so proud of their children and so anxious to cooperate, they would have rebelled against such situations long ago.

Some music directors send tickets to members of the board of education and the faculty. This is commendable, except that it may not include the group most interested in the children—their parents.

We're not idealistic to the point of believing all can arrive at the Utopia of "no need to raise money" today, or even tomorrow. We believe, however, that the basis of charging admission to school events should be scrutinized with care. As long as you are willing to raise money for your musical needs, who's going to stop you—except you?

### *Programs*

School concerts are for children, parents, fond relatives, and—all credit to them—the interested teachers who loyally attend to watch their pupils in a situation different from the usual classroom.

Since we can predict the audience, how does it happen that we very often plan a program that just doesn't click? Too often it's over their heads, it's over or under-rehearsed, it's too long or too short, it has long lags where nothing happens. Or the lights don't go on between groups so the audience knows what's coming next . . .

Here are a few things that will help your concert:

1. Choose music that pupils will enjoy rehearsing over a period of time. It has to be a challenge, but not discouraging in its difficulty. Consider its "wearing" qualities.

2. Include a few familiar numbers. The audience hears a number only once—they can't be expected to grasp its beauty or intricacy on such short acquaintance.

3. Include some program notes, either written or oral.

4. Keep the program moving. Avoid long periods when nothing is happening. The audience may enjoy staring at the band, orchestra, or chorus, but this may also be embarrassing.

5. Enough is enough. Don't let your program run too long; after all, it's an amateur performance.

6. Allow plenty of time for an intermission. Some of your audience will be children—they need to stretch their legs.

7. Assume that you will have at least one crying baby in the audience. This is probably a brother or sister of one of the youngsters in your group, so don't let it throw you. In ten years or so, that baby may be on the stage!

### *Concert Manners*

There are manners for concerts just as there are manners for the Soph Hop. How about letting your pupils know what's expected of them in the way of behavior? *You* may take such things for granted, but they may be in the dark. For instance, how about acknowledging applause? How will you do this? How will your group? What about acknowledging soloists and accompanists? What about encores?

If you explain exactly how you will proceed in such matters, the performers will be more at ease and will enjoy their performance more than if they are wondering just what to do next. In other words, prepare them for what is going to happen. Tell them why waving at Uncle Will in the second row is not the thing to do (when sitting on the stage waiting for the concert to begin). Let them see how one gum chewer can affect the appearance of an entire organization; how one sloucher can make a hundred singers look like a sloppy, poorly prepared choir.

There *are* reasons; why not give them?

## • FOOD FOR THOUGHT

1. Plan a series of events designed to present the entire school music program to the public.
2. Why should the music program be financed by the school?
3. Conduct an informal survey among your acquaintances, asking them, "How's the music program in your home town?" Notice what aspects of the program are mentioned *first* in their replies.
4. Where should the line be drawn between the performing organizations as school-community property and as educational experiences?
5. Interview and/or write to teachers of various areas or subjects, asking how many out-of-school events their pupils participate in during a school year. Include an athletic coach, an English teacher, the advisor of the school paper.
6. Appoint a committee to write up a school policy with regard to the public appearance of performing organizations. Make sure it is so clearly stated that a new teacher would find it easy to understand.
7. A comparison:
   (a) List all the reasons you can think of to justify the continuance of music contests. Then check to see whether any of the reasons cannot be met by participation in festivals.
   (b) List all the reasons you can think of to justify continuance of festivals. Then check to see which of the reasons cannot be met by participation in contests.

# 14 • The administrator considers the performing organizations

## *The Public Sees the School*

The music department of the school is one of the most effective public relations agencies that the school has available for its use. In every community the citizens enjoy music which is provided by school music groups. More than any other one department of the school, the music department represents the school to the lay public. More than any other teachers, the music teachers meet the citizens of the community. This places a very heavy responsibility on the music department. A school concert is more than a concert. It is the school program being shown to the citizens. How the students look, how they sound, how they behave represents for many people the way the school looks, the quality of work produced by the schools, and the discipline of the school.

Many people are involved in the performing organizations in music. The sum total of the reactions of all those people represents the public relations value of the public performance.

## *The "Performing Organization Quintet"*

THE PUPILS. Since all performing organizations in schools are made up of pupils, and since pupils are our major concern in school, the first responsibility of the music director and the school administrator must be the protection of the health and welfare of the pupils. How much activity can these students participate in? Were we to leave the decisions entirely to the students with no guidance on our part, we would find that no amount of work and no number of personal appearances seem too much for the enthusiasm of the vigorous music makers. Always the adult must remember that these pupils are growing. The time when performing music groups are most popular is the time when there is a period of rapid growth for many students. They need ample rest. They need release from constant high-pressure living. This is where the teacher must show his knowledge of child growth and development. He must make sure that the planned program of school activities does not violate what he knows about children and youth and their well being.

What are the demands being made on the pupils by this program? What are the total demands made on the pupil by the combined programs of the school? These questions are basic.

In the elementary school the problems are not so great. Elementary education in the last two decades has moved away from the public performance by groups of children for large groups of adults. The popular pattern, and wisely so, is for the type of activity in music or drama in which a whole class participates; it is given for another group of children or for a small parent group during the regular school hours. The elaborate May Days with weeks and days of rehearsals and yards and yards of crepe paper costumes are being supplanted by informal play days on the school grounds. Every child participating in regular classroom activities with a small and interested audience—this is the widely accepted ideal in increasing numbers of elementary schools. It has developed because of what we have come to know about the dangers of over-stimulation of children and the need that elementary children have for long hours of rest and freedom from pressures.

Elementary teachers have been helped in coming to this highly desirable type of performance because of the fact that elementary children seldom produce the kind of music that adults call entertainment. Everyone enjoys watching the children's faces aglow with excitment. Ten-year-old boys, scrubbed and polished, are a delight to see, but few program committee chairmen within the community ask to have groups of elementary children present music programs. This is not true on the secondary level. From the junior high school age on, the students do produce music that adults enjoy. This, coupled with the fact that school performing organizations charge no fee, makes them the recipients of many invitations. It has been said in the previous chapter, but it cannot be said too often, there must be group decisions on the number of times music groups from the secondary school can perform. One of the first decisions a faculty must make relates to the physical well-being of the pupils. The chief administrator, the school principal, the school nurse and school doctor, the music teachers, the guidance teacher, and two or three representatives from other departments would be a minimum group to arrive at a decision. If there is an organized parent group in the school, one or two representatives from that organization could be invited to be a part of the group. In schools where students have learned to share in thinking through the problems of the school, student representatives could bring a pertinent point of view to the discussion of the questions—

How many hours of rest should our students be able to have each school night?

How much free recreation time do they need?

How much demand does our homework schedule make on the students' time?

How much time does that allow for us to schedule after-school or evening rehearsals and performances?

What groups will want to use that time? Drama? Speech? Music? Athletics?

Decisions reached on these questions can then become the

basis for later decisions about the nature and extent of public performance.

A concern for the mental and emotional welfare of the pupils is also the responsibility of the teacher. Within recent years we have come to know that emotional problems of children, if they are not handled wisely, can become the mental illnesses of adults. Many situations in home, community, and school cause emotional disturbances in children and youth. It is unfortunate when the performing organizations of the school, which should be ways of providing pleasant, satisfying experiences for students, are the cause of emotional disturbance.

The choir of Forest Junior High School prepared for the spring concert. About two weeks before the concert a group of the girls got together and decided they wanted to wear formal gowns. When they asked the director he agreed that they could put it to a vote. Formal gowns won out with a big majority.

The problem here is not with the emotional upset of the homes when the girls demanded new dresses, or where frantic mothers fixed over older sisters' dresses, but with the very real emotional problems faced by Ada. Her family belonged to a religious group which did not believe in the type of dress represented by formal dresses. Ada found herself cut off by her family and her religion from a pleasant experience for which she had prepared herself. At fourteen she was not old enough to be willing to be different. At fourteen a hasty decision by a group of students made her the victim of two conflicting cultures. It is easy for adults to forget how acute the problems of dress are with adolescents. Early decisions made concerning clothing to be worn in public performance can prevent students from anticipation of and preparation for an event in which they will be unable to participate.

The band of the secondary schools in Eastville was in reality the community band in the summer. All the Volunteer Firemen's Parades, all the small town fairs were occasions for the Eastville high school band to march and play. Edgar Parrey, the director, knew that the older band members had summer jobs and couldn't be counted on for summer engagements. In March, April, and May he made recruiting drives into the seventh and eighth grades to recruit new band members. All summer long the eighteen new members came out to march and to practice three times a week. All summer long they paraded and played (music being what it is, it is only fair to say that they paraded better than they played).

When school began the older band members returned and on the first Thursday of the school year at band practice, the director announced, "Now you know the bus that takes us to football games only holds forty-eight people so we will have to drop twelve of the new members from the band this fall. The following people will no longer be in the band . . . ."

The problem here is not with irate parents who had purchased instruments and changed family plans so that Junior could be in the band; the real problem is the emotional upset that comes when youth is let down by an adult, particularly when the adult is a hero, as all band directors are to new band members. Was the director's desire (due perhaps to community pressure) for a good-sized marching band worth what happened to twelve adolescents?

The performing groups in music can do much for students. They can give confidence, poise, opportunity to develop talent, fun, and ways for community service. It is most unfortunate and altogether unnecessary if, through lack of foresight, planning, and consideration on the part of school or community, they react against the students' physical or emotional well being.

PARENTS. The parents are important members of the performing organization team. Parents have plans for the home life of the children and frequently the performing organization plans are in conflict with the parents' plans. In our complicated pattern of living today it seems unlikely that conflicts in dates and time will ever be completely eliminated, but they can be minimized. As has been suggested earlier, a meeting early in the term of the parents who have children in the chorus, band, orchestra, or ensemble can be used to clarify the objectives of the year's work and to outline the tentative schedule of activities. At a meeting the question of clothing can be discussed. The situations which might require extra money can be described. Since secondary-school students are prone to tell their parents, "We have to have a dollar," or "Everyone is getting a new formal for the concert," it might be well to have the parents understand what requests may be made by the director; they can then decide for themselves how to meet the demands of their offspring.

A letter or a brief bulletin to parents is a good follow-up to a meeting. It puts necessary information in a tangible form. A useful bulletin will tell the parents:

(a) how often the group meets, and where and when.
(b) how the members are chosen.
(c) whether or not the activity carries credit; whether or not it will be graded on the report card.
(d) the regulations regarding clothing.
(e) the rules and regulations that the students and teachers have agreed upon for the operation of the group.
(f) the planned schedule for the organization.
(g) the amount of money necessary for full participation in the group.

When bulletins or letters are sent to the homes they should carry the signature of the music teacher, the music director, and the administrative officer. This gives authority to the communication and identifies the program of the music organization with the total school program.

In rural or suburban areas parents frequently are required to play the role of transportation agents when school events are held after the regular school hours. This becomes a very real problem in many homes, particularly when there is one car and three or four family members with varying interests and activities. The teacher of music who spends some time thinking through the transportation question with his group may be able to have greater pupil participation in the music activities. Are car pools the answer? Are there two or three parents who would plan with the other parents for this? Is the answer a special bus?

The parents in one large rural school system thought so. They heard complaints that children from the rural areas couldn't take part in many of the school activities. Their project for a year was hiring special "after-school buses" which left one hour later than the other buses and took home the pupils who wanted to be in activities that rehearsed or practiced after school hours. On the nights of concerts, games, plays, and other school functions, the special buses were used to transport participants. This plan avoided the necessity of many cars making the same trip, saved many family arguments about taking the car, was highly satisfactory from a safety point of view, and permitted wide participation in school activities. For two years the parents operated this auxiliary transportation system; then the School Directors came to believe in its value and provided for it in the regular school budget. Increasing suburban living has made transportation of students to and from school activities a major concern of parents.

When we are considering the role of parents in the successful music activities programs, the question of Band Parents Organization is worthy of serious consideration. Band Parents Organizations flourish in all sizes and types of schools. They are buyers of instruments and purchasers of uniforms. They are transporters of band members and staunch supporters of many music activities. They range from informal groups of parents to highly organized groups with officers, dues, and regular meetings.

Are they desirable? At the present time it appears that there is great enthusiasm for them, particularly in smaller secondary schools. Only a few voices are raised in criticism. The administrators and music directors who face the question of whether or not to encourage an organization of band parents (or chorus mothers or orchestra fathers) should consider the matter from many points:

(a) Will this organization help the program of music education or will it be a pressure group to further one isolated segment of the program?

(b) Will this organization run counter to an existing organization of parents in the school or will the parents continue their interest in the over-all school group as well as in the music parent's organization?

(c) Is the chief purpose of the group to earn money for a performing group, or is its purpose to help parents learn about the music program and ways of helping their children with their music education?

(d) If the purpose is to earn money, is this the wisest way to finance a part of the school program, or should the energy be used in establishing the activity as a budgeted item through regular school finances?

(e) If the purpose is to learn about the music program, could its object be achieved by having a music-study group within the framework of the existing parent organization?

(f) Is the organization of such a group an activity that will bring the music department closer to the total school program, or will it serve to isolate music?

(g) Is the organization being formed to further the interests of an individual or a small group of individuals?

(h) How will the organization be viewed by faculty members? A "special interest" group is always a difficult group to assimilate into a large organization. It will pay the music director and the administrator to study the question of a music parents' organization very carefully.

Parents, along with grandmothers and aunts and uncles, are the chief consumers of school music. This audience needs consideration when music concerts are planned. Even the most interested parents fall by the wayside when the senior operetta is followed by the band concert, the music festival, the orchestra concert, and the spring choral festival, all within a few days of each other and all requiring paid tickets. A small audience is discouraging for both the music teacher and the participating group, but small audiences are inevitable if the music department's public appearances are not well spaced throughout the school year. Before we blame parents for non-attendance at

school music functions, we need to examine our schedule, our offerings, and the cost.

TEACHERS. All teachers on the faculty have some relation to the music department and the public performances of its various groups. The music director and music teacher have, of course, the most important relationship. The public frequently knows a music group by the teacher's name—Miss Willert's Quartet, Mr. Loew's Choir, Mr. Purcell's Brass Quintet, Mr. Stravin's Annual Music Festival. This means that the teacher's reputation for skill in teaching and musical ability depends on what the group does in public performance, although that may be only a small fraction of the work he does in the music department. Each public appearance of the group must represent the best that the teacher can produce.

Studied consideration of the number of public performances that a group can do well should be a part of the initial planning for music organizations. To accept invitations for more public appearances than a group can prepare for is to invite the audience to say, "I don't know what's happened to Mrs. Dowland.

Her trio doesn't sing as well as it used to." Music teachers have another way to save their professional reputations. Could the organization have its own name and not use the teacher's name? When the organization uses a chosen name, rather than being known by the teacher's name, the teacher may lose some individual recognition but he also is saved from some individual criticism. Wouldn't it be wise to connect the school's name to the organization rather than a teacher's name? The girls' octet at Farmers High School is known as "The Farmers' Daughters." The saxophone sextet at Woodtown is known as "The Six-Teens." Secondary-school pupils enjoy belonging to a group with a name. Teachers need to be identified with a school, not a small group.

Teachers, even music teachers, are people. Teachers need to have lives of their own. They need evenings to bowl, to read, to study, to go to the movies—even to rest. They cannot schedule two or three music rehearsals each week and one or two public performances and maintain their own mental and physical health.

The one who is the only teacher of music in a small school most often tries to carry a load beyond reasonable size. Many small schools try to have programs as varied as large schools, but there is only one person to take care of all of the activities. The inevitable result is the lowering of standards of performance or the exhaustion of the teacher. How much can one teacher do well, and within the limits of a well rounded life? That question must be decided in each small school.

Teachers other than music teachers are concerned with the performing organizations because the members of the organizations are members of their classes. They are concerned when evening rehearsals interfere with class assignments. They are concerned when students must be excused from their classes to participate in music activities. In some schools there is a running feud between the music department and the teachers of the other subjects because of these two concerns. Is there any way in which these irritations can be eliminated or lessened?

Inter-faculty planning of activities is one way. If teachers know in advance when students will be participating in evening activities, the homework can be adjusted. Careful scheduling can eliminate some of the requests that students be excused from classes. But emergencies do arise, and the demands made on students with musical talents are many. The music teacher can help maintain good feeling if he will personally request the teacher to excuse a student from class. Frequently the classroom teacher's only notification is from the student: "Miss Meister, I won't be in class today. I have to sing at Kiwanis Club." Small wonder that Miss Meister resents the whole proceeding. Had the music teacher taken time to see Miss Meister and explain the circumstances, the request would have had professional status. And while Miss Meister may not have been pleased, at least she would not feel that she had been "ordered around" by "the music teacher and his pet soloist."

If the school is so big or the duties so many that personal contact is impossible, a printed form should be developed which could be signed by the teacher requesting the excusal and sent to the teacher from whose class the student is to be excused. This is one of the many situations in school where good professional manners can smooth a rough situation.

THE SCHOOL. The performing organizations are school organizations. They do not represent the music department and the music teachers alone. They represent the school, the faculty, and the administration. The administrator of a school has the final responsibility for all groups in the school. The music department has a direct responsibility for the music organization. This calls for close cooperation between the music director and the principal or superintendent.

The administrator must assist the music director in the formation of a policy concerning the schedule of the performing organizations, or he must assist the new music director in interpreting a policy which already exists. When the policy is formulated both must be ready to adhere to the policy. The superintendent cannot say "Yes" to a community group if the music director has said "No" because the school policy dictated "No." Neither can the director say "Yes" when a request is made to him by a personal friend if the school policy does not permit acceptance of the invitation. Mutual agreement and respect are necessary when there is mutual responsibility for school activities.

The administrator who, in absence of a mutually agreed upon school policy, says to the music director, "You make the decisions—it's your department," must be prepared to stand behind the decisions the director makes. If he wishes to be fair to the director, the adminstrator cannot insert a decision of his own into the midst of a controversy.

The administrator who depends upon the performing music organizations to serve in a public relations capacity for the school has a responsibility to help the music teachers open channels to the community; at the same time, he has the responsibility for protecting the music department from exploitation. Dr. Shoeman, Superintendent of Fieldbrook Schools, sent this letter to the service clubs, patriotic organizations, women's clubs and other groups that in previous years had requested music programs from the school:

Dear Friends,

Last year the music department of Fieldbrook Schools was pleased to help you with your program. This year we have a new director, Miss Lucy Woten, who has come to us from Cove High School. This will be a busy year for her as she becomes acquainted with our school and our community. If you have any requests for the services of our music department, will you please fill in the lines below and return this letter to the school so that we may plan our yearly activities.

Name of Organization ____________________

Type of Music Desired ____________________

Approximate Date and Time ____________________

Occasion ______________________________________________

Person to Contact ______________________________________

Phone _________________________________________________

Sincerely

Carl Shoeman
Superintendent of Schools

Another type of letter was sent by Francis Vaughn of a neighboring school:

It is the agreed policy of our school to permit our music organizations to accept invitations for only a limited number of public performances during the year. Requests for services of soloists, ensembles, band, orchestra, or chorus must be made in writing and sent to the high school office. The requests will be referred to the music activities board of our student-faculty group and you will receive a reply directly from that group.

This procedure has been approved by School Board action.

Francis Vaughn
Principal

The two letters show different philosophies of service, but they have one common purpose—to protect the students from over-activity and to protect the music director from a too-demanding public.

The administrator of a small school and the music teacher have to work out together the answer to the question, "How much of a music program can we reasonably have?" Personal pride may lead a principal to want all the music activities in a school of two hundred that are found in a school of two thousand, but good judgment should lead him to develop a program that his one teacher can handle well. Frequently he may have to curb the enthusiasm of a beginning teacher who wants to do everything and in September feels equal to it!

There are more opportunities for things to "go wrong" in the performing organization programs than in any other area of the curriculum except inter-scholastic athletics. The administrator does well to lend his guidance and leadership to the development of sound policies and practices.

THE COMMUNITY. The last member of the "Performing Organization Quintet"—we have already counted pupils, parents, teachers, and school—is the community. "This is what the community wants" becomes the final word for many teachers when decisions are to be made.

Who is the community? How do you find out what it wants? *Participation is one criterion.* Do the parents want their children to play and sing? Does the community attend music events?

*Support is a second criterion.* Does the community insist that music be financed as science or mathematics are financed? Or must music organizations earn their way with Candy Sales?

There is another way of finding out about the community and what it wants. Lucy Woten invited six citizens to come to her office and talk about music. She invited Miss Lock, a church organist, Sam Ventorn, the director of the Legion band, Miss Tristan, a piano teacher, Mrs. Hassler, the president of the Civic Music Club, and Dan Gregg, a Barbershop Quartet member. She asked them to discuss this question—"What do you want in music in this community from the schools? What do you think we do well? What would you like to see done in a different manner?" She listened while these people talked, and learned in a direct way what people who were interested in music thought about the performing groups within the school.

Many communities do not know about the music program in the schools. Music teachers can plan interesting ways of telling about the program. A window for "American Education Week" could show materials and methods used in music. A clever speech telling about music teaching, and using one or two pupils to demonstrate is always acceptable. A community that knows the music director and understands the philosophy of music education can become a community that is free from undue pressures for "the biggest and best band at any cost."

The performing organizations of a music department have so much to give to individuals, to schools, and to communities that it is worth our united effort to secure those things which will insure good relationships among all concerned with the program.

## • FOOD FOR THOUGHT

1. Present the arguments for a choir dressing in robes, evening clothes, or uniform clothing from the viewpoint of a parent, a music teacher, a junior high school student, and a senior high school student.
2. Is a Band Parents' Organization a pressure group? Present the arguments of a school principal, a music director, an English teacher, the president of the Parents Association, and a band parent.
3. Should school music organizations furnish programs for groups in the community? On what basis?
4. Should pupils be "expelled" from performing organizations? Under what circumstances? By whom?
5. Prepare a policy of public performance for a senior high school music department.
6. Write a handbook for orchestra members in junior high school.
7. Write a letter to the parents of your band members, telling them of the plans for the band during football season.

# 15 • Housing, equipping, and scheduling music

## *Housing*

Over in Fall School District, Tom Fiddler sits down after school and writes a letter to a former college instructor. Propping a piece of paper on an instrument case that rests on his knee, he begins:

Dear Dr. Reid,

School's out and I have a few minutes before a faculty meeting. I suppose you're wondering why you have not heard from me since I took this job. To tell you the truth, I've been looking things over and trying to assimilate all the aspects of my work.

When you think of me, I want you to visualize this: The school is so crowded that I have to teach my music classes on the stage. But where is the stage? It's part of the gym. You can guess, I'm certain, what is going on in the main part of the gym while I am having classes on the stage—Phys Ed classes, naturally! Well, we do close the curtain, but it *is* disconcerting to have a basketball bounce off the keys of the piano during a song. (This is only a slight exaggeration!) . . .

To mention other extreme cases, there's the teacher who reports teaching instrumental music in an empty coal bin during the opening weeks of school. He adds humorously that he had a narrow escape the day they filled the coal bin and forgot to notify him: " . . . got myself and the pupils out in hurry, but

I lost a music stand and a clarinet swab!" And another teacher, who says " . . . I give lessons in the lumber storage room adjacent to the shop . . . ."

Now we know that no administrator would willingly assign teachers and pupils to such housing facilities. We know schools are overcrowded. We also know that there are many new schools with entire wings—classrooms, rehearsal halls, practice studios —designed for the teaching of music. The teachers who have an ideal situation in which to carry on the music program are fortunate indeed. But they are in the minority. For the older school buildings were not designed to house active music programs. The situation is akin to that of a young married couple who purchase a two-bedroom home and then proceed to have six children—until they can afford a bigger place, it's going to be crowded and inconvenient.

On the one hand, we might say that the school should not attempt to develop a music program if it cannot be suitably housed. On the other, we might say that there are few music teachers who will restrain their programs to fit inadequate housing facilities, or few administrators who would encourage them to do so. So it is not unusual for the pupil "families" of the music program to outgrow their housing facilities; indeed, it is not unusual for a music teacher to begin his work in a school building where no particular space has been designed or designated for the music program.

Fortunately, it is almost axiomatic that a good housing situation does not necessarily make a good school. Many strong music programs have been built under the least favorable conditions, and contrariwise, weak programs exist in some schools with fine housing. The teacher is the key factor.

There are, however, pertinent reasons why every teacher should have a favorable physical situation in which to teach, and these apply equally to the music teacher. We can applaud the ingenuity and determination of Mr. Jenkins, who gives lessons in the school bus parked alongside the school. But was a bus seat designed to encourage correct posture in a young instrumentalist? Does Mr. Jenkins have an opportunity to do his best teaching? Do his pupils have a chance to achieve as much as they could under better circumstances?

Here are indications of some important reasons for good housing. The music program needs a suitable physical environment for the welfare of both teacher and pupils. It has particular needs because of its particular characteristics. Perhaps you can learn to play the piccolo in a broom closet, as one boy did, but you can't learn to play the 'cello!

Miss Stanley has a choir of 102 members. They have no place to rehearse except the stage of the auditorium. Miss Stanley doesn't mind carrying music and other equipment through the halls to the stage, or setting up chairs and taking them down, even though it takes a few minutes from her rehearsal time. She doesn't complain too often when the chairs disappear, as did the chairs of Dave Speres. Occasionally such occurrences are the last straw, and she says, "Take a study hall, boys and girls—sit in the auditorium." (She can't rehearse her choir if they sit in the auditorium, because there's a study hall already assigned there; the place is three-quarters full.)

Miss Stanley feels discouraged about her opportunity to work with these boys and girls. "Unless they feel they are making progress, they can't be expected to put forth their best efforts. We have only two periods a week to rehearse, and when one of these is broken up, we have difficulty keeping the continuity from class to class. Now I know as well as the next person that it's necessary to give and take, but why a stage set should be erected on the stage three weeks before the play, so that I have to crowd 102 youngsters into a room designed for 35 or give them a study hall, I'll never know. One teacher told me I shouldn't have such a large choir, but my principal says I'm doing a good job trying to meet the needs of my pupils. Well, I wouldn't be if I kept the choir to 35."

Other music teachers say:

"I can't see why the principal doesn't understand that I NEED A DESK . . . ."

"The storage closet for music is on one side of the school building; the choir rehearses on the other side. I need a storage closet in or adjacent to the rehearsal room. I've been asking for it for five years . . . ."

"We have nice new band uniforms that cost plenty of money. But you should see the postage stamp of a closet where I'm supposed to take good care of them. . . ."

Some teachers say that they are asked to conduct general music classes—junior or senior high school level—on the stage of the auditorium. "I have to hold my general music classes in the auditorium; naturally the high school principal and the janitor come in to plan PTA or other evening meetings, or other individuals arrive to set up the stage for plays during my classes." Or, "The principal thinks the music class should meet in the auditorium while health class meets in the music room. He seems to think music is more of an entertainment than a regular class." Still another, "Even if I didn't mind teaching a class on the stage of the auditorium, I would be handicapped by lack of a chalkboard, storage facilities, and desks or chairs so that the pupils can do some writing. I think the impermanence of the situation affects the attitude of the class, also."

So far we have not heard from the elementary music teachers, but they have problems, too. At times they need space for rhythmic activities. These activities should be based on free, untrammeled motion. Unfortunately some teachers are working in schools where desks are screwed to the floors. And the question of the classroom piano! One teacher says, "For some reason, the piano is kept in the Teachers Room, and I'm not allowed to move it (even if I could!). Consequently, no piano accompaniments are possible for classroom work, even though I know the children would enjoy them."

It is fair to assume that no administrator would handicap his music teachers deliberately. Having hired them and given them a job to do, it is certain that he would prefer to have them function so that the music program accomplishes its objectives.

But music is only one part of the school program, and music teachers must bear this in mind, since it means that the administrator is involved with other aspects of his school. In the many ramifications of running the school as a whole, it is easy to overlook certain needs that, if satisfied, add immeasurably to the welfare and efficiency of the music staff.

For teachers have their school needs, as well as children. In our discussion here, these revolve around music teachers and their work; they can be met only through the mutual cooperation of the administrator and his staff. If an administrator or supervisor has read through this book to the present chapter, he already understands the music program to an extent that will justify the stated or implied requests of the teachers whose situations we have noted. In any case, whenever music teachers have to make shift with what they consider to be substandard, inadequate housing and equipment the reasons usually have to do with lack of understanding of the music program's nature.

*Minimum Requirements*

The scope of a music program determines what basic housing and equipment is necessary. If we are beginning with very little, in a system where there has been limited musical instruction, just what will be required depends on the teaching experience and ability of the instructor and the projection of the program. Do the administrator and the music teachers have the time and the inclination to plan together such minimum housing and equipment? If not, a short circuit results; a teacher in such a situation may say, "It seems that the music program at this school must really prove its value before it will be given money to go ahead. How you prove the value of your program without the necessary equipment certainly stumps me. It's like being ordered to learn to walk a tightrope without the rope—one will be supplied after you have mastered the technique."

We'll begin with some modest requests and work from there. One teacher wanted a place to "stay put" and do some planning, yet he had to share a desk with a piece of office equipment. Now, does this teacher really need a desk?

He has reports to complete, resource materials to list, lesson plans to outline, requisitions to make out for teaching materials. He really needs *more* than a desk; he needs office space for conferences. He does more than visit classrooms and conduct rehearsals; he is a *teacher*.

An adequate teaching situation may have been a log hut seventy-five years ago, but not in most public schools today. The log hut just won't do the job of the desk in meeting the responsibilities of today's teacher.

In the elementary school, music is often a part of the classroom, and as such is taught there by the music teacher, the classroom teacher, or both. In newer schools where there is an all-purpose room, the class may use this room when space is needed for rhythmic activities, musical plays, or phases of the program that will best be served by a free space area. In some schools the piano is kept in this room, with the teacher taking the class to the piano rather than moving it from one room to another.

But whether such activities are carried on in a room planned for the purpose or in a room adapted on a temporary basis by such simple devices as pushing back the chairs, it should be understood that they have a functional purpose—helping children grow in musical understanding. Therefore attention should be given to needs in these areas.

"Resolved, That Music Classes Should Meet on the Stage of the Auditorium." If we put this in the form of a debate, it would be difficult to gather many reasons, if any, to bolster the affirmative. Do English or social studies classes meet on the stage, or even in the auditorium itself? If they do, evidently the music teachers don't know about it. Now obviously this is a poor teaching situation. Furthermore, these classes are usually junior high general music classes, a most difficult area of teaching music so far as age groups are concerned, as has been noted in preceding pages. It follows, then, that this is the area in need of a stable and favorable environment as well as a well-prepared teacher.

If the room scheduling officer understands the nature of the music classes, it will be evident that they need a room of their own, and a room in which the teacher can build a musical environment. A bulletin board, for example, may not be very important in itself, but it can serve as an aid to learning, a means of class participation, and a channel for building class interest and continuity from one period to the next. Remember, that "next" period may be two, three, even six days away. Besides this, the teacher who must move around with him all the books, instruments, and other equipment that make the music class interesting and lively for this age group will be sadly inefficient in terms of wasted time.

Why does a music teacher need a chalkboard? Well, a good teacher, when mentioning the name of a composer, will place that name on the chalkboard so the children can *see* it. Musical themes and excerpts from songs will be placed on the board, along with other elements of the musical score, and placed there for a musical purpose. We hear a great deal, today, about the failure of teachers to develop a satisfactory level of skills in their pupils. Skill in music is related to visual and aural recognition of the score. In developing the visual aspects of this skill, a chalkboard is of inestimable value. We suspect that some of the college freshmen who spell bassoon "bazoon," Chopin "Shopan," cornet "coronet," and Waltz of the Flowers "Walls of the Flowers"* were taught on the bare stage of an auditorium. It may be possible for a superior teacher to do a passing piece of work under such conditions, but it is certain that both teacher and pupils would achieve much more in a room equipped for the task.

The music room serves *all* the purposes of teaching music; for example, when an opportunity arises to explain a musical skill, such as a way in which folk songs may be accompanied, an Autoharp may be needed. "Johnny, run over to the music closet on the second floor and get the Autoharp," means a delay of five or ten minutes. By the time Johnny returns, the period may be over. But if the teacher and class are in a room where children regularly come for their musical experiences, it takes only a few minutes to reach for the Autoharp, explain the accompaniment, demonstrate, and have pupils accompany a simple song.

These general music classes—the ones we have said often end up on the stage in an auditorium or gymnasium—seem to constitute an area some administrators have little time to investigate. Music teachers actually wonder out loud, at times, how the principal knows what is going on in their classes. "I know he's busy, but in two years' teaching I've never had a classroom visit from my principal. How does he know what I'm trying to accomplish, or whether I actually need the materials I order?" This type of remark is no complaint; it may represent a desire to establish a channel of communication or

*Elmer C. Wareham, Jr., "Use That Blackboard," *Pennsylvania Music Educators Association News,* October, 1954.

a realization that help is needed. It may, too, indicate a need for expressed understanding of what is being accomplished by the seventh, eighth, or ninth graders.

Perhaps the administrators feel they observe enough of the music teacher when he is in action with a performing group. Or perhaps the lack of visitation indicates satisfaction with the program. There are administrators who are honestly concerned about the wisdom of requiring music of all junior high pupils— "The classes are too noisy, they create discipline problems, the children don't like them, and it would easier to drop them from the curriculum." Whatever the attitude, music teachers would like to know that administrators are aware of the conditions under which they work and the content of the courses they teach.

These are no longer the classes where children spend the period singing aimlessly from a community songbook, passively or impatiently listening to records played on a portable phonograph. Today's teachers are planning classes specifically aimed at capturing the interest and attention of pre-adolescent and adolescent youth. They are attempting to meet the musical needs of all the boys and girls in their classes.

This is a tough job in itself, and it may very well become impossible when the class and teacher are pushed from pillar to post where a meeting place is concerned. We have never heard a scheduling officer say, "Music classes are not very important— they can meet anywhere," but because they are sometimes placed in any available free space, both teachers and pupils may receive the impression that this is the school attitude. Since every teacher has chosen to teach music because he thinks it is worthy of inclusion in the school curriculum, the attitude that it isn't, even when implied, is a blow. Teachers, unlike golfers and racing horses, do not need a handicapping system!

Mr. Bell, principal of Ringer Junior High School, says, "Still, in spite of what you are saying, would you prefer to forego the music program until you have everything right in the way of housing and environment?" Mr. Bell, if the music program had waited for such a millenium, we would still be waiting today. Like other teachers, the music educators hope for and work toward an improved situation. All items pertaining to housing and equipment are raised by them not as complaints, but as questions—"What can we do to help our teaching in such respects?" One teacher said, during a discussion of undesirable teaching situations, "All through college I heard that overcrowded home situations and unstable environment were causative factors in producing delinquency. When I hear about some of the teaching situations of you people, I begin to think that comparable conditions in the schools may be causing delinquent music programs!"

Here are some recommendations for adequate housing. Let's consider these to be minimum recommendations. Those readers who are living a plush life in new buildings complete with music wings may skip to the next topic!

1. In the elementary schools music may be carried on in the regular classroom where space is provided (or can be arranged by shifting furniture) for the rhythmic aspects of the program that call for freedom of child movement in terms of the whole body. This rules out rooms where furniture is fastened permanently to the floor. (Today's classroom teacher would prefer to have it unfastened, anyhow.)

2. If there is only one piano in the school, encourage the music or classroom teacher to exchange classrooms occasionally so the children may enjoy the experience of singing with piano.

3. In setting up an instrumental program for the elementary schools, list the possible locations suitable for group or individual instruction. Let the instrumental teacher inspect and choose from these locations. Then help him to arrange, decorate, or otherwise adapt this space so that it takes on a physical atmosphere conducive to learning about an instrument. Even the darkest room will benefit from a gallon or two of paint and a few murals on the wall. There are teachers and classes eager to

take on such an improvement project, and it can be a true educational experience.

4. General music classes in the junior high school should be taught in a classroom large enough to accomodate the class comfortably. It should be equipped with chairs that not only can be used for the usual classroom activities such as writing or working with text materials, but also can be moved aside for other activities such as folk dancing. These rooms should have bulletin and chalkboards.

5. Rooms, halls, or other space designated for the rehearsal of musical organizations should be assigned to them as a regular meeting place. These organizations should have priority on their assigned rooms, halls, or stages where they are meeting. Storage cabinets for music, instruments, and other equipment should be convenient to the rehearsal space.

Where such space is used by several groups, the responsibility of each group for leaving it in proper condition for others should be clearly understood. For example, an instrumental group can clear the room of music stands at the end of a rehearsal to prepare the room for a health class.

When it is necessary to change the regular meeting place of such an organization for a special occasion, the teacher should be notified well in advance and should understand the reason for the change. "Where do we go today?" heard as pupils mill around in confusion indicates lack of good planning.

6. Adequate ventilation is one of the problems of large instrumental and choral organizations that rehearse in a comparatively small room. Examine the facilities for ventilation before assigning a rehearsal room; where boys and girls are singing or playing instruments the air may easily become foul and the temperature too high. Isn't it foolish to teach good health practices one period and demonstrate poor ones the next?

7. Lighting facilities should be at least average in situations where boys and girls are working with the musical score. Spend-

ing a few hundred dollars to install good lighting may save many times that amount in eye glasses and medical bills.

8. When any musical group is to present a program, arrangements should be made for rehearsals in the place where the performance is to take place. This affords an opportunity to arrange the organization and its equipment in the most advantageous manner. It also develops self-confidence on the part of the group members. Since they are relatively inexperienced as compared to professionals, the importance of this procedure cannot be overstressed.

9. When a new building is being planned, the special requirements of the music program should be considered by the planning committee, along with the special requirements of other areas of the program. Some school administrators follow the wise course of allowing members of the music staff to visit new schools where facilities for the program have been well planned. Some items to consider in such visits are:

(a) Position and acoustics of the music rooms in relation to the rest of the building. Music, as we all know, is sound producing!

(b) Acoustics of the auditorium in terms of performing organizations.

(c) Size and location of music classrooms, rehearsal rooms, practice studios, recording booths.

(d) Position relative to easy stage access and access to outdoor drill fields for bands or other instrumental groups that perform at such events as football games.

Whether a school is in a relatively strong or weak financial position to provide for the housing of its music program, careful planning and foresight will prevent many of the problems cited in the preceding paragraphs.

## *Equipment*

A music teacher, after listening to his fellow graduate students discuss their problems of housing and equipping public school music, remarked to the instructor of the class: "We have no major problems in our school. The administration and the school board are behind the music program one hundred per cent! This may be unbelievable, but it's true."

It seems wise to include the above statement at this point, just in case readers get the idea that we are not aware that such situations exist. We know they do, and many of them. But the situations where problems are so acute that they trouble either the music teachers, the administrators, or both, and no solution has been reached, are our chief concern. Wherever an unsolved problem exists, it interferes with the efficiency of the teacher and affects the children he teaches. However negative these problems may seem, they cannot be solved until they are recognized. So—let's bring them into the open.

Henry Hall says that he has asked his principal for one music stand for three years and still does not have it. Total cost? Five dollars. Another teacher says, "I often mention buying a different set of music books. My principal always gives me the same answer: she'll talk it over with her aunt. Her aunt gives violin lessons (in another town). Therefore, she's supposed to be an *authority* on public school music?" Another teacher writes, "What can I do to solve the problem of no recordings available and, the administration says, no appropriations available for buying them. Still, I'm expected to carry on a good, balanced music program. Should teachers be responsible for purchasing these materials of teaching out of their own pockets? I wonder, because I don't see geography teachers buying maps and globes for school use."

Another teacher cites the same basic problem, but from a somewhat different angle: "There seems to be difficulty in getting orders for materials, repairs, etc. through the administrative office. They are not refused—they just don't get very far. Now this does not seem to be intentional. My principal is a very fine man to work for. How can I get the orders filled without making myself a nuisance—that's the problem."

All of these problems, and many, many others that come

from the troubled voices of conscientious teachers, seem to stem from that familiar source, a lack of understanding of the nature of the music program in *all* its aspects, and a failure to realize the necessity for certain equipment. If the majority of requests were for carillons or concert grand pianos, we could say immediately that they were unreasonable. Some teachers say, however, that it seems easier for the instrumental department to obtain several thousand dollars worth of instruments or band uniforms than it is to obtain a new set of basic song books for the music classes.

Does this illustrate a general lack of understanding? We think it does, if the music program is to serve all the children of a school. That song book for Henry, fifth grade pupil, is just as important to his musical growth as a bassoon may be to the growth of tenth grade Horace, member of the concert band. Why is it easier to obtain the bassoon? Perhaps because the public sees Horace playing his bassoon. They don't see Henry singing from his song book, so they seldom, if ever, have an opportunity to know just what that small bit of equipment has meant in terms of his musical growth.

Now in using this example we do not mean to imply that something is wrong with spending large sums of money for band and orchestra instruments. Such instruments are expensive, and a thousand dollars doesn't go very far. If a school can afford a well-equipped band, fine! But not at the expense of a comparatively hidden segment of the school program. The music educator who manages to get a disproportionate share of school funds for any one segment of the program is as much at fault as the administrator who recommends, or the board that approves, such a request.

### *Basic Equipment*

To think through this question, let's examine the basic music equipment needs for the entire school.

1. In any music class, with the possible exception of the early grades where experiences are not oriented to the musical score, song books are needed. These are usually basic song series texts, particularly planned for use by school children. There are books to place in the hands of the children, and manuals to guide teachers in helping children use these books. While it is true that a teacher who is fairly good in developing the music experiences of her class may not need such a manual, it is just as true that the majority of classroom teachers who have either average or below-average ability in this area will find such manuals helpful and time-saving in terms of planning.

We do *not* suggest that a teacher be bound by any song book or manual. The newer song series, however, include many suggestions for teaching songs, developing understanding and skills from these songs, and correlating with other subjects, such as reading or social studies. Few classroom teachers have the time to look up such materials and procedures. It is important to mention this, because teachers have been heard to say that the school will not purchase teacher's manuals. The teacher who requests such a manual is probably an interested, alert individual who wants to do all she can to help her pupils learn about and enjoy music. This, then, seems to be a reasonable request, as is a request for song books to place in the children's hands.

An order for a teacher's manual from one teacher may do little to indicate a legitimate need for or use of the book. If, however, the music specialist or supervisor, together with the classroom teachers, general supervisor, and the administrators examine various song series and manuals, evaluate them in terms of music program objectives, agree on what is needed, and make recommendations for the purchase of certain books, the request will impress any reasonable administrator, even though he has paid little or no attention to sporadic requests for such items as one pitch pipe, with no reason indicated for its need.

2. Every school needs at least one piano. Although not every *classroom* can have a piano, the music specialist and class-

room teachers should have the opportunity to get their classes to a piano, or to get the piano to their classes. In addition to accompaniments, many musical activities of the class can be enriched and made more meaningful through the use of this instrument.

Even teachers who have had little or no experience with piano can help children create musical effects, interpret and imitate ideas and concepts. "How does thunder sound—like a single piano tone or a group of tones played with the closed fist?" "Will these be high or low tones?" "At what end of the keyboard will we find them?" "Should they be loud or soft?" "Let's find the tones that sound the way the big clock in the center of the town sounds when it strikes the hours." "How would you use the keyboard to show us the way an elephant moves?" "Let's have two children find some tones that sound well together." "If we play only the black keys, it sounds like music from a certain part of the world. Tell us some of the countries where you would hear such music."

These suggestions and questions, and the experiences that develop from them, illuminate and illustrate the process of developing musical understanding of such factors as tonal relationships, mood, rhythmic movement, and dynamics. Yet all of them may be used with children at any level of experience, with or without pianistic technique. The piano need not be silent most of the time because no teacher can play it. And it certainly will not be of much use if it is placed in some out-of-the-way corner and hauled out only for Christmas or May Day Festivals.

Have you ever watched a class examine the inner workings of a piano? Questions fly thick and fast—"Why are some strings longer and thicker than others? Why does it sound different when you step on the pedals?" And many more, all developing naturally from the curiosity of children, and all leading toward insight into the ways in which music is made.

Yes, schools need access to pianos, and the classroom teachers will appreciate help learning about the many ways in which the piano may be used. Pianos are expensive pieces of equipment, however, and they should have the regular services of a piano tuner. We have seen too many school pianos that obviously had not been repaired or tuned for years. Tuning should be done as a routine procedure twice a year—not just prior to a concert. A piano badly out of tune is worse than no piano at all. The football coach will not allow his players to use a ball unless it is pumped full of air and correctly laced, because they cannot play good ball with it. The out-of-tune piano cannot make good music; it will have a detrimental effect on the musical concepts children are forming. Don't use it, but explain why.

Any piano that must be moved from place to place, even from one side of a stage to another, should be equipped with a roller device to prevent injury to the instrument or to the individuals who do the moving. The piano should be equipped with a dust cover. Not only is the cost of these accessories small compared to that of the instrument itself—it will be worth many times the initial investment in keeping down the size of the repair bills.

3. Elementary and junior high classrooms now find extensive use in their musical activities for such instruments as Autoharps, bells, and classroom rhythm instruments. These comparative newcomers to the music class have great value. The Autoharp, as an example, for some children seems to satisfy a hidden longing to make music. Perhaps these are children who do not have the drive, stamina or talent to learn such demanding instruments as piano, trombone, violin. Perhaps they are children to whom such opportunities have been denied. Whatever the case may be, an attitude of intense interest is revealed in the faces of such children when, by pressing a chord bar and strumming the strings of the Autoharp, they find themselves making real music. And again, as with the piano, much musical understanding can be developed through the use of this simple instrument.

Teachers who are unaware of the many ways in which bells, Autoharp, and rhythm instruments may be used to enrich the singing, listening, and rhythmic experiences of children should investigate this area. Children like to *think and do,* and such instruments, used creatively, are an ideal avenue for combining the two. Certain of the rhythm instruments can be made as group or individual projects. Beautiful drums with excellent tone have been made from such materials as nail kegs, wood containers, rubber inner tubes or old drum heads discarded by the instrumental teacher.

One interested school principal found that boys who had been sent from their regular classrooms to his office because of behavior problems were often interested in doing something with their hands while they thought through their problems; he gave them the opportunity to work on such a project as a classroom and school contribution. Furthermore, he lent a helping hand as they worked, finding that it was easier to establish communication under such circumstances. Not many boys will resist the chance to work with tools and fashion a useful, interesting object. We feel that such a procedure, although not arising from a direct musical need, is well worth while.

4. Every teacher should have access to a phonograph and recordings suitable to her class. As with the piano, not every classroom can have its own machine in the majority of schools; perhaps several teachers will share one. Many makes of portable phonographs are available today, and classes look forward to their turn to share the phonograph and records.

Some elementary classroom teachers have found the use of records so valuable that they bring their own machines and records to the classroom and build a record corner where children may play music at a low volume level, just as they go to the book table and choose a book to suit their individual interests. In a classroom where children are working in different groups and where there is what one teacher described as a "busy, happy, hum of activity," children will not be disturbed by music played softly.

If the school is to purchase phonographs, a primary consideration is that they should have good tone. A machine with record changer is unnecessary, although it is wise to show children how to place the needle on the record and explain why this should be done carefully. In one classroom an understanding teacher noticed that Charles, who was not achieving a high academic level, seemed to be quite expert at handling records correctly, that is without touching the grooves. She asked him to supervise the class record collection, much to his delight. Again, this was not a direct musical activity, but Charles, in his newfound status, took great pride in the task and increased interest in the musical content of the records. Eventually, he made a card catalog of their titles and composers. Of course this involved reading, writing, and the use of numbers. Yes, it was a by-product of music—but important.

5. For schools that have a large budget, fascinating musical instruments of excellent tone and attractive appearance have

been made available by companies specializing in this field. Drums of all descriptions, do-it-yourself instrument kits, and the "Pogo Cello" are examples of some of these interesting and valuable additions to the music teacher's tools.

In certain schools having a limited budget, the teachers have been amazingly resourceful in collecting objects that serve as accompanying instruments but are either free for the asking or very inexpensive. The use of inexpensive water glasses filled to different levels in order to produce various pitches is well known to most music teachers. While horse-shoes are not common in some sections of our country, in others pupils are using these as triangles to produce a bell effect. Pieces of metal having good tone quality are sometimes rescued from trash heaps, attics, or cellars and find a place in such classroom collections. Sets of tubular chimes may be made by cutting metal pipes in different lengths.

The assortment of such materials is limited only by the imagination, ingenuity, and inventiveness of the teacher, although the assistance of a muscular helper and access to a workshop of tools is a big help. Even the school that can afford to purchase adequate equipment should consider the educational advantages of encouraging pupils to fashion some of their own.

6. There are small pieces of equipment, such as staff liners, staff-lined paper, and metronomes, that may look like extras when they appear on a requisition form. Actually, these are as necessary to the music teacher as maps to the social studies teacher. Furthermore, in schools where there is extensive correlation or a flourishing core curriculum, the music teacher may even order maps and the social studies teacher a song book or two.

7. Does your school own and use a tape recorder? If not, you and your pupils are missing an opportunity that is likely to be one of the most revealing experiences in building musical values through self-criticism. Many schools own, but do not use to the fullest possible extent, tape recorders. Perhaps some mu-

sic teachers may be afraid of what this tool may reveal; they confine its use to recording concerts—the finished product. To justify its expense —and an inexpensive tape recorder will not record and play back music satisfactorily—this instrument should be used to stimulate musical growth.

Children grow from day to day, week to week, month to month. They need to know how they are growing, what they are accomplishing, what they have achieved this week or month beyond last week or month. The expense involved in purchase and upkeep of a tape recorder is justified if it is used in some of the following ways:

(a) Record classroom singing so children can hear and discuss the *sound* of their singing. Encourage suggestions for improving singing tone, diction, expression of mood or spirit of song, dynamics, and tempo. This affords a positive basis of procedures—self-motivation and understanding of the goal. Record again after progress has been made.

(b) Keep the recorder running *throughout an entire* choral or instrumental rehearsal. The director of the organization should then study the tape, isolate problems, locate good features of rehearsals, evaluate his rehearsal techniques. This will serve as a basis for setting up the next rehearsal. It is time-saving, it prevents useless drill through diagnosing errors and devising remedial procedures, and it allows the director to concentrate on the sound of his organization without the usual distracting features of the rehearsal situation.

(c) Play tapes of rehearsals for members of the organization and ask that they evaluate their playing or singing. Encourage them to listen to the whole composition being performed, not only their particular parts.

(d) Use with pupils during individual or group instrumental instruction as in (a). It is good procedure to keep recordings of progress on a monthly basis, as the pupil then has, along with the teacher's comments, an aural progress report in the form of his own playing.

(e) In classes, or in musical organizations, it is sometimes interesting to tape a song or composition performed by the pupils, then allow them to compare it with a professional recording of the same music. An analysis of the differences will reveal many ways in which the pupil group can improve their performance.

Great care must be exercised to impress upon pupils that they are *not expected to reach a professional level.* In other words, the tape recorder should be used as a positive means of encouraging pupil growth, not as a negative means of criticism. It is very likely that the open-minded music educator will find, through the careful use of this teaching aid, many ways to improve his teaching techniques.

(f) Teachers who attend graduate classes, in-service clinics, or other professional education sessions, may find it useful to take along tape recordings of their own classes or musical organizations. Competent, impersonal evaluation of such tapes is a good method of promoting one's growth as a teacher.

8. Remember the teacher who said he had ordered a music stand more than once and never got it? He wanted this for his instrumental program. He needed other working materials, too. Here are some necessary items:

(a) Folding chairs that will not only permit, but also encourage, the pupil to develop correct playing posture. We specify folding chairs so they can be stacked to clear a space for other classes, or easily transported when necessary for concerts.

(b) Music stands (reason obvious).

(c) Podium for director.

(d) Storage cabinets for music, either permanently built in or furniture-type.

(e) Risers for concerts. These improve both the appearance and sound of an organization. They also make it possible for parents and relatives to see the member of the family whose presence on the stage has brought them to the school. If you, the director or the administrator, don't know how important this is, listen to and watch these parents as you sit among them at a concert.

(f) Folders for music. Two types are needed, those for the current repertoire and those for filing the music library.

(g) Some schools permit the music instructor to sell such items as strings, reeds, and rosin as pupils need them. This service is non-profit, of course, and is done for the convenience of the pupils.

(h) The big items—instruments. The school should own as many instruments as it can afford, for the simple reason that more boys and girls will have an opportunity to learn an instrument. Is it fair that only those who can afford to buy an instrument can learn to play one when an instrumental program is being maintained through public money? Schools most often purchase the larger instruments such as tubas, bassoons, and string basses. It seems fair to say, however, that they should also purchase enough instruments of each family so that all children may have the opportunity to try out instrumental music if they so desire. Once a child has progressed to a point where he wishes to own his instrument, many parents will purchase one, and the school's may then be used by another child.

Yes—this is an extreme recommendation. Each school will have to decide what it can buy. We believe, however, that all aspects of the school program should be open to all children regardless of financial means.

(i) Money must be available for instrumental repairs and reconditioning.

(j) Uniforms. These should be the property of the school, purchased and paid for by the school. If money is raised for uniforms through tag days, bake sales, solicitation of merchants, and other such methods, it comes from the public. If a community can afford to supply money in such a manner, it can also afford to pay it through taxes. Why not be direct about it? Let music groups and their equipment stay within the province of the school. No community group should have a grip on any school organization, but sometimes a group, having contributed generously to the uniform fund, feels it has a claim on it in terms of service.

9. The choral program has needs that are similar to those of the instrumental program. It needs chairs, stands, storage cabinets, risers, podium, folders for the same reason. It also may need choir robes for performing groups, and these, too, should be paid for by the school. This is not a brief dismissal of the choral needs; the fact is that the basic needs of the choral and instrumental programs are similar, and for similar reasons.

10. Both choral and instrumental programs need a repertoire of music. Because the members of these organizations are students, they should play and sing many compositions in a school year, not all of which they need perform publicly. This is important; any student who has had the unhappy experience of rehearsing the same few numbers month after month will reflect his discontent with such a situation, as will his music director.

Furthermore, the same music cannot be used year after year. Scotty, who joins the school orchestra as a ninth grader, won't grow much in musical experiences if he plays the same numbers in tenth, eleventh, and twelfth grades. Of course a few numbers will be played several times during these years, but not, it is to be hoped, over and over again.

### *Building The Budget*

"I don't understand why the music department needs so much money," remarks Mr. Bass, administrator in the Harmonyville School District, "Their requests for money have more than doubled in the last three years." His wife, sitting nearby in their home as he works over his budget for the next school year, replies, "Well, they seem to be building an excellent music department. One of the ensembles played for the Music Club last month . . . you know we give them twenty-five dollars every year to help buy music."

After this brief exchange of comments, Mr. Bass goes back to his budget. His wife, however, used the key word to the problem—"building"—when she answered him. Three years ago the music program was practically non-existent. Then a new music director appeared on the scene. He at once set about building a music program. As he examined materials available in Harmonyville Schools, he came to the conclusion that nothing much had been ordered for many years. He found, too, that what was available was in very poor condition. As his music program attracted more boys and girls, new materials were needed in increased quantity. In three years the pupil participation in music quadrupled.

This is the reason for the increased money requested. Mr. Bass is pleased with the new music program; the community is pleased. The new teacher, however, has been so absorbed in his work that he has overlooked the need for communication in a vital area—the school budget. He forgot to say why he needed more money, and he was too busy to sit down and write up a progress report on his work in terms of pupil participation.

Mr. Bass, anxious to please all teachers, simply asks them to turn in their budget needs by a certain date. Then his balancing act begins. It's a tough one, too, because he would like to give teachers the best of working materials.

Trouble is, the music department never gets around to finding out what the English department needs, the social studies people don't know what the commercial teachers need—each group is in its own little groove, and Mr. Bass is right in the middle in his. Remember the song about music going 'round and 'round? Well, right now the Harmonyville budget is doing just that, because no one knows who needs what the most. Here's a real short circuit in the lines of communication.

"How do you find out what money is available for buying music equipment and supplies?" asks Lois High, fresh from teachers' college. "You don't," says "Hi" Downs in a weary voice. Hi's been teaching in Tipe City for three years. "You just ask for twice as much as you need, and hope to get one-quarter as much as you ask for!"

Tut, tut, Hi. You're going to be even wearier if you continue this approach. School budgets are no guessing game. A certain amount of money comes in, a certain amount goes out. Your administrator has to apportion this money as fairly as possible. Perhaps he is expert at this job, perhaps he isn't. In any case, let's advise Lois to inquire, to learn something about school budgeting. Then she can help decide what is important in the way of purchases, for this year, for next year, for the following year.

Most of us face exactly the same problem in our personal finances. We can't afford everything we want, so we decide what items have priority and wait for others. Music teachers should not assume that they can have whatever they want, or that their need is greater than that of any other school area. Neither should an administrator expect teachers to guess at what they have in the way of budget allotment. The spending of school funds is a serious business, and should be conducted in a business-like way.

"My principal's all for music, so we get whatever we want," says a teacher. We question, "Does the commercial teacher get all he wants, too? Or are his pupils learning their work on old, outmoded typewriters? Does this principal like art equally as well as music, or do the art classes take turns using the water colors?" Few principals, we are sure, are inhuman enough not to have their personal favorites among the various school curricula, but few indeed will carry such personal likes so far as to reflect them in the matter of allotting funds.

Dream on, my friend. We have a feeling that every teacher in your school would say, "My principal's all out for my subject, so . . . ." This seems like a happy situation, but again, a matter that should be on the basis of cooperative planning is operating blindly though blissfully. A sounder basis of teamwork would result in a more intelligent understanding of the entire school's needs.

Every teacher who is applying for a position should inquire about the method of allotting funds to the music program. He should be more concerned about the method of operating the budget than about the amounts involved. Here's why: if music receives more than its share, misunderstandings are likely to result; in some cases ill-will is engendered.

"Look at that," says Mrs. Byrd as the music teacher leaves the Teachers' Room laden with musical equipment, "does *she* ever have drag with the boss!" Mrs. Byrd thinks music got more than its share of the budget last year, just from what she sees. At the spring faculty meeting, when the music teachers ask for a schedule change, Mrs. Byrd is going to be against it.

Petty politics? No, human nature. Mrs. Byrd is just as interested in her teaching area as the music people are in theirs, and she thinks she's been shortchanged. Mrs. Byrd is shooting at a target she doesn't understand, but her aim is good and she has the range. Her ammunition may do damage.

Now, whose fault is this? We're going to lay it squarely at the feet of the school administrator. His teachers do not know how he arrived at the decision to buy this new, shiny music equipment. Mrs. Byrd has no idea why certain items she requested were approved and others failed to materialize. Neither does she know that certain items requested for music failed to materialize. Did music receive more than its share? We don't know—neither does anyone except the administrator. This situation should be labelled, "HIGH EXPLOSIVES—HANDLE WITH CARE!" Trouble is, no one will ever see this label, and someone is sure to jar the package sooner or later. It may be a small explosion, but the fall-out will be terrific.

Let's bring the budget out into the open and stop the snap judgments made on a basis of what shows the most. Give music its share, no more, no less; give Mrs. Byrd's area its share, too. But most of all, see that all the teachers are aware of the process through which allotments are made. This is democratic procedure, and it's all Mrs. Byrd really wants.

Why not devote a faculty meeting to budget problems? Invite a committee to sit in with the administrators and exchange opinions, make recommendations. No, it won't solve all the problems. It may create better understanding and improved relationships. And it will initiate an approach to problem solving. This is enough to accomplish as a beginning.

## *Scheduling Music*

"Jane, just look at this schedule . . . ."

You don't know Jane, who has just been asked to look at the new music schedule. But she's a music teacher in some American school, and she has scheduling problems. These you do know. Either you've had them or you've heard about them.

We wish it could be stated that some electronic brain had found a way to solve all scheduling problems. But not yet, so you will have to continue depending on human brains. These differ, schools differ, music programs differ. Result? You must custom-build your music schedule.

The major problem in elementary school scheduling is taking pupils out of class for instrumental lessons, music festivals, choruses, or other groups. This can be a Pandora's Box. If all children participated in these activities, the problem would not exist. Because the music program cuts through grade levels and classes, because it involves certain pupils and not others, it perplexes us.

When children begin instrumental study, they must leave the classroom for instruction. The only solution is for principals and teachers to adjust this so that the children are out of the room when something they can afford to miss is taking place. Perhaps this is when they are working at the desks in a study period. The music teacher cannot say when it should be; the classroom teacher must decide. She is responsible for the welfare of her charges. In this case we believe it wise to ask her to suggest a time, then work out a schedule with the school administrators.

This is easier said than done, though, since the instrumental teacher will have other pupils, other classes, and other schools. He must inquire from all the teachers as to their preference for released-time instrumental instruction, then work out the best schedule he can, preferably through a series of conferences with the teachers involved. This way they will understand the situation; most of them will be willing to do some shifting in order to cooperate.

Exactly the same principle applies to taking children from class for other musical activities. Imagine the reaction of Mr. Cambee, whose class has been planning to give the culminating activity of a unit of work this afternoon. He has just received a notice saying, "The following pupils will be excused from class at 2:30 P.M. to attend chorus rehearsal for the PTA meeting . . . ." Ten names are on that list. He'll have to change his plans, the class reaction will be poor. He should have had a voice in deciding *when* these children should be excused, *whether* they should be excused, and even *if* the chorus should be formed. He's been bulldozed, and he resents it. So would you.

You can't make a schedule of classes, lessons, concerts. You make a schedule of *people,* big and little. So don't sit down in a quiet room and work out the day's rounds in terms of economical starts, stops, and assignments. Get around and talk to the individuals you work with. Ask them to help you make a workable schedule. Use all you can of their ideas. It may not be as neat and efficient a program, but it will work better, because more people want it to work. They've built it.

### *The School Bus Is a Factor*

When it is necessary to take pupils from classes for instrumental lessons in the secondary school, do it as we suggested for the elementary school. If possible, it's even more important here, because now you are taking them from the classes of specialists. They undoubtedly like music, but they have no inclination to lay their own subjects on its sacrificial altar. Why should they?

The history teacher thinks history is fully as important as horn; chances are, he's certain it's *more* important. It's no good using the principal as a battering ram, either. "The principal says John, Henry, Sue, and Mabel may be excused" may bring about compliance, but it also builds hostilities.

The school day has only a few hours. If music is part of the curriculum, it should be scheduled on school time. In many schools we cannot teach music groups before or after school, because the bus schedule deposits and removes them in no uncertain fashion. You may have to work on borrowed time—borrowed from another teacher. We don't approve of this, but it's being done in various schools. Effort is usually made to see that pupils miss a class something like once a month. How well it works depends on the people who work it.

If this is the only arrangement a school can make, we hope it doesn't trap the pupils. A teacher who resents it can find ways to make life unpleasant for the "borrowed" pupils; for example, giving tests when the lesson is to take place. Who's to blame? Everyone who made the schedule. Who is hurt? The pupil, caught between two adults. Think of him, walk softly, and forget the "big stick."

Musical organizations are the biggest problem in scheduling organized groups of pupils. They include pupils from several grade levels. All of these pupils are taking certain subjects taken by pupils not in the organization. To clear several rehearsal periods a week without closing down classes tests the skill of any administrator.

Mr. Core, principal, says, "You're the music teacher; show me how to do it and I will." The music teacher replies, "It's your job, not mine. I'm no specialist in scheduling." Another impasse!

## *Suggestions for Scheduling*

Here are a few basic principles for custom-building your schedule:

1. The schedule may be built around the most difficult

subjects, those that include large groups of pupils on more than one grade level. Physical education and music are two examples.

2. Where activity periods release pupils for musical organizations, use them. Remember, though, that the groups should meet regularly.

3. Today's high schools teach everything from diaper-changing and bottle-warming (for prospective baby sitters) to chemistry and physics. Pupils must make choices. Teachers can't have all the pupils they want; pupils can't have all the subjects they want. Let them decide, with the advice of parents, teachers, and guidance officials. What's best for the pupil is best for the school. The larger the high school, the greater the choice. The smaller the high school, the tougher the choice, because many of the same pupils want to be in the same activities. How far can you stretch one pupil?

4. Schedule music on school time. Yes—we said it before. But we think it's the school's business to take care of music if it's part of the curriculum. In so doing, we take care of the pupil.

### *Large Classes Once a Week*

The general music program has two problems that are of concern to many music educators. First: Remember the music class with over sixty boys and girls? This is a spirit breaker for music teachers.

The average teacher who meets her class five times a day and knows them well finds thirty or forty children at a time all she can teach, and even this size means a definite limitation of attention to individual needs. Pity, then, the music teacher who finds herself assigned 60 to 120 pupils to teach in one class, and who sees them only one or two periods per week. "All I can do with the 120 youngsters I have is sing some songs. A lot of the time I police the group," wrote one discouraged teacher. "My principal says there's no other place to send them, so it's a good chance for them to have music."

This is certainly a negative approach, and serves to keep the teacher in a state of quiet desperation. If music is a subject worthy of inclusion in the curriculum, and if general music is that segment of the program reaching the most children, it deserves better treatment. The teacher should be able to start work with a fair chance of success. Do administrators think of general music classes as large choruses? There are still teachers who find this to be the case. Yet these teachers are eager to share their knowledge of music with boys and girls who are ready to explore and learn. It seems reasonable to expect that the same learning situation be set up in music as in English or social studies classes; the ratio of one teacher to 30 or 35 pupils is recommended. The chorus, band, or orchestra is a different situation; let's not confuse these in our planning.

Now, a second problem: Sam Young teaches in Jonson Junior High. "One of my biggest headaches is music classes that meet only once a week," he says. "I see them for fifty minutes and then they're gone for a week. In between they do fifty-six different things and it's hard to make anything stick." Sam, you have plenty of company, and all of it feels the way you do; it's tough.

Some teachers make the best of the situation by developing a three or four-week unit and, through careful planning and out-of-class assignments, maintain a thread of continuity. An example of such a unit might be investigating the instruments of the orchestra or voices on radio, records, or television. Incorporating such work into the class, it is possible to keep a fair level of interest running.

Other teachers feel that under such conditions each lesson must be a unit complete in itself, limited in scope—the hit-and-run type of teaching. It seems difficult to accomplish enough in terms of tangible results to give either pupils or teacher satisfaction through mastery of materials, though. Even at its best, once a week teaching appears to be like froth on the sea; it evaporates or is blown off easily.

## *Credit for Music*

Music teachers frequently raise the question of accrediting music courses. When music is part of the curriculum, regularly scheduled, it should receive credit on the same basis as other school subjects.

It is sometimes pointed out that music classes do not meet often enough to receive credit. If this is the case, it is an argument for scheduling their meetings more frequently; if a class that meets once a week, for example, does not represent sufficient time for credit, it scarcely represents enough time for adequate learning to take place.

Another frequently raised objection to accrediting music courses and organizations is that they do not require homework. This cannot be considered a valid criticism if we remember the time required for individual practice and extra out-of-school rehearsals, to say nothing of the time spent in concerts and other public appearances.

One recommended procedure appears in a bulletin released by the Maryland Department of Education:*

> Recommendation: When schools offer courses meeting only twice a week, it is suggested that a course grouping be offered called "Broad Musical Experiences;" for example, under such a heading a pupil might schedule band and chorus, one course meeting twice a week, the other meeting three, and receive the same credit as a single course meeting five times a week. Courses requiring homework, outside obligations, and individual home practice similar to home study in other subject areas and which meet five times a week should receive one credit per year.

It may be that the failure to allot credit for music originated in its extracurricular meetings. However that may be, music

*Maryland State Department of Education, *op. cit.*

should be accepted as an accredited subject in today's schools.

### *Teacher Load*

"Why doesn't *he* have a Home Room?" wonders Mr. Anderson as he watches Mr. Cope disappear into the band room. "I suppose it's because he's a MUSIC teacher."

By the time Mr. Anderson reaches the word "MUSIC" in his silent commentary, Mr. Cope is wrestling with a broken 'cello string, a bent clarinet key, and reassuring Johnny who forgot this was the day for orchestra and left his trumpet home. He's also about to set up chairs for a class of elementary school pupils who come in early for instruction. (They could set up their own chairs, but the period lasts only thirty minutes, and by the time they get their instruments and music ready, only twenty-five minutes are left.) Yes, he could have prepared the room after school yesterday, but an adult group used it last night, and it looks that way. All of which goes to show that music teachers have a few responsibilities that differ somewhat from those of others.

Mr. Cope's schedule calls for him to meet the elementary pupils before their school day begins, at the high school adjacent to the grade school. High school begins forty-five minutes before grade school, so this gives him an early start. As soon as he is through with this group, he drives as fast as the law will allow to his next assignment, three miles away. He has ten minutes to get there. When high school classes end, he is *six* miles away, still teaching, because the grade schools close later than the high school. He spends about half his time teaching in the high school band room, however, and so his fellow teachers wonder why he doesn't have a home room.

Someone should tell them.

### *Here's Where I Get Off!*

John Clair left the teaching profession last year. People asked him why. He told them. "My wife said she only caught fleeting glimpses of me from one Sunday to the next, except at football games when the band was playing. One evening when I came home I heard my little boy saying to the kid next door, 'My Daddy does so live here!' Sure, I liked my job. But my family . . . ."

John's wife had reason to worry. During football season, the band kept him busy. On Memorial Day the band played, also on such occasions as Hallowe'en, Fourth of July, and the night Santa Claus arrived in town to usher in the Christmas shopping season. In between he led singing at the PTA, took groups out to play for various service clubs, churches, and other community organizations. Then there were evening rehearsals for the spring concert. When the last senior had been handed his diploma, John was still waving his baton over the orchestra as the audience filed out. This year they asked him to bring the band to basketball games. John got another job.

Yes, lots of music teachers do all these and more. The question is, should they? How thin can you spread one music teacher?

When John took his job no one told him that he could and should draw the line somewhere. He wanted to be successful. The more he did, the more he was asked to do. Perhaps if he had discussed the matter with his administrator, a reasonable agreement might have been reached. The fact is, not all his activities showed on his teaching load. But they should have. He should have been asked to turn in a full report of all his in-school and out-of-school activities. He should have turned it in even if he wasn't asked.

The teaching profession couldn't afford to lose John Clair. We hope it won't lose more like him.

## *Classroom Load*

Miss Ferm, music teacher, feels tired! She feels this way at the end of every week, after she has rapidly visited X number of classrooms. Even so, she visits each one only once a month, and then there isn't time to stop and talk with individual teachers. She'll be late to her next room, and she doesn't want to upset the teachers' schedules. Most of them really look forward to her arrival; they're waiting for her.

A heavy, close schedule such as Miss Ferm's may look like efficient use of teacher time. In reality, it's the opposite. The teachers with whom she works carry on their own classroom music nineteen out of twenty days a month. She should have time to talk with them, identify individual problems, get to know the children in their classes. She needs time to stop in the Teachers' Room at recess and rub shoulders with these teachers—rub off a little of that "supervisor" label. But she has to get on to the next stop.

Here is a prescription that may help next year, if filled by her administrator and taken by Miss Ferm on the opening day of school:

*Add the number of classrooms Miss Ferm is expected to visit. Add a fair amount of time for travel from one to another. Now divide the result by two, thus allowing for teacher conferences and time to plan for the individual needs of teachers and classes.*

This prescription will result in economical use of teacher time. It is *not* who gets there "fustest"—it's who gets there "with the mostest." And still on her feet.

## *"Consider the Lilies . . ."*

Despite the evidence before their eyes, some people classify music teachers with the lilies—neither spinning nor toiling. Perhaps this is because they are frequently seen on the run, going or coming. Yes, they like their work; they'll tell you, "Never a dull moment." But all the same, they lose out, because they are cast in the role of the music teacher morning, noon, and night. With a reasonable load, they will have time to mix with other teachers, lead an adult life with other adults, be people as well as "music teachers."

When the teaching schedule is made out, here are some factors to be considered:

1. Out-of-school-hours work. Include both school and community work—band trips, community service, taking instruments to be repaired.

2. Wear and tear on teacher in traveling among many assignments. Call this a "fatigue factor."

3. Pupil load. An organization of one hundred members may meet only twice a week, but it's more work than a class of thirty pupils meeting four times a week. Think in terms of one hundred individual pupils instead of one organization.

4. Responsibility for maintaining amicable relations between school and community.

5. Right to enough time for a normal home life.

Music teachers should be faculty members as well. Let's give them a chance.

## • FOOD FOR THOUGHT

1. What would you do to improve housing facilities in either the school system you attended as a pupil or the one in which you now teach?
2. Would you prefer to carry on an extensive music program poorly housed or a limited one well housed?
3. Give three reasons why music classes are sometimes assigned to meet on the stage of the auditorium. Under what circumstances is this justifiable? How can teachers make the best of such a situation? What can the administrator do to help?
4. Discuss planning a music department for a new school on three different bases: (a) Unlimited budget, (b) Moderate budget, and (c) Minimum budget. In each case describe the the community for which you are planning.
5. Choose any geographical area with which you are familiar and list five items that would be easily available for making

or improvising musical equipment. Why should such equipment have good musical tone?

6. Enact a scene in which you appear before the school board to present and explain your music budget, planned for a three-year period of time. Include in your budget specific items, approximate cost, and the company or dealer from which they are to be obtained.
7. Dramatize a meeting in which the principal, dramatics teacher, and music teacher are discussing sharing the school stage. Use this as the situation: The senior play will take place April 5; the band concert is scheduled for April 15. Have a committee summarize the results of the conference.
8. Write a letter to your administrator explaining the reasons why pianos in the school system should be tuned at regular intervals. Include approximate cost and indicate when tuning should be done.
9. Poll the class as to scheduling practices in the school each knows best. Appoint a committee to analyze these practices, report their conclusions, and make recommendations for improvement.
10. Make out what you consider to be a fair teaching load for any of the music positions described in previous chapters. Include out-of-school responsibilities as well as in-school.
11. Rate the school system with which you are most familiar on the following chart. How many of these items should be rated "Always" in order to have a favorable situation? Add four items to the chart.

| | Always | Sometimes | Never |
|---|---|---|---|
| Administrator Explains Budgeting to Faculty Members | ______ | ______ | ______ |
| Teachers Explain Reasons for Ordering Equipment | ______ | ______ | ______ |
| Teachers and Administrators Plan Room Assignments Together | ______ | ______ | ______ |
| Classes Are Changed from One Place to Another without Warning | ______ | ______ | ______ |
| Music Department Receives a Fair Share of the School Budget | ______ | ______ | ______ |
| Music Department Has to Raise Funds for Buying Certain Equipment | ______ | ______ | ______ |

# 16 • The administrator works with housing, equipping, and scheduling

## *Administrative Roles*

It is said that in the old western town of Leadville, Colorado, there was a sign in the dance hall that read:

Please Do Not Shoot The Pianist
He Is Doing His Best

When we consider the position of the administrator in today's schools we wonder if we should not borrow one of those old signs and place it on the door of the administrative offices!

The administrator must be a supervisor of teachers, a guardian of pupils' interests, a public relations counsellor and the watchdog of the people's pocketbook. In his various capacities he must make the decisions that affect every member of the professional staff of the school. Not the least of these are the budget allotments for instructional supplies, the assignment of space within the school, and the scheduling of classes. In the previous chapter the importance of wise scheduling, adequate housing, and good equipment for the music program have been discussed. In the final analysis these are the responsibility of the school administrator and will depend upon his decisions. But before final decisions are made there are important steps that can be taken by both the music director and the school administrator.

## *The Budget*

You can't do it because of "The Budget."
"The Budget" won't allow it.

What is this "Budget" that looms like a dragon to separate us from the things we would like to do in school; from the equipment we need? The budget (with a small "b" this time) is a plan that allows us to get the maximum value from the tax dollars that are available for school operation. The man who is responsible for making the budget is not a giant who guards the dragon, but a man who is expected to achieve the best possible schools with the least possible money. The best plans are made when all the pertinent facts are known by the planner. The budget planner needs to have all the pertinent facts before he makes the budget.

This is where the music director can take a first step toward insuring consideration of the needs of the music department when the annual school budget is made. He can assemble the pertinent facts, put them in easily understood form, and see that the facts are available for the administrator. Do you need more money for the music department budget? Why? Can you answer these questions:

1. How many pupils were enrolled in music classes last year?
2. Was this an increase or decrease over the previous year?
3. What enrollment is anticipated for the new term?
4. How many pupils participated in performing groups during the year?
5. What per cent of the pupils in the school were enrolled in some music class or activity?
6. What was the amount spent for supplies and equipment for music in the preceding year?
7. How much was that per capita?
8. What amount per capita do you suggest for the new term? (More about this point later.)

Who has time to work out the answers to these questions? The music director who wants to make sure that he has done everything he can do to secure adequate budget allotments for his department will *make* time for them. "We need more money for music," is a request that can be easily by-passed. Everyone in the school "needs" more money for something. Accurate facts and figures that show why money is needed are specific and show that thinking has preceded the request.

How do you get the administrator to receive the figures and give consideration to them? Budgets are made in the late winter or early spring. Lines of communication should be well developed by that time. If there are no lines of communication it will be difficult to open them with a budget request. During the months that precede budget making, if the administrator has not taken the initiative and conferred with the music director about the music department, the music director himself should try to find ways and means of establishing communication.

In most schools the administrators are willing to discuss budget needs, and are grateful to the teacher who presents factual data to support his requests. Administrators want to have good schools. They try to use the budget money wisely, and seek the assistance of their staff in making decisions. Who should take the first step to bring about the working relationship that results in a planned expenditure of funds, with each department of the school receiving its fair allotment? There is general agreement that such cooperative action should come from administrative leadership. If it doesn't come that way, the next best thing is for the music educator to assume some initiative and approach the administrator: "Mr. Snyder, I know you are beginning to work on the budget, so I've brought you some figures that I've worked out for the music department. When you have had time to look at them, I'll be glad to discuss them with you."

### *The Schedule*

Next to "The Budget" the second enemy to educational progress is "The Schedule." John can't play in the band because "The Schedule" won't permit it. The chorus can't rehearse until after school because of "The Schedule." Miss Ravell accepted a position in a neighboring state because last year she couldn't stand her "Schedule." The general music classes have one hundred students in them because of "The Schedule."

What is this formidable schedule? A plan that makes it possible for us to do what we need to do and want to do within the limits of the school day and week and year. As the budget is a responsibility of the chief school adminstrator and requires a large block of time in his work year, so the schedule in the secondary school is a responsibility of the principal and is a job which requires much of his time.

How can the music teacher help the principal in the scheduling problem? He can analyze the present schedule and discover the points at which the schedule causes difficulty with the music program. He can invite the principal to visit the classes, sections, or activities which are not functioning well because of the schedule. Then he can show what schedule change he believes will improve the situation. This approach to the problem will let the principal see the situation as the music teachers see it. He then is in a position to do the work that only he can do—view the music scheduling in light of the entire school program and plan the schedule that best fits all the needs.

One of the main difficulties in scheduling is our failure to examine critically the current schedule we are using. Some schools use the same pattern over and over, even though for five years everyone has been muttering about the length of the noon hour. The school principal should provide the opportunities for all the teachers to tell how well the schedule meets their needs or where it "pinches" their program. But if the principal does not ask for such criticism, the music teacher can say, "We haven't been able to accomplish what we hoped to accomplish in the eighth grade music class. The lunch period cuts the class into two parts and there are eighty-nine pupils in the group. Will you come up to room 210 at 11:30 some day this week to see the class?"

After the principal has visited, or in a few days if he fails to come, the teacher can say, "Here is my idea of what we could do in scheduling eighth grade music next year. I think it will improve the work we can do." *Schedules are made in offices but they are lived out in classrooms.* The music teacher should accept any opportunity extended by the administration to tell how the schedule works in the daily program, and if the opportunity is not extended he should find a tactful way of giving both the criticism and a possible solution to the administrator.

In the classrooms of the elementary schools the scheduling problems are not so severe. Most classroom teachers develop their own schedules and the schedules are flexible. Music is introduced when music fits into the activity and on the days when the special music teacher or supervisor comes it is no great problem to change things around as the day's activities demand. The greatest scheduling difficulty in the elementary school is in the schedules of the music teachers who travel from room to room and from school to school. In their zeal to accomplish much they overschedule themselves and as a result are always in a rush with never an opportunity to talk to a teacher, consult with a child, or take care of their own physical needs. If there are 330 minutes in a school day, ten 30 minute classes cannot be scheduled. There is the lunch hour, and at least five or ten minutes are needed between classes. Eight 30 minutes classes would be the most that could be comfortably scheduled, and six would probably be wiser. Principals and superintendents need to be alert to the schedules of beginning teachers who move from room to room. They need help in planning efficient but unhurried music schedules.

### *Equipment and Supplies*

The big question is, "How can we get what we need and want?" Exhibits at conferences, advertisements in magazines, college classes, and his colleagues all help the music director to know what he wants. Complaints of teachers, lack of equipment needed to do specific work, inadequate supplies all tell him what he needs.

Not knowing how to get what he needs and wants budget-wise, the music director frequently turns to bake sales, tag days, and a series of concerts to earn money with which to equip the music department. If music is a part of the school, the text books, instruments, and other supplies needed for good instruction should be a part of the school budget. How can the music director get his needs from the budget? Will there ever be enough money?

Perhaps here is where more thought should be given to what we want and need. All of us are susceptible to the pull of advertising. Each of us likes new text books. What do we need? What do we only *want?*

A five-year plan is a good working basis for planning for equipment and other teaching aids. Such a plan must begin with an inventory. What do we have? How old is it? After he knows what he has the music director begins to build his equipment, supply, and book stock by planning what should be purchased for each of the next years, so that at the end of that time the department will be well equipped. The values of such a definite plan are many. First, it keeps the director from buying carelessly; second, it gives continuity to a program if there are changes in staff personnel; third, it enables the director to keep a constant flow of new materials to the department; and lastly, it shows the school administrator that thought and planning have preceded ordering.

Two other things will help the music director in securing the materials he needs. Each order should be accompanied by exact information as to where the material can be purchased, the address, and the approximate cost. Many times a music teacher will say, "We need records," or "We need more books for eighth grade," or "We need choral music," and is no more definite about the order. The next term he is heard to complain, "I ordered records and never got them." Specific ordering is a help in securing the needed supplies.

Another way in which the music teacher insures acceptance of his requests is to be sure that the administrator knows why the items are needed:

> 50 music books, grade 8, to replace the *Red Music Book* purchased in 1935.
>
> 1 complete recording of *Porgy and Bess* to use in the elective course on Modern Music.
>
> 3 music stands to be used in the three new rooms on second floor.

The music director who presents definite planned requests is the director most likely to receive from the school the supplies and equipment that he needs.

Related to the question of ordering equipment is the problem of taking care of books and other equipment which have already been purchased. Music departments are notorious offenders in this matter (this is an administrator's observation). Music strewn around, books piled in corners, stacks of records on top of the piano—conditions like these force administrators to wonder if there is any use in ordering supplies for the music department. Reasons for poor care of materials are easy to name: large classes, small rooms, busy schedules. Yet each of those causes for carelessness is also an argument for orderliness. When many students use small rooms every period of the day, neatness helps to keep the program functioning smoothly. The music director who fails to receive the materials he orders may well take a look at the appearance of his music rooms.

### *Housing the Music Department*

What can a music teacher do if he is assigned to teach in an auditorium—or a broom closet? On the surface, very little. Administrators assign rooms, and if broom closets must be used, someone must be assigned to teach in them. It is true that frequently the music department is the department that is required to make the greatest adjustment to poor housing. Why? There appears to be no really valid reason. The ones most often used are, "We don't have to teach music; it's nice but not really important." "You don't need a classroom for the music class. They can sing anywhere."

Is there a way in which the music director can help in this housing problem? He can look around and see what changes could be made in the rooms that he uses. He can look at the school and see if he can find rooms that would be better suited to music teaching than the rooms currently used. He can work with the music teachers to plan what they believe would be good music rooms. Then he can ask for a conference with the administrator and present his ideas. Sometime repairs will be scheduled, sometime a new building may be built, sometime rooms may be reassigned. It is advantageous to have the person who will do the assigning and make decisions on renovation and building know what your ideas are. Most work in housing is done in the summer when teachers are not available for consultation. Administrators must hear from teachers during the school term.

In an ideal situation there would be an administrator who recognized all the needs of music education, who would ask the teachers what they needed, and order all that they asked. But there are few ideal situations and most administrators, like the dance-hall pianist, are doing the best they can. The situation can be improved if the trained music faculty will make ways to get their specific needs to the attention of the educator responsible for the administration of the school, and if the administrators in turn will initiate cooperative procedures in budgeting, scheduling, and purchasing.

## • FOOD FOR THOUGHT

1. What dangers are inherent in having students or their parents raise money for band instruments?
2. What do you believe is an adequate per capita cost for music equipment and supplies in a high school for 500 pupils in an industrial town?
3. Do you believe that in most schools music gets its fair share of the budget? Defend your position.
4. Make a five-year plan for buying the equipment for a junior high school band.
5. Make a five-year plan for buying recordings for teaching about the orchestra.
6. Draw a floor plan of what you would consider to be an adequate music department for a senior high school of 800 pupils.

# 17 • Teacher personnel

## *Getting a Job*

Hilda Weber is applying for her first job. She is sitting in the office of the Personnel Director. We won't listen in on the interview, because Hilda is not going to get this job. Why? Hilda says she will teach senior high school music only. The position open includes some junior high music as well. The Personnel Director wonders how specialized you can expect to be in your first year's teaching.

Somewhere there's exactly the kind of position Hilda Weber wants. Chances are, though, she won't get it the first year she teaches. Maybe not the second or third year either—because Hilda doesn't know where *it* is. She narrowed her field too much, too soon.

Early in the teaching career of every music educator there is a real need for broad experience in many areas of school music. The reason for this is simple: If the program is continuous in nature, elementary through senior high, vocal and instrumental, the best way to understand how it "meshes" is to see its different aspects. And the early years, when the teacher is particularly receptive to ideas and impressions, are the ideal years for such experience. Putting it bluntly, you work hard, you meet many adults and many children, you learn an immeasurable amount about your work.

What kind of a job will give you this broad teaching experience?

Probably you'll find it in a smaller town, one that can't afford a number of specialists. It may include helping the classroom teachers with elementary music, teaching some junior high music classes (perhaps an English or social studies class, too), directing the school band, or teaching a string class. You may have to travel around among four or five different school buildings. You'll be busy.

This kind of experience fills your need to understand the problems of all the school people—pupils and teachers. You can wave your baton over the "select few" forever and you won't understand why the elementary schools are not sending you neat little pupil packages marked, *"Can Read Music."* Likewise, you can teach music in one elementary school forever and still puzzle over why the secondary music teachers *expect* such neat pupil packages to be delivered.

## *Performer or Teacher*

Of course, we are assuming that you are interested in a career as a *music educator*. Some applicants for school music positions are really PRIMARILY interested in careers as performing musicians.

"Well, what's wrong with that?" asks James George.

Just this: if you are first a music educator, you are chiefly concerned with the musical progress of your pupils and the development of your school's music program. If you are a musician first, you are chiefly interested in your own musical prowess.

"Well, I can do both," says Mr. George. Maybe so. But the needs of schools and children are time-consuming, and it's inevitable that, sooner or later, we place the musician first or the educator first. In other words, you can't teach from 8 A.M. until 4 P.M., work with groups and individuals several additional hours a day, and still get in a few hours' practice on your major instrument.

Let's take the case of Miss Wagner. She has a nice voice. When she went to college, her family thought she might have a career as a professional singer. So did Miss Wagner. But it wasn't long before she found that neither voice nor musical talent would enable her to make the grade. About this time she had her tonsils out, so she had a good excuse for changing from music to music education—at least, she could let her friends assume that the operation had an effect on her voice. (Not enough to stop her singing, of course, just enough to interfere with a singing *career*.)

Miss Wagner made it through the music education courses. She never quite got over looking down her nose at those creatures who actually *set out* to be TEACHERS, and she never really accepted herself as one of them.

Still, teaching certificate all in order, she secured a position in a city system. Why? So she could continue to study voice and also join the community opera association and continue her "career." This, too, might have been a wonderful experience, except that Miss Wagner allowed it to absorb her entire interest. School's out—you could see her whipping into her car and away—for a voice lesson, an opera rehearsal, a session with a dramatics coach on how to faint in five easy lessons.

Meanwhile, back at the school, things were going from bad to worse in her classes. Her principal pointed out ways for her to help the situation, but these all meant spending extra time on planning, talking with pupils, doing some studying. She couldn't take the time from her operatic activities. When the county teachers had their annual Institute and there were workshops in music, Miss Wagner took off for New York to hear—you guessed it—an opera.

Miss Wagner, of course, is no *one* person we know. But there are music teachers like Miss Wagner, in one way or another. Who suffers? Their pupils.

What is your job—a pay check or a teaching career? If it's

the latter, your pupils must come first. Yes, you *can* combine the careers of musician and music educator. But if the educator is the large part, you are going to achieve the most satisfaction from the music your pupils make and enjoy, whether it is the first grade youngster singing his first recognizable tune, or the high school orchestra playing part of a symphony. And the more you know about the many aspects of your work, the bigger the share of satisfaction you cut for yourself.

So—consider the job with many facets. Specialize later.

### *Interviews*

Make it easy for a prospective employer to interview you. If you have been informed that you will be considered for a position, have your credentials forwarded to the proper officials. Prepare a written summary of your educational background, professional experience, family status, avocational interests, and any other information that will help an employer decide whether you are a suitable candidate for serious consideration.

If you want to find that one "best" position for you, learn some techniques of being interviewed. Remember that you are expected to be communicative, but you are not expected to monopolize the conversation. By asking some questions, you can keep things moving and yet still remain in the position of being interviewed.

Here are some items of information you should try to investigate before the interview is over:

1. Is the school philosophy compatible with yours?

2. Is music included in the over-all school philosophy? Or is it in its own little corner, pumping away at its own lifeline?

3. Will this position be challenging to you? Will it result in professional growth?

4. Will it be possible to achieve tangible results, or are there limiting factors that make this questionable?

5. What has been done with music in the school up to the

present time? (Remember, it is often difficult to take the place of a very strong teacher who has built a flourishing program.)

6. What materials are in use? Will it be possible to secure needed materials and equipment? What funds are available in the school budget; how allotted?

7. How is music scheduled and housed?

8. What is the attitude of the school faculty toward the music program?

9. Is school and faculty morale high? Does it reflect good leadership?

10. Is there a definite salary schedule in the district? How are raises awarded? Do the teachers accept the salary schedule as a fair one? We assume, of course, that the matter of salary will be a pertinent factor, as will the "livability quotient" of the community itself.

It would be rare, indeed, for an applicant to find a job that rates 100 per cent on the items listed above. Once you have such information, however, you have the basis for making an intelligent decision.

### *Deciding Which Job*

How well do you adapt to different situations? Jane, who grew up in a major city and attended a large high school, was unhappy teaching in a small rural town. Norma, who had attended a consolidated rural high school, took the same position the following year and found it just what she wanted.

Lew Fisher had two offers of positions one spring. Although there was a six hundred dollar difference in the salaries offered, he took the position with the lower salary. Why? "There were some factors in the higher salaried position that made me think I wouldn't have as good a chance to reach the children," said Lew. "These had to do with scheduling music. And the administration seemed to think it wouldn't be possible to change these conditions. I'd rather be happy working for less money than unhappy working for more. I don't want a job for just one year. I want to work at building a program for a period of several years."

Such considerations are important. True, there is no law requiring a teacher to remain in a particular position for more than a year (unless so specified in contract). Many teachers feel, however, that the first year in a strange community is a period of getting acquainted with school and community, and that the knowledge thus gained is reflected in the following years' teaching. This means that the teacher who remains in a community for more than one year is likely to make a larger, more substantial, contribution.

If you are a beginning teacher, consider the various geographical areas of the country, their need for teachers, their advantages and disadvantages. In a day of rapid transportation and a mobile population, in a day when teachers are in demand, there is a wide choice for you when you select your first teaching job. Of course, some individuals will prefer to remain in their home town or state because of home and family ties. Most teacher-education institutions will help students in locating and choosing a position; many of these institutions have teacher placement bureaus where information can be obtained regarding teaching opportunities in a wide range of localities.

If you are offered a position, it is highly advisable to make a decision either for or against acceptance within a short period of time. The reason is simple; the school needs a teacher. You've been offered the position—if you decline, another candidate must be located, interviewed, and evaluated. The less time available for this process, the less likely the school to find the best-fitted teacher. A prompt decision is not only courteous; it is professional procedure.

### *How Many Hours in a Working Day?*

The time to find out about your working hours is when you have your interview. If you don't care how many nights a week you will be expected to take the chorus out to sing, the band to play, then don't bother to inquire. If you feel that you should have a reasonable estimate of the in-school and out-of-school hours you will be expected to keep, better inquire. This can be important, so unless you are willing to devote an unlimited proportion of your life to the job, an understanding should be reached—before you sign that contract.

### *Say "Thank You!"*

After you have obtained a new position, write a few notes to the people who helped you get it. When you ask a busy individual to write a reference for you, it seems like a small request, but it may mean almost an hour's work writing the letter and sending it off. Doesn't it stand to reason that this person would like to know whether you got the job? If you hope to call on him for future references, it is certainly good policy to acknowledge his help.

Furthermore, he may be called upon to write references for literally hundreds of individuals. Letting him know you appreciate his help will make this a more rewarding task.

### *Keeping a Job*

Having settled into your teaching position, you can help yourself succeed by learning exactly what is expected of you. This means details of when you should arrive at the school, dates when report cards are due, what to do about pupils who loiter in the halls, whether or not you may send a pupil to the locker room for a forgotten book or instrument after classes have begun—all these and a host of other details will help you in your job efficiency. Some schools have handbooks for new teachers. Inquire about student handbooks, too. Teachers should know what is expected of pupils and whether they are *told* what is expected of them.

A primary procedure is to listen a great deal and talk very little the first months in the new position. Nell Minor, after a week in her new position, told her landlady that the music program was practically at rock bottom. "I can't imagine what the pupils have been learning," she remarked as she corrected a music test.

Nell's landlady said nothing at the time, but it wasn't long before the remark circulated around town. Parents and pupils alike felt Nell had been somewhat precipitate in her judgment. Whatever Nell thought, she should have kept her criticism to herself; since it implied that she rated everyone but herself down, it effectively put her on the spot, too. Nell just talked too much without thinking how it sounded!

Criticism of school procedures comes under this heading, too. Almost every music director who takes over a band, orchestra or chorus has been told by its members, "We always did it *this* way," when he gives instructions. If a director makes an issue of such matters, he will engender friction. It's far better to say, "Let's try it my way for a while, then decide which way we think better." If the new way is really an improvement, the pupils will be ready to admit it after a few weeks' trial. Why do they mention the methods or procedures of former music directors? Probably because of loyalty. Since no organization can do without this, better not attack its source!

The situation in which a new director fails to give definite instructions is equally dangerous, however. When music must be distributed, uniforms issued, chairs set up, large groups of pupils taken to and from an outside location for marching drill, certainly there must be guiding rules and regulations. A few hours spent in planning such procedures will result in more productive teaching during the adjustment period.

### *Stay in the Background*

Since you are a music teacher, you may be in the spotlight more than other teachers. This has been mentioned in a previous chapter, but it belongs here, too. You will be called upon to lead singing in school and community, perhaps in church. You may be asked to direct a church choir or serve as organist. If you have a band, you'll march down the street with it. When there is a school concert, you'll be up on the stage. You will make contacts with more pupils and townspeople than most of your fellow teachers. More people will know your name.

Because you are in a relatively prominent position, your colleagues will notice you. They may envy you your prominence, not stopping to realize that it is really part of the job, and in some ways almost an occupational hazard. Unless you offset this effect, some resentment (conscious or unconscious) may be aroused. Offset it by scrupulously carrying out all school responsibilities, whether or not they have to do with music. Offset it by minimizing your own share of the limelight and giving credit to other persons: pupils, parents, teachers, administrators. When you have a printed program for a school concert, see that it includes names of all persons who have had anything to do with it.

Perhaps you think you do most of the work yourself, but looking a little deeper into the matter, you'll see that many persons are partly responsible:

You couldn't have the concert without the parents, who get the children there in spite of interrupted meals, who make up the audience, and who see that your pupils are properly attired for the occasion.

You couldn't have the concert without the support of the administrator and the school board. You wouldn't be teaching music in the school without their support; not for long . . . .

You couldn't have your concert without the cooperation of many other teachers and school officials, who cleared the date and place for you. The school custodian, for example; his cooperation is invaluable.

Isn't it human nature to appreciate being given credit for your efforts, even though they are relatively small?

Remember, too, that when an audience applauds at a concert, they are applauding a *musical group*. When you acknowledge applause, indicate this. Include the members of the organization. Put *them* in the spotlight more than yourself. Some directors who are conscious of this take time to develop group techniques of acknowledging applause. And a few words spoken by you in acknowledgment of the cooperation of parents and others will not only be appreciated—they will build good will.

Whether you fervently wish that, as choir, band, or orchestra director, you could be concealed from the audience by an expanse of potted palms, whether you are by nature shy and retiring, you must look confident when you stand before your boys and girls. They depend on your confidence to build theirs at the "moment of impact"—the performance. But the audience appreciates your directing applause to the youngsters on the stage. They'll see that you get a fair share, too.

### *Maintain a Sound Teacher-Pupil Relationship*

Music teachers, working as they do with large numbers of students in musical organizations, often have more contact with these students than do teachers of academic subjects. They accompany them on trips, they see them in out-of-school rehearsals, they often have individual and informal opportunities for meeting. The music teacher who drives the boys' quartet to play for the T Club meeting will learn more about them during the fifteen-minute drive than the math teacher may learn in a month of class relationships. All the knowledge of individual differences thus attained will help the teacher in his work.

If, however, this pupil-teacher contact reaches a chummy level, the seeds of difficulty are growing. George Cliff, a popular, competent instrumental teacher learned this the hard way. The band room became a gathering place for any of his instrumental pupils who had a free period. George enjoyed this. It made him feel popular. "Helps me get to know them, too," he told his wife. Many of the students who came to the bandroom had legitimate reasons; instruments to be checked, music to be sorted, help needed with a difficult solo passage. Then there were those who came to loaf—Hank, who appeared every morning around 11 A.M. and liked to sit with his feet up on Mr. Cliff's desk, munching a candy bar.

What Mr. Cliff (or George, as the students were soon calling him) didn't know was that smokes were being sneaked in the band uniform closet (someone had a key made), excuses passed on to teachers ("Mr. Cliff needs me in the band room this period!"), and informal jam sessions being conducted when "George" was off teaching in the elementary school. Things became so noisy that eventually Mr. Cliff was summoned to the principal's office for an explanation.

What was wrong? Mr. Cliff forgot that the band room was part of the school, subject to the same rules and regulations as to its use. As long as his band members had legitimate reasons for being there, as long as he could really supervise them while they were there, no one objected. When George was afraid to jeopardize his popularity by saying, "There are times you may not be in the band room without permission or supervision," he laid the foundation for trouble.

It appears that music teachers need to stay within the bounds of good judgment and cooperative action with other teachers, particularly because they may enjoy greater popularity—and also greater opportunity for criticism—within the school.

Another outcome of the "Let's be pals" attitude may be the violation of professional ethics. Mr. Cliff found that he was listening to pupils' remarks about and criticism of other teachers, sometimes as part of the free-for-all band room gossip sessions, and other times because pupils made direct remarks to him concerning his colleagues. When the band room is used as a clubroom, it is difficult to control such matters. Mr. Cliff was caught between his desire to be loyal to fellow teachers and his desire to be popular with his pupils.

### *Professional Ethics Are Important*

Not only does the matter of teachers maintaining an appropriate relationship with pupils pertain to ethics—all relations concerning the professional matters should be carried out from an ethical viewpoint. Let's consider the case of Miss Hessy, who wanted to attend a string clinic. Her request for time off from school duties to attend this clinic was granted, but on condition that she pay her substitute. The principal explained that since she already had had six days absence with pay to attend festivals and clinics, he felt that any further absences should be her own financial responsibility.

Now, disregarding the obvious fact that a written policy with regard to this matter would have prevented the situation, let's consider Miss Hessy's next move. Filled with indignation because her professional training was not to be nurtured at school expense, she went to the president of the school board, who happened to live in the same block. We don't have to know the outcome of her visit. Her action was unprofessional, because it involved going over the head of her administrative superior.

In deciding to accept a position, we decide to work on a team. If conditions prove to be unacceptable, we can either put up with them, change them through group action, or leave. Whether or not Miss Hessy was unfairly treated, she should have kept her action within the school itself. Going over the head of the principal seldom brings sound results; it often does result in bitter and strained relationships. And again, where such relationships exist, the welfare of children becomes a secondary consideration.

Their welfare can be endangered, too, when teachers disagree, or when a parent and a teacher disagree.

And when such situations are allowed to continue, keeping a job in the community becomes either hazardous, unhappy, or both.

Is it worth it?

## *Those Temperamental Music Teachers!*

The day of the temperamental music teacher is past. The music educator isn't in this category today. Yet something of the stereotype of "temperamental musicians" still figures in the thinking of many school administrators and teachers. What this means is that the music educator, even though he is working with comparatively large groups of pupils, even though he has contact with more teachers and community residents than do most of his colleagues, must display a greater degree of self-control and equanimity than they do. If he doesn't, that old tag of "temperamental, egotistic musicians . . ." may return to haunt him. If he is late to school more than a few times, if he forgets an assignment or a report, the same thing may happen.

Closely related to this is the problem of handling large groups of pupils. If such groups are overly noisy, the attitude of other school personnel may not be that large groups make more noise than small groups; it may be that "music teachers" are not very expert at establishing group control.

In any case, if your classes annoy those of others through movement, activity, or even the making of music, you may hinder the effectiveness of your program.

See that you manage your classes so that they do not cause unfavorable comment in terms of their "nuisance value." See that the administrator knows where you are—that is, if you teach in more than one building, rehearse a marching band outside the school, take a class to a nearby church for an organ demonstration. A parent who calls to say that her son should come home at once may not understand why the principal's office can't locate him. The principal may find this difficult to understand, too.

## *Leaving the School*

Having decided, for good and pertinent reasons, that you are about to leave a school system, there are some procedures you should not overlook:

1. Be sure to submit your resignation within the period of time stated in your contract. A replacement will be needed.

2. Be sure to thank the people who have helped you with your work.

3. Be sure to leave your materials and equipment in good condition. It is wise to make an inventory of all books, instruments, and similar items both when you take a position and when you leave.

4. If you are responsible for any school funds (such as income from concerts) be very sure such funds are accounted for with school officials.

5. Summarize for your successor the work you have done, suggestions for carrying on, and any items you think may be of assistance in beginning the next year's work. Give a copy of this to the administrator plus a copy for your successor.

### *A Word to Administrators . . .*

One of the more puzzling phenomena of personnel policy—or perhaps lack of policy—occurs when a school system is in need of an elementary music specialist, for example, and someone with only an excellent *instrumental* teaching background is employed to fill the position. This could also happen in the case of a secondary general music opening. It rarely seems to happen, though, that an instrumental position is assigned to someone without instrumental experience.

If a definite position is open, every effort should be made to secure the teacher with appropriate training and background. The instrumental teacher who is excellent in his own field may be relatively inexperienced in working with elementary teachers and children. On the secondary level, many unhappy instrumental and choral specialists are struggling with general music classes they would prefer not to teach, classes they know they are not equipped to teach.

Administrators and school boards should not assume that a music teacher can teach all phases of the program equally well. Some teacher-education institutions graduate instrumental or vocal "specialists"; teachers who have had student teaching experience only in their major field (vocal or instrumental, let's say), and little course work in others. Other institutions, where students do have courses and student teaching in all areas, will still turn out certain individuals who are highly competent in one teaching area and relatively weak in another.

A teacher may be competent in the field of instrumental music and fail to understand the problems of the elementary music program as it affects many classrooms. And of course, the elementary "vocal" specialist may fail as an instrumental teacher. In employing teachers of music, the specific responsibilities of each individual position should be considered and matched against the qualifications and experience of the candidate. This is an administrative responsibility, for teachers do not hire teachers. It's important because the welfare of many children depends upon the judgment of the person who does the hiring. All possible efforts should be made to get the right person for the right job. And a certificate to teach music does not mean ". . . teaches all phases of music *well.*"

In examining the credentials of the candidate, administrators would do well to check his experience in the particular field of music represented by the job vacancy. A blanket statement to the effect that he taught music in the schools of a certain system and did a fine piece of work may be perfectly true, but was it elementary or secondary, instrumental or vocal music? And what proportion of each? Did he belong to both instrumental and choral organizations on the college level—or did he concentrate on one field?

Administrators would also do well to check the teaching philosophy of the candidate. Is it a *music education philosophy,* and is it compatible with the general philosophy of education in today's schools? Or is it centered around building highly skilled performing organizations that will work in the interests of only a small per cent of the school population?

While the majority of administrators will be happier with the music educator whose philosophy is in keeping with that of the school in which he is to work, there may be a few who want the other type. Whichever is desired, the candidate should be encouraged to identify himself in terms of one or the other.

## *Give New Teachers a Fair Chance*

Give your teachers an opportunity to do the best work they can. Is your school hidebound with traditions? Do you proclaim

that you think the old ways are the best ways? Have you kept up on new developments in the various curricula areas?

If you know a new teacher is coming into your music department, full of new ideas and methods, if you do not want such ideas and methods in your school, the time to tell this to the teacher is during the interview—not after school begins.

Such ideas and methods may bring badly needed new blood into your music program. The adminstrator who is willing to do a little guiding here will help the teacher make a good adjustment.

Because a teacher has taught twenty years does not always mean that he or she is a better teacher than the one who has taught four years. As we have said, it does mean that this individual has been accepted in the role of the teacher by the community. But the administrator who refuses to let younger teachers make a contribution because of less experience is deliberately placing a gag on their desire to contribute. They may have some very good and acceptable ideas. Look at it this way: if you were stricken with appendicitis plus complications, would you want the surgeon who had operated the same way for twenty years, or would you want the surgeon with the latest techniques? Fact is, you'd do well to have two of them as a team.

Can you make a team of the older and the younger music teachers in your school? They can't always do it without your help.

## • FOOD FOR THOUGHT

1. Describe three different music positions with which you are acquainted. Which of these would be best for a beginning teacher who wants a broad experience in music education?
2. Should a music educator put his own status as a performer ahead of his service to his pupils? How does the work of the performing musician differ from that of the music educator in the public schools? How can the beginning teacher keep a balance between both sides of his activities?
3. Make a folder of materials to present to a prospective employer.
4. Draw up a check list of information you want to obtain from an employer before you accept a position.

5. Enact a conversation between a music teacher new in the community and his landlady in which landlady questions the teacher on what he thinks of the music program in the schools.
6. Analyze the methods in which school music directors you know acknowledge applause at concerts. Relate this to the way pupils are included in the acknowledgments.
7. Draw up five criteria for establishing a sound pupil-teacher relationship.
8. Why is it important to leave things in good order when you have resigned from a school system?

# 18 • The administrator's role in guiding music personnel

## *A Trouble Spot*

Every subject matter area of the school has some personnel problems that present particular difficulties. They are the problems which, if they remain unsolved, cause school men to become used car salesmen, good teachers to find jobs in distant states, and school administrators to look about for someone to replace certain members of the faculty. Music has its own areas of difficulty. One of these is the problem of discipline in the music classes on the secondary school level. This problem has been mentioned several times as various aspects of music education have been discussed, but because the lack of discipline in music classes and activities is such a major problem in many schools it seems advisable to gather together all the parts and look at the total picture. Why is discipline a major problem in many music classes? Whose responsibility is it? What can be done about it?

## *Freedom and Control*

Students feel free in music classes. We want them to. Students who do not feel free will not produce music. One of the fine distinctions which adolescents must learn is the line that divides freedom from license. Whose responsibility is it to teach the meaning and responsibility of freedom of action? Clearly this is the teacher's responsibility. This must be taught by each teacher and taught as it applies in that class. The home room teacher may have taught the meaning of discipline in home room, but the music teacher must teach what discipline means in the music class. How can it be taught without endangering that essential freedom which is basic to all creative activity?

Most music teachers will agree that music is not the place for rigid regimentation and severe teacher dictums, but too many stop there without finding what to use instead. Janice Kodal has found the answer in the use of student participation in the government of music classes and music activities. Her music groups are organized into committees, each of which has its distinct contribution to make to the orderly conduct of classes and performing groups. There is an attendance committee which checks on pupil attendance, a supplies and equipment committee, a special problems committee, and a rules and regulations committee. One representative of each committee together with the teacher comprise the executive group.

When Miss Kodal is absent from the room at the beginning of the class (and this is one of the common causes of poor discipline in music classes), someone from the attendance committee takes charge—this was one of the things suggested by the rules and regulations committee and approved by the group. If books are used in the class session, someone from the supplies committee sees that they are collected and stored. Another member of the same committee checks with the teacher to see what recordings she will need the next time the class meets. If Joe fails to appear for a scheduled performance of the chorus, the rules and regulations committee talks with him and then the representative takes the suggestions the committee makes to the executive group where final decisions about the penalty Joe must pay are made. Of course all these things do not just happen, and they do not always operate smoothly, but they do teach freedom and responsibility, both of which are essential to music and democracy.

### *Schedules and Discipline*

Earlier it was stated that the failure to be in the room when the music students reported was one of the common causes of lack of discipline in music classes. This points out two other situations which make discipline difficult. One of these is the scheduling of music and the other the inadequate housing of music departments in many schools. In one large junior high school the general music classes meet in the auditorium. Lois Telman is scheduled to meet classes the first, second, and third periods. All the supplies are kept in a small room at the end of the hall. When Lois needs materials for use in the music classes she has to make the trip to the room and back to the auditorium when the class begins to arrive—an invitation to disorder in any junior high school. Willis Tartin is trying to teach instrumental music along with his schedule of general music. There is not time enough for all the individual help needed, so Willis "steals" a little time from general music by putting a record on the record player and telling the class to listen while he crosses the hall and for ten minutes helps an eager sophomore try to play a trombone. As you might expect, during that ten minutes the principal stops in to see what the noise is all about.

Lois and Willis are not prime offenders in these undesirable school situations. The culprits are over-scheduling and poor housing. Here is an area of discipline that is clearly an administrative problem. If Willis is to teach instrumental music he must have time for it; if Lois is to use supplies and equipment in her classes she must have a place to keep them in the room where she teaches. This must be provided by an administrator who is alert to the relationship between discipline and schedules and class meeting places.

"The only answer our music teachers have to discipline problems is to throw people out of the chorus, band, or orchestra," complained a high school principal. "Every week some parent calls up to say his child has been put out of the band after he has bought a new horn for $65. And our guidance counsellor says that she always has someone in her office who has been put out of a music group. Why can't they take care of their problems?"

Certain music teachers would probably answer the question in these words, "Membership in musical organizations is voluntary. Lots of pupils want to belong. There isn't room for those who won't behave. If they can't cooperate, let them leave." That philosophy may produce good orchestras but it won't teach a student how to behave. The pupil learns how to behave in an orchestra by behaving in an orchestra, not by sitting in a guidance office. This is the teacher's responsibility and the teacher is helped in achieving the desired results when he has planned with the group for standards of behavior and set up with the group ways of achieving and maintaining the standards. There may be, in a year, one or two pupils whose conduct is such that they cannot be continued as chorus, band, or orchestra members. The decision should be based on the sober judgment of the group. Hasty expulsions done in anger breed further discipline troubles.

It is a paradox that lack of discipline should be a complaint directed against music departments in many high schools. The chorus, the band, the orchestra are examples of the best discipline—a total group, with each individual important, achieving a commonly agreed upon goal. Teachers who can direct a chorus know all the techniques necessary for good discipline anywhere if they will apply them to the whole program of music. In schools where the music teachers use their skill in working for good group dynamics, the administrators and guidance counsellors frequently find that the music teacher can succeed in reaching students who are difficult to reach.

### *General Music Classes*

The general music classes in junior high school are a source of difficulty in music departments. Part of the problem is that like general science and general mathematics, general music may lack definite meaning and direction. Part of the problem is that the junior high school age is a difficult age for teaching anything, and general music is no exception. Part of the problem is that in large school systems these classes usually fall to the lot of the beginning music teacher because the experienced teachers do not want to teach general music. Part of the problem is that they have become a catchall so that any student in eighth grade who has no other class the third period finds himself in general music class that period. Music in the junior high school is one of today's biggest problems in music education. It requires much attention from administrators so that classes are better housed, scheduled, and of a better size. It requires study by music teachers so that the right curriculum can be found. The answer is not the one that is being offered rather freely by some school people: "Let's give up regular music classes after sixth grade."

### *An Elementary School Problem*

Music teachers who work in the elementary school are seldom troubled with serious discipline problems. However, one of the most difficult interpersonal situations in music education appears in this field. That is the situation of the young person who graduates from college and who on her first job receives the title of "supervisor." She is in need of personal counseling from someone in an administrative position as she begins her work. Someone who knows the teachers in the elementary schools needs to help her make the adjustment to working with experienced teachers and being in a position where she must lead them in their teaching of music. That someone, perhaps the elementary principal or supervisor, can help the beginning music teacher learn the ways of working with children from the experienced classroom teachers while at the same time the classroom teachers learn from her the new techniques of teaching music. The statement, "She can't tell me!" can be avoided and a

good working relationship established. Without help from someone this situation can defeat an enthusiastic beginning teacher.

*The New Teacher*

Closely related to this situation is another teacher-music specialist relationship which may be found on either the elementary or secondary level. This is the situation in which a music teacher with recent education finds himself a member of a music department in which all the other members are older and have a philosophy of music different from the beginner. Shall he teach as he has been taught to teach, or shall he teach as all the others do? If he conforms he will not be happy about his teaching. If he does not conform he may be unhappy in his teaching situation. One reason for lack of progress in many areas of curriculum is, that in the absence of real guidance, most beginning teachers find it easier to conform than to be different. Administrative guidance, supervisory counseling is needed to help the music teacher follow the methods he believes in without offending other faculty members.

*Building a Staff*

1. Careful employment interviews in which mutual understanding of the philosophy of both general and music education in the school is reached—

2. Adequate supervisory guidance to help the beginning teacher through the first months of service—

3. Administrative planning for teacher load and for class scheduling and housing—

These are necessary to reduce staff turnover, to attract the best beginning teachers, and to keep teacher morale high. Without these the school music program will fall short of its objectives and be a source of personnel problems within the school.

## • FOOD FOR THOUGHT

1. What additional reasons for difficulty in discipline in music classes have you observed?
2. What dissatisfactions with school personnel practices have caused music teachers whom you know to change their teaching positions?
3. In the school that you know best, is there in your opinion adequate guidance and counseling for the beginning music teachers?
4. What factors in your school keep teacher morale high?
5. How much is teacher morale influenced by an administrative philosophy? By physical surroundings? By teacher-teacher and teacher-pupil attitudes?

# 19 • Evaluating the school's music program

## *Why Evaluate?*

The simplest answer to "why evaluate" is this: To progress, it is advisable to investigate the past and present standing of our program. From this orienting point, we determine our future course. It would be possible to go "from nowhere," but with an

organization as complex as the modern public school, this seems unwise.

The status of the music program in any school is far from intangible. Music can be assessed as to its effectiveness, just as other subjects can be. It can and should be evaluated, in order that it may serve the best interests of school and community.

Furthermore, it should be evaluated frequently; otherwise, how can intelligent decisions be made as to its needs?

## *How to Evaluate*

School faculties that work closely together will have no difficulty evaluating; a type of informal evaluation is going on most of the time in such situations.

When it is time for a more extensive evaluation, faculties are usually divided into committees; they then complete extensive reports on various phases of the program.

For our purposes, we have compiled a list of questions that can be answered by groups of music teachers, individual teachers, and administrators. These questions are intended only as stimulators, for each school should devise its own rating form after considering its own problems. Yet all schools will have certain questions in common.

## *Some Evaluating Questions*

| | Yes | No | Don't know |
|---|---|---|---|
| 1. Is the staff working together to build a balanced, cohesive music program from elementary through senior high school? | ____ | ____ | ________ |
| 2. Has the music staff evolved a workable philosophy, agreed to objectives, and are its members working in terms of these? | ____ | ____ | ________ |

| | Yes | No | Don't know |
|---|---|---|---|
| 3. Does the music staff understand the general educational philosophy and practices of the school as a whole? | ____ | ____ | ________ |
| 4. Is opportunity provided for new music teachers to become acquainted with the philosophy and practices in your school? | ____ | ____ | ________ |
| 5. Do the members of your music staff work well together? | ____ | ____ | ________ |
| 6. Does the music staff work well with other teachers? | ____ | ____ | ________ |
| 7. Does each music teacher work in an area (instrumental, vocal, general music, or combination of these) for which he is well prepared by education and experience? | ____ | ____ | ________ |
| 8. Does any one portion of the music program overshadow others? (Band, Choir, General Music, etc.) | ____ | ____ | ________ |
| 9. Are the music teachers' pupil loads approximately the same as those of teachers in other subject areas? | ____ | ____ | ________ |
| 10. Is the class load of the music teachers about the same as that of other teachers? | ____ | ____ | ________ |
| 11. Does the class visitation load of the elementary music teacher allow for (a) Adequate travel time? | ____ | ____ | ________ |
| (b) Time to consult with classroom teachers? | ____ | ____ | ________ |
| 12. Does your school system sponsor in-service training to provide assistance for elementary classroom teachers? | ____ | ____ | ________ |
| For music specialists? | ____ | ____ | ________ |

| | Yes | No | Don't know |
|---|---|---|---|
| 13. Do your elementary school music specialists understand the nature of their job (are they to supervise music, teach music, be on-call, traveling, or helping teachers?) | ____ | ____ | ________ |
| 14. Do the elementary teachers understand the music specialist services available to them? | ____ | ____ | ________ |
| 15. Have the elementary music teachers established a good working relationship with classroom teachers? (a) Do elementary classroom teachers leave the room or otherwise ignore the music teacher when she arrives? (b) Do classroom teachers carry on the music program between visits of music specialists? | ____ | ____ | ________ |
| 16. Are decisions with regard to releasing children from classrooms for music activities made with the assistance or knowledge of their classroom teachers? | ____ | ____ | ________ |
| 17. Does the senior high music curriculum provide courses for pupils who are interested in specializing in music (other than performing groups)? | ____ | ____ | ________ |
| 18. Do both junior and senior high music curricula provide courses for those pupils who are not interested in belonging to performing groups and who do not intend to specialize in music (average-consumer courses)? | ____ | ____ | ________ |
| 19. Does a proportionate share of the music budget go to the support of each phase of music, elementary and secondary, vocal and instrumental? | ____ | ____ | ________ |

19. (*continued*)

    (a) Elementary music, classroom . . ——— %
    (b) Secondary music, classroom . . ——— %
    (c) Elementary music, instrumental ——— %
    (d) Secondary music, instrumental . ——— %
    (e) Secondary music, choral . . . . . . ——— %

| | Yes | No | Don't know |
|---|---|---|---|
| 20. Is the music program allotted a definite share of the school budget? | ___ | ___ | ______ |
| 21. Are the music teachers informed of the amount of school funds they may use in planning their program? | ___ | ___ | ______ |
| 22. Is the entire school staff cognizant of the method by which various departments receive funds for purchase of material and equipment? | ___ | ___ | ______ |
| 23. Are music teachers visited by school officials before their proficiency ratings are filed? | ___ | ___ | ______ |
| 24. Does the individual teacher know what particular proficiency rating was assigned him, and how it was assigned? | ___ | ___ | ______ |
| 25. Is the general music program meeting the needs of the segment of the school population not in performing organizations? | ___ | ___ | ______ |
| 26. Is the general music course planned in terms of consumer rather than performer needs? | ___ | ___ | ______ |

## *Try Evaluating Yourself*

The following questions are intended for the music specialist as a type of self evaluation. The really daring teacher may try rating himself on these items and then inviting his principal to rate him. Comparing the two ratings may prove to be an informative experience, if done in an objective manner.

| | | | Yes | No | Don't know |
|---|---|---|---|---|---|
| 1. | Am I (Is he) | teaching in terms of understandable objectives? | ____ | ____ | ________ |
| 2. | Do I (Does he) | plan my work with fellow teachers when possible? (For example, social studies, English, art, others) | ____ | ____ | ________ |
| 3. | Do I (Does he) | know pupils as individuals and plan with this in mind? | ____ | ____ | ________ |
| 4. | Do I (Does he) | know group characteristics of classes and plan accordingly? | ____ | ____ | ________ |
| 5. | Am I (Is he) | as concerned with the planning of General Music Classes as with the planning of my performing groups? | ____ | ____ | ________ |
| 6. | Do I (Does he) | consider the best interests of the school as a whole in determining the planning of the music curriculum? | ____ | ____ | ________ |
| 7. | Is my (Is his) | classroom management satisfactory? | ____ | ____ | ________ |
| 8. | Do I (Does he) | plan a variety of musical experiences for music classes? | ____ | ____ | ________ |
| 9. | Am I (Is he) | aware of the developmental characteristics of children and plan according to these? | ____ | ____ | ________ |
| 10. | Am I (Is he) | well informed as to new teaching materials and methods? | ____ | ____ | ________ |
| 11. | Do I (Does he) | requisition supplies and materials in a businesslike manner? | ____ | ____ | ________ |
| 12. | Do I (Does he) | turn in reports and complete other work on time? | ____ | ____ | ________ |

| | | | Yes | No | Don't know |
|---|---|---|---|---|---|
| 13. | Do I (Does he) | plan out-of-school musical events or trips well in advance and clear all dates with administration? | ____ | ____ | ________ |

## *Testing Children in Music*

This topic conceals all possible kinds of questions. Testing children for what? Ability to sing in tune? Knowledge about music? Knowledge *of* music? Appreciation? Interest?

These questions arise from many discussions of the various ways teachers test children in music in order that they may place a grade on a report card. Since little help has been given music teachers in how to test, and since they are responsible for assigning grades to pupils, let's not "shoot the pianist"; assigning a specific mark in music is often far from simple.

Still, it seems odd to find a mark of 88, 72, 94, on the report card of a first grade child. Granted that this is a traditional marking procedure, still, you'll find it most often based on the child's ability to sing. And isn't singing only one phase of musical ability? Is "88" a true mark?

Other bases for marks in the upper elementary and junior high grades seem to center on singing ability plus the ability to memorize *facts about music*. Therefore it sometimes becomes possible to earn a fairly high grade in music without having had much experience with music itself. To clarify this, let's examine a few test items.

Item: The violin belongs to (a) the string, (b) the woodwind, (c) the brass, (d) the percussion, family of the orchestra.

This could be taught as a fact to be memorized. It could be taught or learned without any association with the music of the violin or the orchestra. It could be a piece of information memorized without musical meaning. As such, it definitely would be of secondary importance.

The sound of music, the significance of music, the function

of music—these are the important aspects. If the child is asked to associate what he has learned about the musical sound of the violin with the orchestra, the question grows from listening to or making music; then we are moving in the right direction. Consider this test item intended for an eighth grade class:

In listening to the symphonic suite Scheherazade, by the composer ........................, we heard the "Scheherazade theme" played by a solo ............ This instrument belongs to the ............ family of the orchestra. The theme representing the "Sultan" was played by instruments of the ............ ............sections of the orchestra. The recording to which we listened was performed by the .................. Orchestra.

Another item based on *musical experience with music* might be:

List three songs we have sung that are in the minor mode.

Such questions indicate that the child has been involved with music itself, not just facts about music. Teaching just the facts, furthermore, requires no special skill in music, and not much in teaching.

Teaching through experiences with music itself, however, is a more challenging task. And if we try to help the child develop his musical skills from a basis of musical experiences, it is still more challenging. Asking why "F" must be sharped in the key of G Major implies that the child has been asked to think during a musical experience. Asking him to give the key signature for G Major implies that he has been asked to memorize. We all know which represents better teaching.

All the facts and all the skills can be taught from the music. It takes better planning on the part of the teacher, but it can be done. Don't do such things as make pupils memorize the name of the bass clef lines and spaces just because it's in the course of study; instead, show them why certain instruments need more than the treble portion of the Great Staff, and show them while they are hearing an instrument that uses those bass lines and spaces.

In some schools the "same old tests" have been given for years. They may be freezing the music curriculum. In other schools, the curriculum is freezing the tests. If either is true in your school, it's time for a thaw. Remember this: Because a child has spent hours singing "do-re-mi" doesn't necessarily mean that he has learned to read music. It may mean that he has learned a sequence of syllable names, and that's all. Look beyond such procedures and try to teach in terms of musical growth. This is our job.

## • FOOD FOR THOUGHT

1. Why should schools evaluate their progress in music?
2. Are objectives really important?
3. Should all teachers agree on procedures, or can some disagreement be a good thing?
4. Should teachers be encouraged to try new ways of teaching, or should the administration encourage teachers to develop similar teaching techniques?
5. Discuss several teachers you know who seem to have superior teaching methods. List the similar ways in which they teach. List dissimilar ways.
6. Draw up a series of evaluation questions designed to help you judge the status of music in your own school system.
7. Draw up ten questions for music class tests that could not be answered unless the children had heard or made the music on which the questions are based.

# 20 • A music director and administrator talk music

## *How Did the School Music Program Develop?*

Superintendent Frederick of Stone City looked up from the draft of his annual report as Frank Roberts, Director of Music, entered the office.

"I've sent for you, Frank, because I am ready to write the portion of my annual report to the School Board that will tell the story of the year's work in music education. You remember that the first staff conference I had when I came here last year was with you. Everyone was all excited about a big music program and you and I had some planning to do. What shall I put in this report? Is what we have done this year in the music curriculum 'expansion', as the newspapers predicted?"

"Well, Dr. Frederick, I think I wouldn't want to say we expanded. I think we did more. We grew, yes, but we developed in a variety of ways. We have more teachers. We have more pupils enrolled in music—but we have done more than that."

"What do you think is the most important thing we've done?"

"Evaluating our general music program in the junior high schools and employing one more teacher at that level was the most important, I believe. Now the class load is reasonable and the teachers have some time and energy to give to rewriting the general music curriculum guide."

"What other things should go in the report?"

"Mention our new student-faculty council for music activities, the plan the instrumental teachers have worked out for gradual addition of instruments for the band and orchestra, the public performance policy we have completed for next term and the workshops Paul Ross set up to help the elementary teachers learn how to teach their students about the various instruments.

### *In What Direction Will it Continue To Grow?*

"Last year when I came I wondered what an expanded music program would mean to you. Frankly, I was afraid. Now I am looking forward to next term. I want you to get the music teachers together so that all of us can begin to plan what rooms we will want for the music department in our new senior high school. After we know what we want, we can meet with the architect."

"I have some plans, too. I think we will need to decide about the music teaching in the elementary school—maybe we are ready for a consultant instead of a supervisor. I'm meeting with the elementary principals on Thursday."

So music education in Stone City will keep on growing. Not into a multiplicity of competing organizations, not into the most important department of the school, but into an important, productive part of the students' education because:

1. A school board planned for the necessary funds.
2. An administrator and music director and faculty worked together to develop a school curriculum in which music had an important place.
3. The students shared in the planning for their music experiences.
4. The community understood the school program.

How will *your* music program develop?

# • Suggested reading

*General References for Teaching Music*

Andrews, Frances M., and Joseph A. Leeder, *Guiding Junior High School Pupils in Music Experiences.* Englewood Cliffs, N. J.: Prentice-Hall, Inc., 1953.

Andrews, Gladys, *Creative Rhythmic Movement for Children.* Englewood Cliffs, N. J.: Prentice-Hall, Inc., 1954.

Cole, Natalie Robinson, *The Arts in the Classroom.* New York: The John Day Company, 1940.

Cooper, Irvin, *Letters to Pat Concerning Junior High School Vocal Problems.* New York: Carl Fischer, Inc., 1953.

Edgerly, Beatrice, *From the Hunter's Bow.* New York: G. P. Putnam's Sons, 1942.

Krone, Beatrice, and Max Krone, *Music Participation in the Elementary School.* Chicago: Neil A. Kjos Music Co., 1952.

———*Music Participation in the Secondary School.* Chicago: Neil A Kjos Music Co., 1952.

Mathews, Paul Wentworth, *You Can Teach Music.* New York: E. P. Dutton & Company, 1953.

McConathy, Osbourne, and others, *Music for Early Childhood.* Morristown, N. J.: Silver Burdett Company, 1952.

Mursell, James L., *Music and the Classroom Teacher.* Morristown, N. J.: Silver Burdett Company, 1951.

Myers, Louis Kifer, *Teaching Children Music in the Elementary School,* 2nd ed. Englewood Cliffs, N. J.: Prentice-Hall, Inc., 1956.

Nye, Robert Evans, and Vernice Trousdale Nye, *Music in the Elementary School: An Activities Approach to Methods and Materials.* Englewood Cliffs, N. J.: Prentice-Hall, Inc., 1957.

Schwartz, H. W., *The Story of Musical Instruments.* New York: Garden City Publishing Company, 1946.

Sheehy, Emma Dickson, *There's Music in Children.* New York: Henry Holt and Company, 1946.

Snyder, Alice M., *Creating Music with Children.* New York: Mills Music, Inc., 1957.

Tooze, Ruth, and Beatrice Perham Krone, *Literature and Music as Resources for Social Studies.* Englewood Cliffs, N. J.: Prentice-Hall, Inc., 1955.

*Materials for Use by Teachers (Also suitable for high school classes)*

Baldwin, Lillian, *Listener's Anthology* (Volumes I and II). Morristown, N. J.: Silver Burdett Company, 1948. (Detailed and interesting material on great composers and their music; Bach to modern times.)

Barbour, Harriet B., and Warren S. Freeman, *A Story of Music.* Boston: C. C. Birchard Company (now Summy-Birchard Publishing Company, Evanston, Ill.), 1950.

Cotton, Marian, and Adelaide Bradburn, *Music Throughout the World.* Boston: C. C. Birchard Company (now Summy-Birchard Publishing Company, Evanston, Ill.), 1953.

Fishburn, Hummel, *Fundamentals of Music Appreciation.* New York: Longmans, Green & Company, 1955. (A comprehensive, concise, nontechnical, but highly informative coverage of music appreciation. Suitable for use in a senior high music appreciation course.)

Kortkamp, Ivan, *100 Things a Choir Member Should Know.* Nevada, Iowa: Published by Ivan Kortkamp, 1949.

McKinney, Howard D., *Music and Man.* New York: American Book Company, 1948. (A music appreciation text that approaches the subject from the basis of cultural backgrounds. Begins with American music.)

Richardson, Allen L., and Mary E. English, *Living with Music.* New York: M. Witmark & Sons, 1956. (A basic text for use in music classes, secondary level.)

Swift, Frederic Fay, and Willard I. Musser, *General Music in the Junior High School.* Rockville Center, N. Y.: Belwin, Inc., 1954. (Basic texts for general music; both teacher's manuals and books for pupils available.)

*Basic Song Series*

*Note:* These include books for pupils on various grade levels and manuals for the teacher. Also available are recordings of songs from the various books designed for different grade levels. For complete information, write to the publisher.

*The American Singer.* American Book Company, 55 Fifth Avenue, New York 3, New York.

*Our Singing World.* Ginn and Company, Statler Building, Boston 17, Massachusetts.

*Music for Living.* Silver Burdett Company, Park Avenue and Columbia Road, Morristown, New Jersey.

*A Singing School.* Summy-Birchard Publishing Company, 1834 Ridge Ave., Evanston, Illinois.

*Together We Sing.* Follett Publishing Company, 1000-1018 West Washington Street, Chicago 7, Illinois.

*Books about Musical Compositions and Their Composers*

Baldwin, Lillian, *Music for Young Listeners (The Green Book, The Crimson Book, The Blue Book) Music to Remember.* Morristown, N. J.: Silver Burdett Company, 1951. (These four books include information on many composers and their music. Records available.)

*Reference Books for Younger Pupils about Musical Instruments*

Balet, Jan, *What Makes an Orchestra.* New York: Oxford University Press, 1951.

Goward, Gladys McFadden, *See How They Play.* New York: Exposition Press, 1953.

Lacey, Marion, *Picture Book of Musical Instruments.* Boston: Lothrop, Lee and Shepard Company, 1942.

Posell, Elsa Z., *This Is an Orchestra.* Boston: Houghton Mifflin Company, 1950.

Stoddard, Hope, *From These Come Music.* New York: Thomas Y. Crowell Company, 1952.

*Publications and Periodicals*

Some informative and timely publications available from the Music Educators National Conference, 1201 16th St., N. W., Washington, D. C.:

*Music in American Education* (Source Book II)

*Music Buildings, Rooms and Equipment*

*Business Handbook of Music Education*

*Function of Music in the Secondary-School Curriculum*

*Music in the Elementary School*

*Musical Development of the Classroom Teacher*

*String Instruction Program No. 1*

*Keyboard Experience and Piano Class Instruction*

*Handbook on 16mm. Films for Music Education*

*Your Future as a Teacher of Music in the Schools*

*Careers in Music*

*The Music Teacher and Public Relations*

*Music for Fours and Fives*

*Keyboard Junior* (for junior and senior high school classes); and *Young Keyboard Junior* (for elementary grades 4-6):

Magazines for use by teacher and pupils (Address: 1346 Chapel St., New Haven 11, Conn.)

Keyboard Junior Magazines also publish many materials for use in the schools, including Radio and TV Music Guide, Film Music Notes, Opera Edition, Conductors' and Composers' Pictures, and other items of interest. For information write to publisher.

*Readings in Administration and Supervision*

Applegate, Mauree, *Everybody's Business—Our Children.* Evanston, Illinois: Row, Peterson and Co., 1952.

Elsbree, Willard S., and Edmund E. Reutter, Jr., *Staff Personnel in the Public Schools.* Englewood Cliffs, N. J.: Prentice-Hall, Inc., 1954.

Franseth, Jane, *Supervision in Rural Schools.* Washington: United States Office of Health, Welfare and Education, 1955.

Hymes, James L., Jr., *Effective Home School Relations.* Englewood Cliffs, N. J.: Prentice-Hall, Inc., 1953.

Sharp, George, *Curriculum Development as Re-Education of the Teacher.* New York: Bureau of Publications, Teachers' College, Columbia University, 1951.

Stoddard, Alexander J., *Schools for Tomorrow: An Educator's Blueprint.* New York: Fund for Advancement of Education, 1957.

Thelen, Herbert A., *Dynamics of Groups at Work.* Chicago: The University of Chicago Press, 1954.

# • Index

C